# Graphic Design Essentials:

## Skills, Software
## and Creative Solutions

Joyce Walsh Macario

To John—for all the love, laughter, and edits.

Published in 2009 by Laurence King Publishing Ltd
361–373 City Road, London EC1V 1LR
United Kingdom
T +44 (0)20 7841 6900
F +44 (0)20 7841 6910
enquiries@laurenceking.co.uk
www.laurenceking.co.uk

351133

Copyright © 2009 Laurence King Publishing Ltd
This book was designed and produced by
Laurence King Publishing Ltd, London

Design: Roger Fawcett-Tang, Struktur Design

A catalogue record for this book is available
from the British Library

ISBN-13: 978-1-85669-599–2

Printed in China

# Graphic Design Essentials:

## Skills, Software and Creative Solutions

Joyce Walsh Macario

Laurence King Publishing

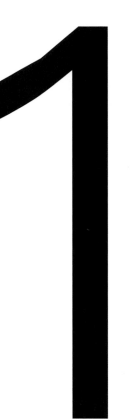

# Introduction

# The Elements of Design

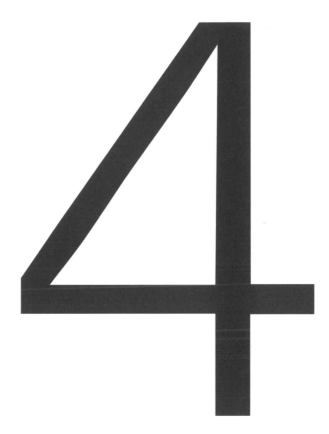

# Typography

# Images

# Layout

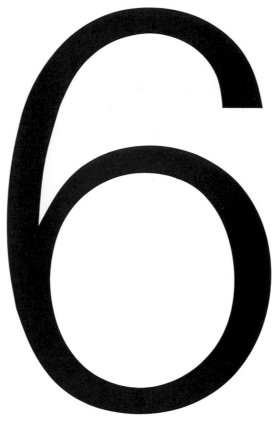

# Logo Design

# Visual Themes

# Information

# Preface

As I wrote this book in a studio a few trolley stops outside of Boston, I occasionally looked out at the tree tops surrounding my third-floor windows and watched several seasons pass. Inside the room crowded with mounds of treasured design books, my dog Archie lay next to me, resting his head on one of the shorter stacks. My husband would tolerantly await printouts in the next room; he'd pause the ball game to look over the latest drafts.

This book is a labor of love, inspired by my students and my own experiences starting out in the design industry. I wrote it to help beginners quickly learn the essentials of graphic design and to reflect the nature of graphic design today: our creative process involves a thorough integration of design principles with software capabilities.

This book is for people who want to create effective graphic design: beginners who have the interest but little knowledge of the field or the related software and are eager to get started. This describes most of the 1,400 students I've taught. The book was conceived and developed with their needs in mind. The goal is to efficiently develop a strong foundation in graphic design and production capabilities, whether students want to pursue design as a profession, or gain skills that will complement other career pursuits such as advertising or marketing. This book can also be used by individuals who are not in an academic program but wish to independently learn the essentials.

Though I wrote this book in my home studio, much of the work that has gone into its development occurred in classrooms. Since 1995 I've developed courses that integrate design fundamentals, analysis, and software skills. Noting the types of contemporary designs that students find inspiring, the book includes many of these, gathered from studios and agencies all over the world, along with explanations of their underlying principles. Having observed how historic graphic designs engage and inspire people who are new to the field, several masterwork examples (spanning 100 years) are showcased. I've also noted which software skills challenge students and the best order in which to teach the most useful capabilities. Adobe Photoshop, Illustrator, and InDesign are introduced with step-by-step software demonstrations that also reinforce design principles and provide professional tips. These skill-building exercises are engaging; in some cases a comical image or inspiring text can help distract from the complexity of the task. Throughout, my underlying goal is to help you, the reader, develop professional software skills coupled with solid design fundamentals.

No experience is necessary to begin. The software skills are presented incrementally, beginning with basics and becoming progressively more complex. You are encouraged to go through the book in order as this will most efficiently build a useful set of skills. Those readers who are more advanced are still encouraged to go through each skill set as they provide design and professional strategies. By the end of the book, you will use Photoshop, Illustrator, and InDesign as professionals do, understanding which software is best for which task. In addition, analysis and design projects provide independent, creative opportunities to develop skills in each topic. With each project, I've included student examples. Aspiring designers appreciate seeing other students' work—they provide insights, showing something to strive for or even surpass.

The book follows a formula: Design Concepts + Examples + Analysis + Software Skills + Projects. This strategy encourages both a successful development of design fundamentals and the capability to produce graphic designs. The text begins with basic design principles and software skills, then builds essential typography, image, and layout knowledge, which leads to more complex topics, software capabilities, and projects by its completion.

The first chapter provides an overview of the book, including images that introduce each chapter topic. Here you'll begin analyzing professional designs to reveal the underlying principles. The first software skill set begins with an introduction to Adobe Photoshop. You'll modify an amusing photo to learn the use of challenging, yet essential, photo-manipulation tools and tonal adjustments. You'll find all of the files used in the exercises on the book's website, www.laurenceking.co.uk/graphicdesignessentials.

The elements of design (color, direction, line, shape, size, texture, and value) are examined in chapter 2 with particular emphasis on color. You'll recognize which elements are used to achieve compelling results and you'll develop the ability to see variations of colors, whether in print or digital form, and to combine colors. The software skill sets provide an introduction to Adobe Illustrator and basic drawing skills while reinforcing color theory. You'll also learn about vector and bitmap images.

Chapter 3 is all about type. We'll explore everything from typography terminology to font selection and formatting strategies. Interesting stories about influential typographers from Baskerville to Brody underlie some of our favorite fonts so I've included them here. The software skill exercises start off with type selection and layout. You'll then learn how to use the Illustrator pen tool to quickly and effectively develop advanced computer drawing skills. The projects in this chapter provide independent, creative opportunities to reinforce type fundamentals and practice newly acquired software skills. Student examples of the type projects are featured.

Images are covered in chapter 4, providing strategies for finding and selecting the most appropriate photographs or illustrations. You'll learn how to acquire digital images from several sources, reproduce images at their best quality, and adhere to copyrights. All of the common digital file types are explained in a clear and useful way. The Photoshop software skills sets cover image fundamentals: cropping, rights, the Rule of Thirds and digital image sizing terminology.

Layout is presented in chapter 5 as an active component of successful design. We will explore establishing effective focal points, path layouts, and grids. This chapter introduces InDesign and builds advanced skills with two exercises in which you'll create a path layout and a grid layout. A path layout advertisement project is presented along with student examples.

Chapter 6 focuses on logo design and provides strategies for developing distinctive marks. By this point, you will have developed a good working knowledge of design principles and software basics, so a creative process is recommended for concept and project development. Software skills include advanced drawing and Pantone colors. The project shows several student designs and provides an opportunity to independently create a logo using your new understanding of logos and Illustrator.

Visual themes are discussed in chapter 7, demonstrating how all of the previously presented topics come together in multiple-page designs such as websites, packaging, magazines, and annual reports. Repetition and variation along with editorial theme examples from several countries are presented. The final software skills exercise is a four-page InDesign project that integrates Photoshop editing in the process to create a CD package design. The final project provides an opportunity to visually interpret your choice of music using these newly acquired design and software skills. Four student examples, along with their design strategies, complete the chapter.

Chapter 8 provides valuable information including shortcuts for Mac and PC and a comprehensive glossary of all of the terms introduced in the book.

The website includes all of the files you'll use in the software skill sections.

# Acknowledgements

I am grateful for my husband John's talent and tolerance for extensive edits, he was a tremendous advantage in this process.

I was fortunate to have the support of publisher Laurence King and art director Angus Hyland for this project; their advice will surely increase the flick factor. My gratitude to the amazing Lee Ripley, publishing director, who made this project possible; my editors John Jervis and Robert Shore who endured extensive emails—and always sent charming responses. Roger Fawcett-Tang who, I'm sure you'll agree, designed the book with wonderful results; Jo Lightfoot, Simon Walsh, Peter Kent, and the LKP team for everything they've done to complete this book.

I am grateful to the reviewers who generously provided thoughtful and useful feedback, they were a significant part of the virtual team that made this book possible.

Many, many thanks to the designers from around the world who kindly contributed their work for this book, I am delighted to share their inspiring work with students.

Many people shared their talents and support during this process, my heartfelt thanks go to: my mom Lois, for a lifetime of art lessons; and my late father, Francis, for encouraging me to write, I'm grateful he was there at the beginning of this project. My brother and sisters: Michael, Lois, Nancy, and Elaine, nieces and nephews whose love is a constant comfort.

Warm hugs to my lovely friends who contributed with their own special flair—Liz Cellucci for her creative zest, Dottie Clark for her thoughtful edits, Jessica Brilliant Keener for her author's insights, and Safoura Rafeizadeh for her design sense.

Special thank yous to Andy Updegrove for his generous advice, and Peter Smith for photographing the student CD packages.

Greetings and much appreciation to my former students who contributed their work and enthusiasm to this project including: Liz Austin, Ashleigh Bateman, Antonios Boskinis, Betsy Brand, Amy Cao, Caitlyn Carouge, Joyce Chen, Alex Cheng, Jessica Chien, Shi-Min Chin, Jessica Darke, Partrick Domery, Alessandra Epstein, Michael Falcone, Brian Forte, Marc Hadjibay, Danny Hayes, Lisa Hayward, Liz Kauff, Kristin Kruger, Kaitlyn LaRiviere, Sicong Liang, William Loo, Kori Mausner, Meredith McClarty, Alexander Moore, Melanie Morris, Antonette Naclerio, Alexandre Nguyen, Nicholas Nikic, Merissa Perasselli, Crystal Pisacano, Jean Marie Post, Kim Rescigno, Kim Richards, Brian Rubin, JC Rubiralta, Haruka Sawano, Emily Schwartz, Evan Silverberg, Jessica Solt, Pam Tamayo, Abigail Terry, Tessa van Charldorp, Samantha Wagner, Angela Wang, and Allie Weinberger. Cheers to Lou Wood, a British design student who taught me a lot—by email.

Wishing you all happiness and success.

Joyce Walsh Macario
Brookline, Massachusetts
June 2008

# Introduction

**Design Concepts + Examples + Analysis + Software Skills + Projects**
*Design Analysis: Environmental Graphics*
**Introduction to Adobe Photoshop**
          **Design + Software Skills 1:**
          **Photoshop Lasso, Layers, and Cloning**
**Major Points Summary**
**Software Skills Summary**
**Recommended Readings**

**Neville Brody**
**Poster for Graphic**
**Arts Message**
**Too Corporation, Tokyo**
**1992**

Britain's Neville Brody is one of the most recognized designers of his generation, known internationally for pushing the boundaries of graphic design. Early in his career he asked, "Why can't you have a painterly approach within the printed medium?" This poster for a graphic arts seminar in Japan demonstrates Brody's digital painting. Brody's work explored emerging software capabilities (Photoshop 1.0 was released in 1990) while testing the limits of legibility and traditional typography. Initially, some critics questioned the commercial prospects of this approach. They were quickly proven wrong. See more of his influential work in the Typography chapter.

Throughout the book you'll notice several historic posters that have helped shape graphic design over the past 100 years. These "hero" designers expressed their passion for type, image, color, and layout in their works. It is my hope they will inspire you as you develop your skills in design.

# Curves ahead

An essential tool for curling your lashes
for more definition. Give them body, give them
volume. Because they ask so little in return.

Look around and you'll see that graphic design is everywhere. It's the most pervasive art form in our society. And when it's good, it's powerful. Graphic design influences our purchases with clever packaging, persuasive advertising, and distinctive branding. It also engages us and enhances our comprehension of text in magazines and books, and on websites and cell-phone displays.

Would you like to produce powerful work such as this? This book will teach you how to analyze designs to understand their underlying strategies. It will provide guidelines for successfully choosing and using typefaces, images, and layouts. And it will teach you software skills with design exercises so that you can create your own influential graphic designs in all forms, from print to new media.

# Design Concepts
# + Examples
# + Analysis
# + Software Skills
# + Projects

We'll use the formula above throughout the book. Each chapter provides explanations of design concepts, along with examples and analysis that reinforce this knowledge. This information is complemented with instruction in Adobe Creative Suite software. The software skills are demonstrated with engaging exercises that reinforce your understanding of design fundamentals. Projects provide you with opportunities for independent creative development using professional design software.

### Adobe Creative Suite

The Adobe Creative Suite (Design Standard edition) consists of industry-standard software: Photoshop, Illustrator, and InDesign. Photoshop is the leading professional software used for optimizing photographic and complex images. Illustrator is used for drawing on the computer and single-page layout for print and screen. InDesign is multiple-page layout software and is used for organizing designs prior to sending jobs to print shops. These three Adobe products share a similar interface that facilitates the beginner's ability to use the software.

A reassuring consideration: in this book software skills are built incrementally. Going through the chapters sequentially, you are provided with sufficient software instruction to perform each exercise. And the exercises reinforce design concepts so you'll build design capability along with technical facility. As you develop these skills your confidence will grow with your ability to produce the ideas that you see in your vivid imagination. If you already know a bit of Photoshop or other program, do the exercises anyway to reinforce the design concepts and build your software skills to a professional level. In the later chapters you will, as most designers do, combine your skills in all three programs to produce designs. Ready? Let's go…

### Functional Fine Art

Designs of words and images are everywhere and, when done well, they're considered functional fine art. The goal of most graphic design is to communicate but visual appeal can be subjective: what you like may differ from what I like. Regardless of style, good design enhances our lives, while bad design impedes communication and comprehension.

Think about examples of graphic design that you've seen today. On these two pages, five examples represent the range we often encounter: books, packaging, logos, magazines, and signs. Magazines, from covers to layout to spilling postcards, are designed to inform and influence their readers. Advertisements—in print, on TV, flashing at you on the Internet—can affect our purchases, whether we think we want a product or not. The design of a web page facilitates our ability to get the information we need, yet we've all experienced poorly organized websites that are incomprehensible. Logos appear everywhere, from handbags to the tops of buildings, as stamps of quality and cost—high or low. Signs direct us to new locations, saving time or painfully causing more steps. From cellphone menus to book covers, graphic designs influence our behavior for better or worse. The design of this book was carefully constructed to enhance your learning experience. Let's look at examples and begin analyzing design to discover the underlying strategies for success.

### Analyze Design

When the reality program *Survivor* came to TV screens, millions were intrigued by this sociological experiment and felt compelled to watch sixteen people trying to survive in the wilderness. But it's the logo that captivated me. This graphic conveys a lot of information very quickly and effectively. At a glance you see the name of the program and a rustic island environment. Now look closely at the images. They are actually very simple shapes—the top half of the oval has a collection of overlapping palm trees; look even closer, the trees are all the same shape, simply placed at varying angles and sizes to suggest density. Notice how the tips of the palms overlap the oval border—this technique creates depth, increasing visual interest. Now look at the lower half of the oval: the image that we immediately perceive as island surf is actually one wavy black line against a blue background—it's remarkable what one line can convey. Limiting the number of colors in a logo is advantageous. Here there are only three: black, vivid blue for the water, and green for foliage. Although limited, this color palette immediately provides information about the environment.

Next, look at the type. It can be described as rough-hewn, suggesting the castaways' experience. Finally, notice how your eyes follow the entire design in a logical path.

You perceived the image and read the text due to effective use of visual hierarchy: the name "Survivor" is largest, then the slogan "outwit, outplay, outlast" is in a simpler, smaller typeface. Your eye is led logically throughout all of the information.

The following season, *Survivor* moved to another hazardous, remote location. The logo design strategy remains the same, yet modifications effectively convey the new locale in Australia. The new color palette is warm—oranges, yellow, and browns. It now looks hot and dry. The illustrations remain simplified—the wavy black line is smoothed, turned 90°, and repeated to suggest the corrugated red earth in the Outback. There's a new graphic element in this logo—notice the notches on either side of the oval. While abstract, these subtly suggest Australian themes, alluding to Aboriginal art or boomerangs. In the logos chapter, we'll learn why simplicity is important in logo design—it enhances recognition and facilitates reproduction.

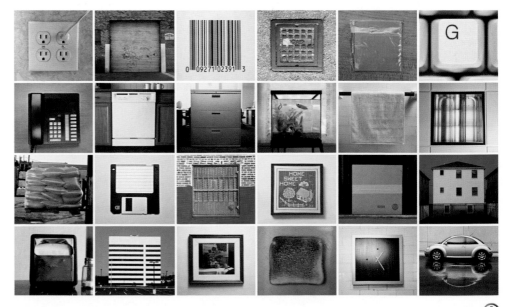

This clever design employs a basic principle (contrast) and an element of design (shape) to create the witty and effective result—more on these strategies in the elements of design chapter.

You'll want to spend some time with this initially simple cover design. Once you've had a moment to explore it, you discover that this two-layer cover presents complex yet engaging examples of guerrilla advertising. Peeking through the letters, the inside cover shows a collage of multiple posters apparently pasted over the years on a brick wall; most are partially torn to reveal earlier posts. All are images of the guerrilla marketing sites featured in the book. The title typeface mimics stencils and is die-cut into the front cover. You'll learn how to choose the most effective font for your designs in the typography chapter.

The Volkswagen Beetle advertisement at the bottom of the opposite page works as well on paper as it does in the television commercial filmed by Malcolm Venville. The print ad is a dense grid composed of close-up photographs of mundane square objects, repetitively flaunting their dullness until we finally discover a curvaceous VW Beetle in the last square. The ad visually conveys the Beetle shape to be more uniquely appealing than a common boxy car.

The brochures below, designed by Loewy for Eurostar, are examples of how graphic design can influence the way we live, our travels, and our impressions of places when we get there. The elegant type, sophisticated photos, and muted colors promise a pleasant experience on the Eurostar; expectations for the train are projected onto the destinations as well. Travelers confirm their accuracy—well-appointed trains provide comfortable travel.

Designers use photographs to immediately communicate a message or set a tone as you see in this *Riot* magazine cover designed by the Australian studio Qube Konstrukt. In the images chapter you'll learn how to choose photographs and reproduce them at their best quality.

Poster design has a venerated history in graphic design. During the last century, posters used type and image to communicate political messages quickly and powerfully. Posters were embraced by the music industry in the 1960s and that tradition lives on in this example created for The Books—a pair of musicians who use found sounds such as tape fragments to produce melodies. This clever design pulls two Os from a tangle of tape: they become reels and complete the band's name. In the layout chapter, you'll learn how integrating type and image ensures your message will be read.

Graphic designers are the primary creators of our visual images of place and time. Take a look at old concert posters to test this statement. When encountering an old poster (or, perhaps more conveniently, an album or CD cover) for a musician you don't know: the typeface, image style, and color palette not only suggest the music genre, they can provide enough visual information to date the recording with some accuracy. In the Netherlands, Attak experiments with iconic graphics, such as those inspired by psychedelic music from the 1960s. In this self-promotional poster the studio has updated the imagery and color scheme to complement the customized typography.

Many graphic designs are multiple-page productions such as websites, magazines, annual reports, and CD/DVD packages. The design cannot be understood at a glance, the audience must flip or click through the pages for the complete experience. The designer's challenge is to be visually cohesive, without falling into redundancy, across all of the pages. This CD package by Sagmeister, Inc. achieves a visually and conceptually cohesive design for the band Skeleton Key. Notice the holes in this design? The album, *Fantastic Spikes Through Balloon*, features portrait-style photos of all sorts of balloon-like objects punctured with a die-cut grid throughout the pages.

The team at Karlssonwilker Inc. have worked with Hattler since 2003 to devise a visually cutting-edge brand that celebrates their music, combining vivid illustrations with clearly commanding type. Methods for achieving successful visual themes are covered in the final chapter when all the information and skills you've learned come together.

**SURROUND CUTS IN STORES NOW**          **THE BASS CUTS TOUR 2004**

## Zoom in

Use the Zoom tool to get a close look at another pigeon in the photo.

Select the Zoom tool, place the cursor to the top left of the pigeon, hold the mouse button down, and drag to the lower right of the pigeon. Let go of the mouse button. You are now zoomed directly to the appropriate area of the image.

## 4 Select the shape

Select the pigeon with the Lasso tool. First, confirm that you have the regular Lasso tool selected—this is the best choice for selecting outlines of organic shapes. The Polygonal Lasso tool is used to select straight edges, the Magnetic Lasso tool is used to drive you insane. (The magnetic version is one of those software tools that promises more than it delivers. In most instances, the basic Lasso and the Polygonal Lasso will work more reliably than the Magnetic Lasso.)

Click at the top of the pigeon. While holding the mouse button down, drag the cursor around the dark edge tracing the entire body, finally ending at the beginning point. Once completely around the bird, take your finger off the mouse. You should now see that the entire figure is surrounded by a dotted line. This indicates that the object is selected.

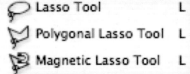

# 5 Copy and Paste

While the pigeon is selected, press Command + C and Command + V to copy and paste. In Photoshop, the first copy appears directly over the original but it no longer shows the dotted outline.

Press Command + 0 (zero) to view the entire file. Look at the Layers window to confirm that you have a new layer that contains only a copy of the pigeon.

If the Layers window is not showing, go to the Window menu and check Layers.

Click on the new layer to make it active.

# 6 Move it

Select the Move tool and position it over the pigeon on the new layer. Click and drag the pigeon up to the top of my head.

## 7 Resize

While the pigeon is still selected, resize it proportionately. Choose Edit > Transform > Scale. Hold down the Shift key, click on a corner control point and drag toward the center to make the pigeon smaller, then press return. Holding the Shift key ensures that the image will resize proportionately, meaning it is not too narrow or too wide. If your finger slips, press Return then Command + Z to undo and try again. You need to press Return to see the resizing results.

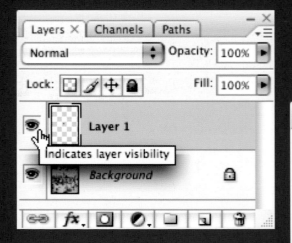

## 8 Switch layers

Behind the new improved pigeon, we can still see the old one. We will now use the Clone tool to remove it. First, click on the eye icon in the left-hand column to make the new pigeon invisible. Then, click on the background layer in the window to make it active.

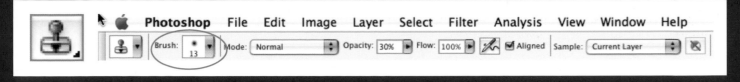

# 9 Clone tool options

Select the Clone tool. In the Options Bar, set the brush size to about 10–15 px (pixels). This setting will select an area of 13 pixels in diameter for you to paint over the background image.

# 10 Cloning

Zoom in to get a better view. Then place your cursor over a clear area of the pavement and hold down the Option key; when the appearance of the cursor changes, click. Pressing Option and clicking the mouse button at the same time selects the part of the image you will paint over the original.

Take your finger off the mouse. Now click and drag over the old pigeon: you will see the pavement cover the old bird. Draw carefully; notice the crosshair that indicates the area you are "painting." If you mess up, just press Command + Z, or Command + Option + Z for multiple undos. Reposition your mouse, then hold the Option key down and click the mouse button to collect a new area of pavement to complete the process.

# 11 Show layer

Once you're satisfied with the cover-up, make the new pigeon layer visible by clicking on the eye icon in the left-hand column of the layers window.

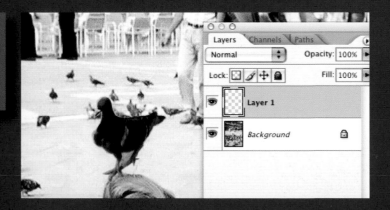

## Photoshop   File   Edit   Image   Layer   Select   Filter   Analysis   View   Window   Help

Tolerance: 32   ☑ Anti-alias   ☑ Contiguous   ☐ Sample All Layers   Refine Edge...

## 12 Magic Wand options

Notice the old background inside the bird legs. You can remove it quickly so that the background photo shows through. Select the Magic Wand tool. Confirm that the options are as displayed here.

## 13 Select with Magic Wand

Click on the area between the legs. This selects similar, adjacent colors. Now press the Delete key.

## 14 Merge layers

Reduce the image to one layer by pressing the Layer palette menu button in the upper right-hand corner of the window. Choose Merge Visible. You can save this file to your desktop using the File menu.

venicepigeon.jpg @ 33.3% (RGB/8#)

33.33%          Doc: 6.40M/6.40M

## 15 View full size
Press Command + 0 to view the entire image.

| Image | Layer | Select | Filter | Analysis | View | Window |
|---|---|---|---|---|---|---|
| Mode | ▶ | | Size | | | |
| **Adjustments** | ▶ | Levels... | ⌘L | | | |
| | | Auto Levels | ⇧⌘L | | | |
| Duplicate... | | Auto Contrast | ⌥⇧⌘L | | | |
| Apply Image... | | Auto Color | ⇧⌘B | | | |
| Calculations... | | Curves... | ⌘M | | | |
| | | Color Balance... | ⌘B | | | |
| Image Size... | ⌥⌘I | Brightness/Contrast... | | | | |
| Canvas Size... | ⌥⌘C | | | | | |
| Pixel Aspect Ratio | ▶ | Black & White... | ⌥⇧⌘B | | | |
| Rotate Canvas | ▶ | Hue/Saturation... | ⌘U | | | |

## 16 Adjust exposure
Should you find a need to adjust a photograph's exposure, Photoshop provides automatic adjustments under the Image > Adjustments menu. Rather than relying on the auto-corrections, the best tool at this point for adjusting exposure is the Curves feature.

Choose Image > Adjustments > Curves.

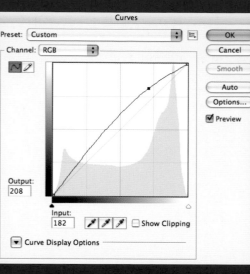

# 17 Curves window

Confirm that the Channel selection is RGB—this setting adjusts all colors in the image. Confirm that the lower left-hand-corner bars display black. If not, simply click on Curve Display Options and choose the Light button.

To make the image lighter, click on the line in the upper-right quadrant. Keep your finger on the mouse and tug ever so slightly up. Notice the change in the image—a very slight movement on the curve makes significant changes to lighten the exposure.

To make your image darker, click on the line in the lower-left quadrant. Keep your finger on the mouse and tug ever so slightly down. Notice the change in the image. A very slight movement on the curve makes significant changes to darken the exposure.

When satisfied with your adjustments, press OK. To start over from the original image, you can press Cancel. Or, press Command + Z and reselect Image > Adjustments > Curves.

# Major Points Summary

— Graphic design is everywhere. Examples include packaging, logos, signs, advertisements, magazines, books, websites; the list goes on… All are forms of communication.
— Graphic design can influence our actions, purchases, and the way we live.
— Good design is functional fine art; it enhances our lives.
— Logos require simplified forms for effective recognition, recall, and reproduction.
— Contrast is used to attract attention to a design.
— Visual hierarchy created with typeface size and style choices improves comprehension.
— Layouts organize content to better communicate the message.
— Integrating type and image ensures the message will be read.
— Visual themes—consistent use of fonts, colors, and style of images—provide cohesion for multiple-page designs such as websites, CD packages, ad campaigns, and magazines.
— Sketches help to communicate visual concepts.
— For accuracy, sketch while observing the object.

# Software Skills Summary

**Photoshop introduction**
— Overview of the toolbox and the most commonly used tools for beginning designers: marquee, lasso, crop, red eye, clone, move, magic wand, paint bucket/gradient, dodge/burn, type, eyedropper, zoom, foreground and background colors, color toggle, and default colors.
— Keyboard shortcuts.
— Skills: layers, proportionate resizing, options bar, curves adjustments.
— Tools covered in depth: zoom, lasso, move, clone, magic wand.

# Recommended Readings

Each chapter combines: design concepts + examples + analysis + software skills + projects on the elements of design, type, images, layout, logos, and visual themes. Additionally, every chapter will provide you with further reading suggestions for each topic.

To see more inspiring design, look for design annuals. These are published results of international contests for the year's best design. Designers use these books, magazines, catalogues, and/or websites for inspiration, to keep up with trends and the studios that are creating great work. The magazine *Communication Arts* publishes a highly anticipated graphic design edition every November, and its interactive annual is published in the September/October issue and on its website.

For sage advice on working as a designer, read Adrian Shaughnessy's *How to Be a Graphic Designer Without Losing Your Soul*.

A complete list of the contributing designers and citations for books can be found in Chapter 8.

# The Elements of Design

2

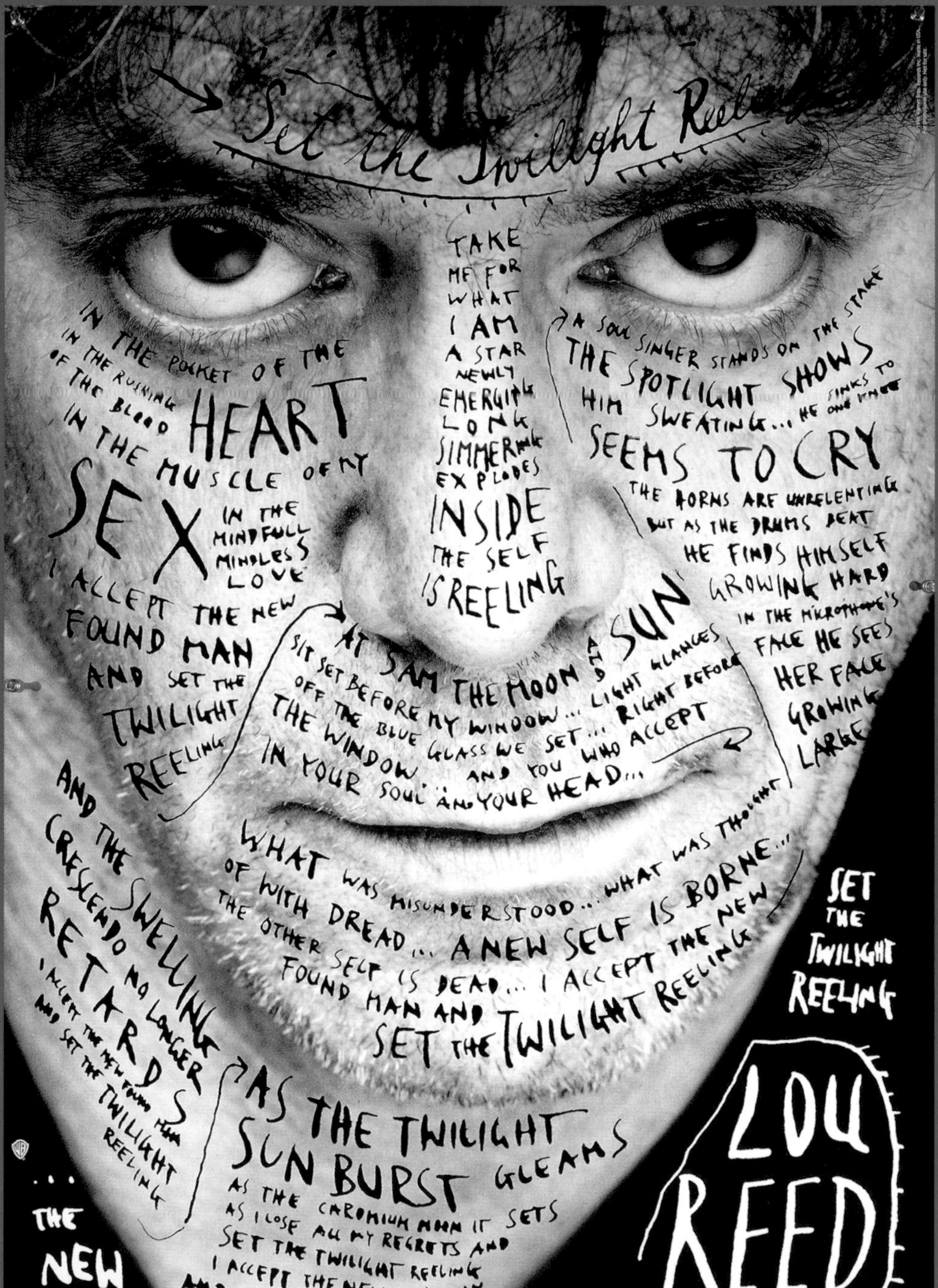

Stefan Sagmeister
Lou Reed poster
1996

Austrian-born New York designer Stefan Sagmeister created this poster for a Lou Reed album. The music had very personal lyrics so he placed the text directly on the musician's face. A few years later, Sagmeister shocked the design community with a unique lecture poster. A color photo of Sagmeister's body displayed the text for the event. All of the copy was cut into his torso with an X-acto knife (an intern did the carving). This concept was meant to express the pain that accompanies some projects. All of Sagmeister's designs express unique conceptual strategies and often an irreverent wit.

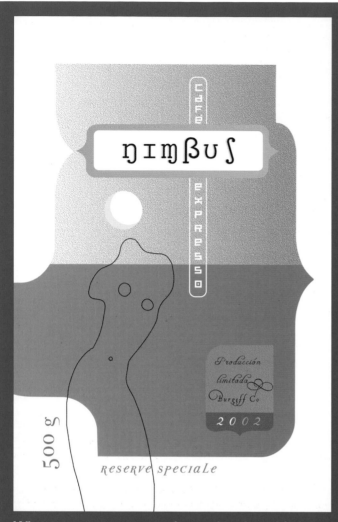

**What captures our attention and makes this label so appealing? Is it the color, the line drawing, the variety and texture of the shapes, or the value modifications within them? Is it the unique placement of the text in vertical and horizontal directions? Read on to learn the underlying design strategies.**

Let's start with a design exercise. Draw a rectangle, any size. Easy for you, right? Now, draw two lines. Are you hesitating? Suddenly, drawing two lines becomes a thoughtful challenge. You've probably not thought much about lines before, but they are a basic building block of graphic design. In other words, an element of design. An element is one of the simplest parts of anything. For graphic design they are:

> color
> direction
> line
> size
> shape
> texture
> value

Designers manipulate any or all of these elements to create effective visual designs.

## Lines

Experienced designers know that all designs begin with four lines—the edges of the page that determine the format. Of course, drawn lines are also used in graphic designs. The formal definition illustrates how varied lines can be: a line is simply a mark made by a tool as it is moved across a surface.

Because lines are basic, yet so varied, the ability to describe them effectively will lead you to more successful designs. There are a great variety of lines, but they all have three attributes: type, direction, and quality. Type refers to whether it is straight, curved, or angular. Direction describes the line's virtual movement on the page. If your lines are horizontal, you can describe them as going east or west. Vertical lines can be described as going north or south. Indulge your descriptive abilities when describing the line quality. Are your lines thick, bold, or stout; thin, narrow, or slender; wavy, rippling, or undulating? A regular line quality maintains its thickness throughout. The quality of a line drawn with a slanted calligraphy pen nib will change, going from thick to thin along its length. Look at the two lines you drew and describe them using these terms.

These two designs use line, but no color or images, to produce intriguingly austere results. This cover design uses line as abstract form to convey meaning. Columbia University's School of Architecture, Planning and Preservation published this collection of selected student projects, the restrained cover design expressing many aspects of urban planning. Pull the elastic that is the black straight line to reveal the title. What do these lines suggest to you?

The logo for the television series *Queer Eye for the Straight Guy* primarily uses lines—no color is necessary to create a simplified-looking yet memorable logo. It's cropped to the point of abstraction—can you see the eyeglasses and *Queer Eye* initials in the lines?

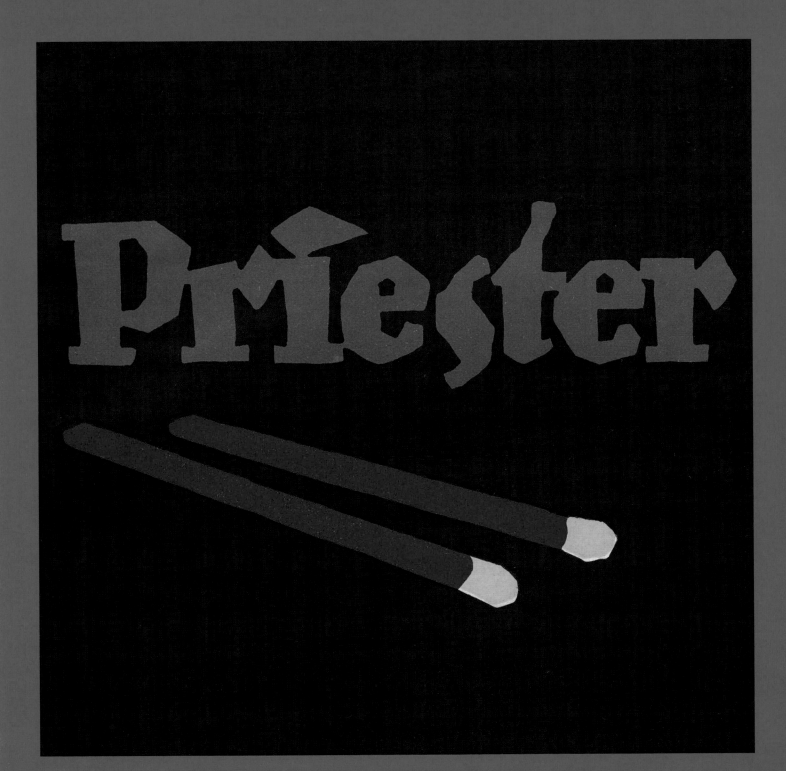

**Lucien Bernhard**
**Priester matches poster**
**1905**

Bernhard was a struggling young artist in Berlin when he won a poster contest with this radically concise design. The Priester matches poster was considered a work of genius and made Bernhard famous. He successfully reduced the style of commercial communication from complex lithographs—think Art Nouveau posters —to one word and two matches. It is Bernhard's bold colors that make the visually simple message powerful. He repeated his formula—flat background color, product name, and simple image—for over twenty years. His designs moved graphic communications forward and continue to inspire new designers with their use of simplified form and bold colors.

# Color

## Color Connotations

Color has an immediate effect on its audience. Before type is read and the image is understood, color makes an impression. Red is passionate, whether in love or fury, and carries a strong visual message. It is favored for designs ranging from sport cars to national flags. Here is a bold banner hanging at an upscale bar and grill on the Vancouver waterfront. Because red is so strong, its intensity sometimes needs to be softened with black to produce a more conservative effect.

Found imagery is emboldened with primary colors in this poster for a Francophone theater in Switzerland. Blue has positive connotations. Dark values of blue such as navy suggest expertise, authority, and a seriousness of purpose. Medium values of blue are associated with honesty and cleanliness. Look at the cleaning products on grocery-store shelves to confirm this point. Yellow is associated with warmth and wholesomeness so it is often used for food-product designs to convey healthful messages. Green is also healthful, indicating freshness and the outdoors. As a term, green represents environmental sustainable products, practices, and organizations.

## Color Combinations

Color is a very powerful and provocative design element, but using multiple colors successfully can be challenging. Let's start with basic color theory and look at the three primary colors, red, yellow, and blue, and the secondary colors, orange, green, and purple.

When these two groups are placed in overlapping triangles to form a circle, the relationships between the colors become apparent. Colors that appear opposite each other on the wheel are called complementary colors. Opposing positions are significant because these pairs of colors have the most contrast when used together. Contrast creates a visual dynamic that is often desirable in graphic design. The following examples and design exercises will help you to recognize the visual power of these color combinations.

Blue and green hues suggest something cool and soothing, while red and yellow suggest warmth, even heat. Notice how illustrator Michael Schwab's bold flat areas of color set meaningful tones in each of these posters for San Francisco's National Parks.

Some people have a natural facility for using color; but it can also be learned. Select colors that are appropriate for the design. Would you recommend the use of hot pink to a client whose business is financial planning? Probably not: for a client in a conservative industry, it might be better to choose darker colors for immediate and appropriate impact. Avoid using only your favorites—experiment. Observe when a design catches your eye and notice which colors are used to create particular effects.

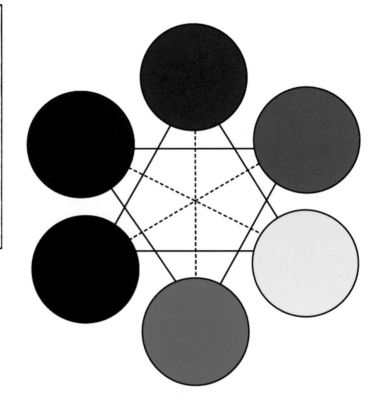

In a series of concert posters for a student band festival, red and green text and irreverent doodles brighten up the photo and, with it, the prospects of latent rock stars. Using a soft green and deep red, the trumpet tree illustration was created for a series of limited-edition posters produced to commemorate New Orleans and raise funds after Hurricane Katrina. On the example below, the unique placement of the copy engages us, but it's the contrasting yellow text that really "pops" against the rich purple tones in this poster for a graphic design exhibition in Mexico.

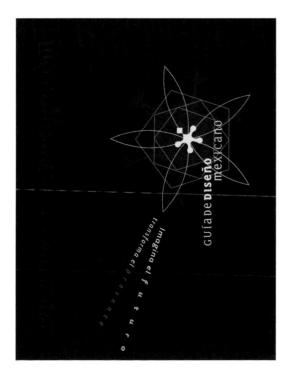

## 2 Choose a color

Select a red. First (a), double click on the fill color. To see a selection of reds in the large square, slide the arrows on the rainbow spectrum to the bottom (b). If your color picker does not appear as in this image, confirm that H (hue) is selected (c). Choose a true, saturated red by moving your cursor to the top right of the Color Picker square (d). Click OK to select red and close the window.

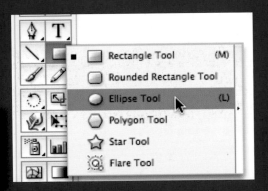

## 3 Make a circle

Place your cursor over the Rectangle/ Ellipse tool, click, and hold. Select the Ellipse tool and release.

## 4

While the Ellipse tool shows in the toolbox, click once on your file workspace. Illustrator will place your object wherever you click, so click in the top center area of your page. Make the height and width 1 inch (2.5 cm), and then select OK.

You've successfully drawn your first object. Admire its bold symmetry for a moment.

### 5

## Make more circles

Now, draw the other colors in the wheel. Reposition your cursor lower and to the left to create another circle.

Next, double click in the fill color square again to bring the Color Picker window into view. Move your cursor along the hue spectrum bar to choose a blue, then select a specific true blue from the large square color field.

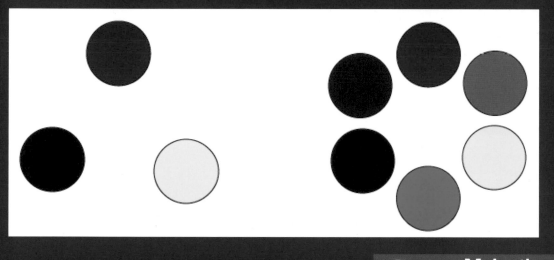

### 6

## Make the wheel

Repeat the above directions to draw another circle and make it yellow. If your virtual triangle looks a bit wobbly, you can move a circle after the color has been changed. Choose the black Selection tool, click over a circle, and while holding the mouse button down, nudge it into position.

**Tip**
A shortcut to the Selection tool is to hold down the Command key. Your cursor will temporarily change to the Selection tool, allowing you to move the circle. Once the circle is moved, and you release the Command key, your cursor returns to the Ellipse tool mode.

Continue to follow the directions in steps 3–5 and add three more circles—orange, green, and purple—to complete the wheel. Position the colors into a wheel using the Selection tool.

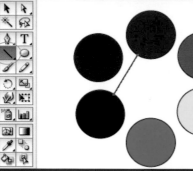

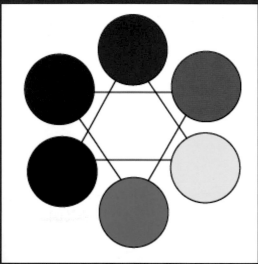

## 7  Draw the lines

Draw black lines to connect the two triangles that indicate the primary-color and the secondary-color groups. First, you will change the fill color to transparent or no fill. Place your cursor over the no fill button at the bottom of the toolbox and click.

Select the Line tool from the toolbox. Place your cursor on the lower-left-hand curve of the red circle, hold the mouse button down, and drag the cursor to the top right of the blue circle, then release the mouse button.

Repeat this step to draw solid black lines among the color groups. Hold the Shift key down while drawing horizontal or vertical lines to make them perfectly straight.

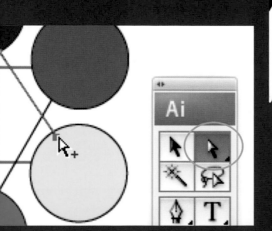

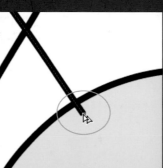

## 8  Make adjustments

If you want your lines to meet perfectly with the black circles, make small adjustments to one end of a line with the Direct Selection tool. Choose the white Direct Selection tool.

First, click off by clicking into the white background area so that nothing is selected. Then click directly on the end of the line you wish to adjust. Click and drag the end of the line into position.

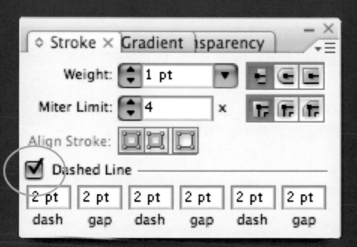

# 9 Draw dashed lines

Draw dashed lines to indicate the complementary color pairs. From the Windows menu, open the Stroke palette. Check the Dashed Line box and fill in values for the dashes and gaps. Start with 2 pts. each, then try experimenting with other values.

# 10 Finishing off

You can make the lines and circle outlines thicker by selecting them and then increasing their weight in the stroke window.

Save your work by using the keyboard shortcut Command + S. Phew. You have completed your first Illustrator drawing. Well done. Now take a break.

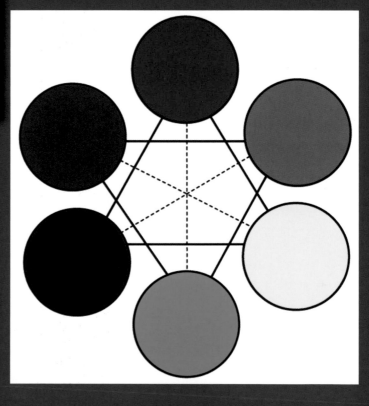

# Design + Software Skills 2.2:
# Photoshop Bitmaps and Filters

## Objectives

Demonstrate the differences between Photoshop and Illustrator image types, called vector and bitmap images. This exercise also shows the compatibility of Photoshop and Illustrator. In addition, you'll use one of the fun features of Photoshop, Filters.

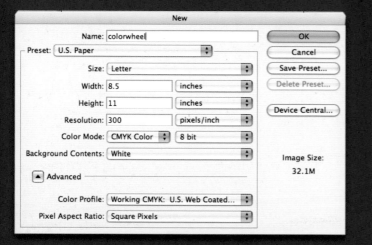

## To Do

Copy the color wheel from Illustrator to Photoshop. Compare the two types of images: vector and bitmap. Then get creative in Photoshop by applying various filters to the color wheel graphic.

Photoshop was introduced in Chapter 1. Now let's expand your Photoshop skills.

## 1 Make a new file

Start Photoshop and open a new file by choosing File > New. Name the file "colorwheel." Set Preset to Letter size, inches (twice), Resolution to 300, Mode to CMYK, and Background Contents to White. Leave the remaining options as the default values. Press OK and a new file will open on your screen.

## 2 Copy the wheel

Return to your Illustrator color wheel file for a moment to copy it into Photoshop.

In Illustrator, click on the file. Use keyboard shortcuts to select the entire image and make a copy.

Press Command + A, then Command + C.

Your image will look like this when it is selected.

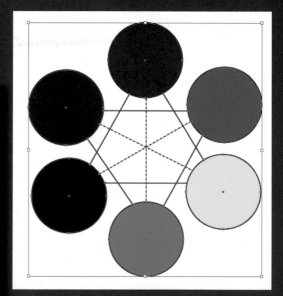

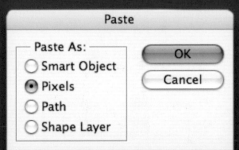

# 3 Paste in Photoshop

Return to your Photoshop file by clicking on the Photoshop icon in the dock. Press Command + V to paste the color wheel into your file. Photoshop may prompt you for a Paste type. Select Pixels, because this graphic will be converted to a bitmap image. Then hit the Return key to place the graphic into your file.

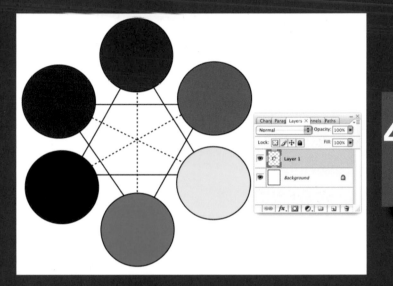

# 4 Layers

Note that the graphic is placed into a new layer. Remember, Photoshop creates a new layer every time you paste an object into a file. Layers allow you to edit graphics independently; it's a good thing.

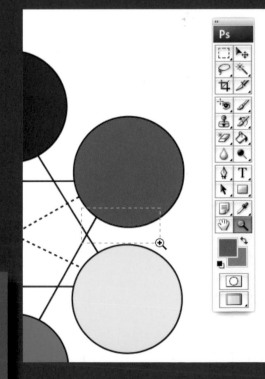

# 5 Zoom in

Use the Zoom tool to magnify the graphic.

Select the Zoom tool from the toolbox.

Click and hold the mouse button down as you drag and draw a virtual rectangle around the area you wish to magnify. Release the mouse button.

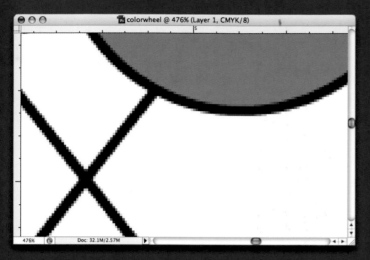

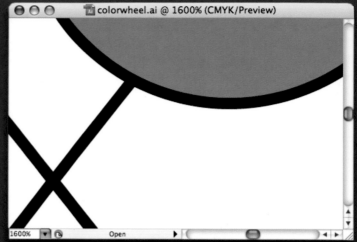

## Bitmap Images

Notice the rather rough-looking edges of the magnified illustration. Photoshop files are bitmap images. Bitmaps are a collection of pixels in a dense grid. Pixels look like tiny squares. A bitmap digital image can display subtle variations in colors, as is typical of photographs. But bitmap images cannot be enlarged without causing problems because a set number of pixels is based on the image resolution. When an image is resized, the number of pixels remains the same. Consequently, as the size of the pixel enlarges, the image acquires a fuzzy appearance. Designs created in Photoshop are bitmap images.

## Vector Graphics

Here is the same graphic magnified in Illustrator. Notice how smooth the image appears in Illustrator. Illustrator creates vector graphics. This term refers to the mathematical interpretation and display of graphic objects. Vector graphics can be resized without losing quality. The crisp lines of vector graphics are highly desirable, particularly in print and logo design, because they never lose their details or clarity. Designs created in Illustrator are vector graphics.

Rasterization is the process that occurs when a vector image is converted into a bitmap.

 **Zoom out**
In Photoshop, return to the full-size image. Press Command + 0 (zero).

## Photoshop Filters

Let's have some fun with Photoshop. The filter menu provides you with countless variations for modifying graphics. While many of the filters may not be professionally viable, they'll provide you with an early opportunity to get creative using the software.

 **Apply a filter**
From the Filter menu, select Filter > Blur > Radial Blur.

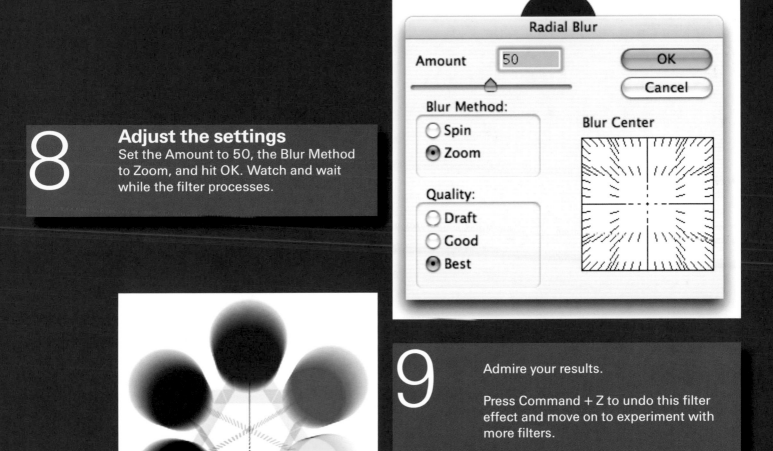

## 8 Adjust the settings

Set the Amount to 50, the Blur Method to Zoom, and hit OK. Watch and wait while the filter processes.

**Radial Blur**

Amount  50    OK    Cancel

Blur Method:
○ Spin
● Zoom

Quality:
○ Draft
○ Good
● Best

Blur Center

## 9 Admire your results.

Press Command + Z to undo this filter effect and move on to experiment with more filters.

## 10 Try another filter

Try the Ripple Filter.

From the Filter menu, select Filter > Distort > Ripple.

Filter   Analysis   View   Window   Help

Radial Blur            ⌘F

Convert for Smart Filters

Extract...             ⌥⌘X
Filter Gallery...
Liquify...             ⇧⌘X
Pattern Maker...       ⌥⇧⌘X
Vanishing Point...     ⌥⌘V

Artistic          ▶
Blur              ▶
Brush Strokes     ▶
Distort           ▶    Diffuse Glow...
Noise             ▶    Displace...
Pixelate          ▶    Glass...
Render            ▶    Lens Correction...
Sharpen           ▶    Ocean Ripple...
Sketch            ▶    Pinch...
Stylize           ▶    Polar Coordinates...
Texture           ▶    Ripple...
Video             ▶    Shear...
Other             ▶    Spherize...
                       Twirl...
Digimarc          ▶    Wave...
                       ZigZag...

## 11 Adjust the settings

Set the Amount to 100 and the
Size to Medium.

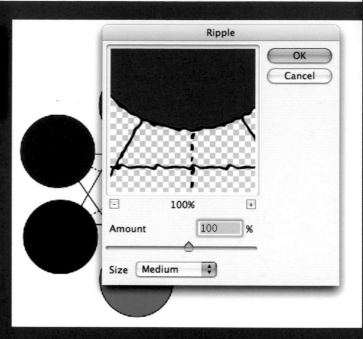

## 12 Experiment

Here are the results. What happens when
you change the Amount and
Size settings?

Illustrator has some of these same
filters. Experiment with the Filter menu
in Illustrator as well. How do the vector
graphic effects differ from the bitmapped
graphic effects?

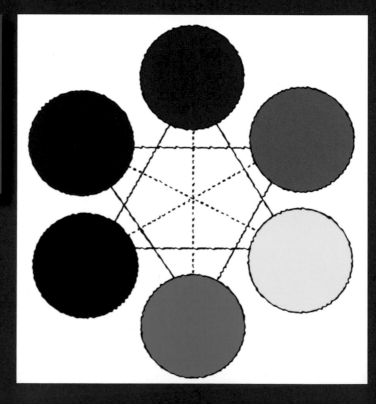

# **Design Analysis:** Complementary Color Grids

**Objective**   Provide a reinforcement of the color theory discussion and develop the ability to see nuances among colors in printed material. In the next Illustrator exercise, we'll use this project to look at the use of color in graphics software.

**To do**   Create two grids for a pair of complementary colors.

1   Search magazines or catalogues for examples of one primary and one secondary color of a complementary color pair.
2   Cut out nine 1-inch (2.5 cm) squares of each color.
3   Arrange each color's squares on a 3 x 3 grid.
4   Place the most "true" of each color into the center of each grid and arrange the other squares around it.
5   Paste the grids into your notebook.

My student Tess's homework is shown here. She used blue and orange, but you can choose any of the complementary color pairs.

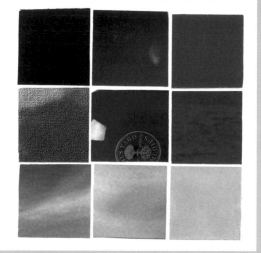
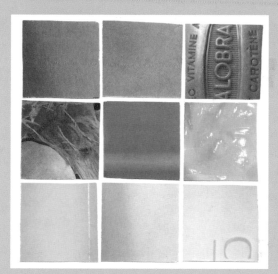

**Obj**
Provi
deve
comp
value
facili
dem

1

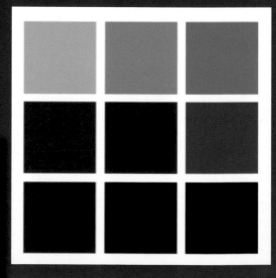

**Color Picker**

Select Color:

OK
Cancel
Color Swatches

H: 208 °
S: 41 %
B: 80 %
R: 118   C: 54 %
G: 162   M: 27 %
B: 204   Y: 5 %
# 76A2CC   K: 0 %

☐ Only Web Colors

### 4 Select colors

Now change the other eight squares to look like the colors in your paper version. Select the second square to change its color.

While the second square is selected, double click on the Fill Color to open the Color Picker window. Move the hue spectrum indicator and then choose the second square color from the large square. Notice the HSB, CMYK, and RGB values as you go through the grid.

### 5 Adjust the colors

Select each square one by one and find the color that most closely resembles your paper squares. Remember to double click on the Fill Color in the toolbox to open the Color Picker window.

As you choose each color, notice the position of the cursor and the corresponding HSB, RGB, and CMYK values. Can you fine-tune the color selection by changing the numeric values?

## 6  Draw a guide

You can draw guides to help you place the next grid. Press Command + R to show rulers along the left and top edges of the file. Then click in the ruler, hold your mouse button down, and drag a guide into position.

hueanalysis.ai @ 100% (CMYK/Previ

## 7  Create the second grid

Repeat this hue analysis process with the other color grid. Select the entire first grid, press Command + C, then Command + P to copy a second grid.

While still selected, move the second grid to line up with the guides you've drawn. Then change the colors to mimic the printed version.

# Typography

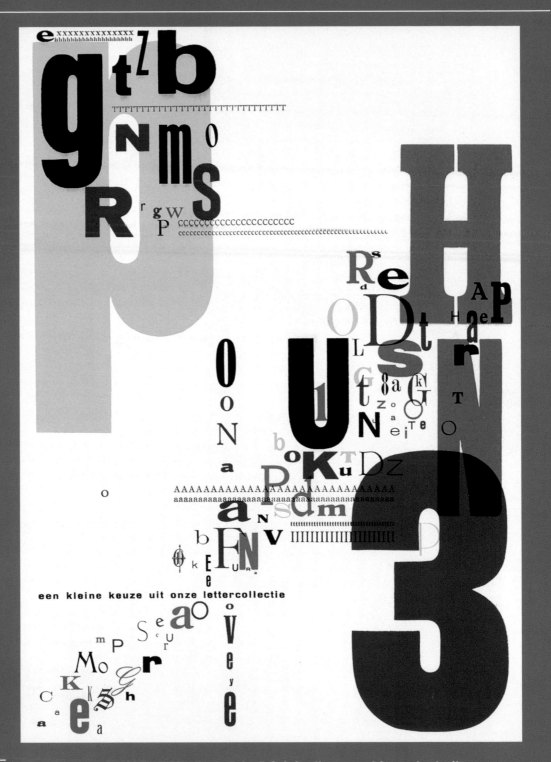

**Piet Zwart**
**Drukkerij Trio**
**(Trio Printers) catalogue**
**1931**

Piet Zwart called himself a "typotekt." Originally an architect, he built graphic designs using type. Zwart, who was Dutch, was influenced by Dada, Constructivism and De Stijl. He was concerned for the reader and legibility so he made his designs bold to attract attention. Zwart typically used brief slogans to allow the audience to get the message quickly. He rarely used images; instead he relied on collage techniques, rhythmically placing letters of contrasting sizes and weights for timeless appeal. This poster uses 134 different sizes and fonts. According to classic typography guidelines this mix really shouldn't work, but somehow it does.

## Transitional

Transitional typefaces have more refined forms than Old Style ones, with more contrast and deeper bracketing to the serifs. Technical developments by the mid-18th century included smoother inks, glossy papers, and stronger metal alloys to support these more elegant designs.

In Birmingham, England, a wealthy young man named John Baskerville took on the challenge of developing printing technology. His inventions advanced the use of more delicate typefaces that could withstand the repeated poundings of the press. Baskerville developed smoother paper and inks so that these finer typefaces could print without breaks or clogs. His designs had an airy quality due to the lightness of the letterforms and the generosity of the page margins. Ever the perfectionist, Baskerville melted down his type after each printing.

Times, another Transitional typeface, is perhaps the most widely used font in English-speaking countries. The characteristics of Transitional typefaces are not readily noticeable: they do not attract our attention. Nothing about their design distracts or hinders our reading; consequently they are highly reliable and legible. Use Transitional typefaces for readability and subtle elegance.

## Modern

The Modern letter style is characterized by a distinct contrast between the thick and thin strokes and hairline serifs abruptly set at right angles to the stems. Giambattista Bodoni's typefaces are in the Modern category because the Italian used the latest technology developed during the Industrial Revolution for the design and implementation of his work.

Celebrated for his accomplishments, Bodoni eventually developed 300 typefaces. Years after his death, Bodoni's home town of Saluzzo, Italy, erected a statue in his honor—pause for dreadful irony—with an inscription carved in Old Style letters.

Use Modern typefaces for their cool, crisp appearance in logos and titles. Brands from The Gap to Armani use them in their logos. This style is not the best choice for large amounts of copy—the extreme contrast between the thick and thin strokes creates an overall irregular appearance on the page.

## Slab Serif

In the mid-19th century, before images could be reproduced easily, advertisements used bold typefaces to grab attention. Stout typefaces were designed with serifs that were the same weight as the vertical and horizontal strokes. At the time this style was developed excavations and artefacts from Egypt were quite the rage. Consequently, this category was originally called Egyptian. Fonts were given Egyptian names such as Memphis to increase their sales. Common examples today are Rockwell and Courier (the typewriter font).

Clarendon and New Century Schoolbook are Slab Serifs with great legibility. With thicker strokes and serifs, they create an overall darker appearance to the page. Many children's books use these bold, clear typefaces to ease the new reader's experience. In your page layouts try Slab Serif titles combined with sans-serif body copy for a clean yet dynamic page appearance.

**Baskerville** | "What I cannot love, I overlook. Is that true friendship?" *Anaïs Nin*

**Bodoni** | "God gave us our relatives, thank god we can choose our friends." *Ethel Watts Mumford*

**Rockwell** | "Treat your friends as your pictures and place them in their best light." *Jennie Jerome Churchill*

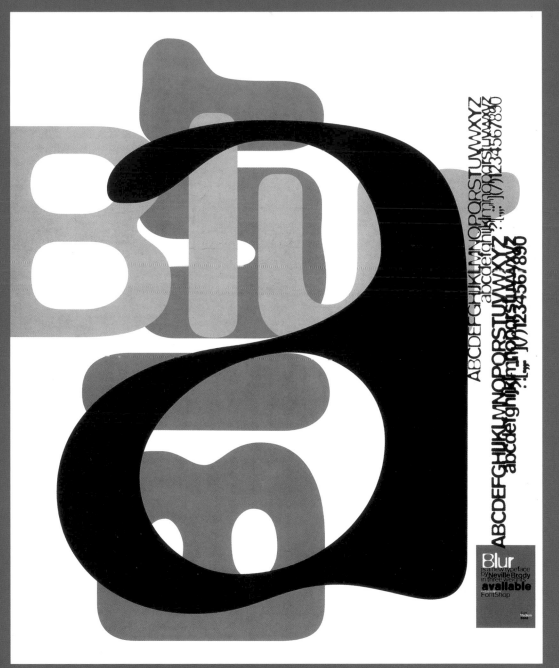

**Neville Brody**
**Postcard for FF Blur**
**Fontworks, UK, London**
**1992**

Neville Brody digitally modified Helvetica letterforms in Photoshop to create the font FF Blur. Rather than simply providing information, fonts can provide immediate emotional expression for text. Believing that design colors the content, Brody became a celebrated art director for magazines, including *The Face*, published in the 1980s, for which he created hand-drawn titles and innovative layouts to enhance the experience of reading each story. His postmodern designs pushed the boundaries of legibility and at the same time he designed many distinctive fonts including Arcadia, Insignia, and Dirty. Brody was the art director for the recent redesign of *The Times* of London. This project included the development of a bespoke font to be used only by the newspaper called Times Modern.

## Choosing and Using Typefaces

There are so many fonts on my computer that my hand cramps as I scroll through the entire list. Does this stop me from searching for the perfect font? No. Next, I go online to my favorite font websites and look there too. With an overwhelming number of fonts at our fingertips, how do we select the perfect one?

Start with a decision about the attitude and tone of your design. Then search for one or two typefaces that match the desired mood. The right typeface sets the proper tone for your design and helps establish a voice for your copy.

## Combining Typefaces—Opposites Attract

A classic approach to selecting typefaces is to use two fonts in each design: one for titles and one for the body copy—one serif, one sans serif. This mix adds visual interest to the page by creating contrast. It also enhances comprehension by indicating visual hierarchy of the text in titles and subtitles.

Why not combine two serif typefaces or two sans-serif typefaces on a page? Because two fonts from the same category will look somewhat similar—as well as somewhat dissimilar. It frequently looks like a mistake when two typefaces of the same category are mixed. See what I mean? Don't distract your readers from the content by making this rookie mistake.

The coolest-sounding type term is also the most useful when combining typefaces: x-height. This is the height of the lowercase letter x. Try to use typefaces that have the same x-heights when combining two typefaces. In this way your design will achieve an elegant unity. A few winning type combinations of serif and sans-serif fonts are Garamond and Universe; Sabon and Frutiger.

Depending on the project, one of the two typefaces may also be a novelty typeface. The purpose of these is similar to the use of colors: a novelty typeface communicates information even before the words are

Caslon Roman

*Caslon Italic*

**Caslon Semibold**

***Caslon Semibold Italic***

**Caslon Bold**

***Caslon Bold Italic***

read. Use the distinctive typeface for the titles, perhaps the subtitles, and even the folios (page numbers). The other typeface will be a serif or sans-serif font chosen for legibility. After all, the goal of most graphic design is to entice an audience and enhance its reading experience.

Most typefaces come in a variety of weights and sizes. A type family contains all the variations of a particular typeface. The chart above shows Caslon in a series of modifications described as roman, italic, semibold, and bold. These can be combined into a unified design because of the similarities in character widths, serifs, and x-heights.

Several typefaces have been developed that contain both serif and sans-serif versions (sighs of gratitude). This greatly facilitates combining typefaces—use just one. These fonts include Lucida and Stone, which was developed specifically for young designers learning to combine typefaces.

## Distortions

Computer software has the ability to make a wide variety of changes to these carefully designed letters. Software allows type to be skewed and scaled with varying horizontal and vertical effects that do not maintain the original proportions of the letters. New designers need to respect the subtle, complex beauty of letter designs. Just because the software makes distortions possible, that doesn't mean we should indulge. Resolve not to modify the proportions of the original typography.

## Fonts to Shun

Certain fonts are best unused—pass up poorly drawn typefaces with unsteady proportions. Avoid overused novelty typefaces as their ubiquity weakens their appeal. Instead of the lovely but overused Copperplate, try classics like Baskerville or Garamond with small capitals. Typefaces that are trendy can make your design look quickly dated. consider the life span of your project when choosing the typeface. Every designer has a dislike for a particular typeface—ask around and heed the warnings.

# Formats

The format of paragraphs affects the overall design as well as the readability of the text.

**Justified** type refers to lines of text in which all of the lines are the same length. The left and right margins are virtually straight edges—gorgeous. This is the common format for books and newspapers. It is considered the most legible format, good for reading with speed and ease—as long as the columns are not too narrow or too wide. A general guideline is to make your columns 50–70 characters wide. Justified copy is considered easier to read than unjustified copy, as the eye always knows where the line begins and ends. It also gives an orderly, elegant appearance to the page.

Life shrinks
or expands
in proportion to
one's courage.
*Anaïs Nin*

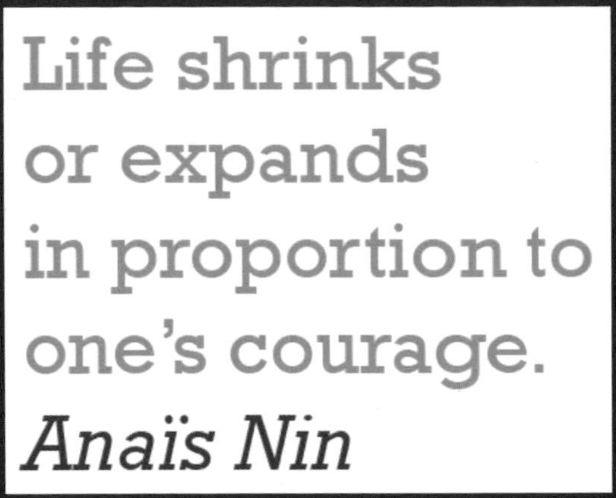

## Objectives
With this exercise, you will build software skills for using type and develop your ability to choose and combine fonts.

## To Do
Set this quote three times, following the typographic rules from earlier in this chapter: "Life shrinks or expands in proportion to one's courage"—Anaïs Nin.

### 1 Draw a text box
Start Illustrator and open a new document by choosing File > New. In the new document window, name the file "typedesign1" and make it letter size. Click OK. A new, blank document will appear on your screen.

Choose the Type tool from the toolbox.

Place your cursor on the file window, then click and drag to draw a rectangle with the Type tool.

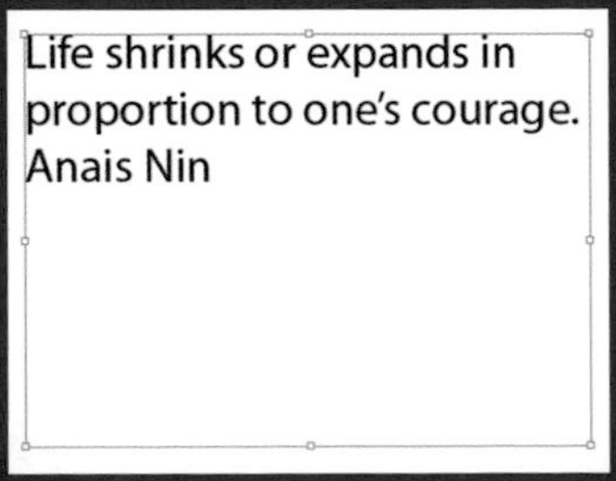

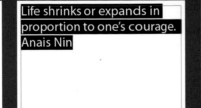

### 2 Add your copy
Type the quote into the text frame, using proper punctuation for this part of the exercise. Then select the text with your Type tool.

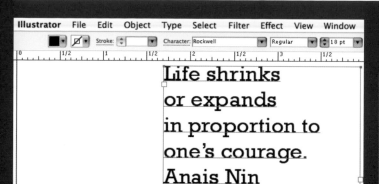

### 3 Format the copy

In the Control Bar typography options, choose an appropriate typeface, set the size to about 18 pts. and the format to left-aligned. (If the Control Bar is not visible, choose Window > Control Bar.) This example uses Rockwell, but if it's not on your computer, choose another Slab Serif font.

### 4 Italicize the name

Select "Anais Nin" with the Type tool, then change regular to italic in the font style window on the Control Bar.

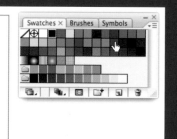

### 5 Change the colors

Select her name with the Type tool and change it to blue by clicking on the blue square in the Swatch window. (If the Swatch window is not visible, choose Windows > Swatch.) Select the quote with your Type tool and click on the orange square in the swatch window.

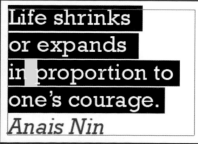

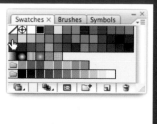

### 6 Add a special character
Refine your text by changing the "i" to an "ï."

Select the "i" with the Type tool, then choose Type > Glyphs.

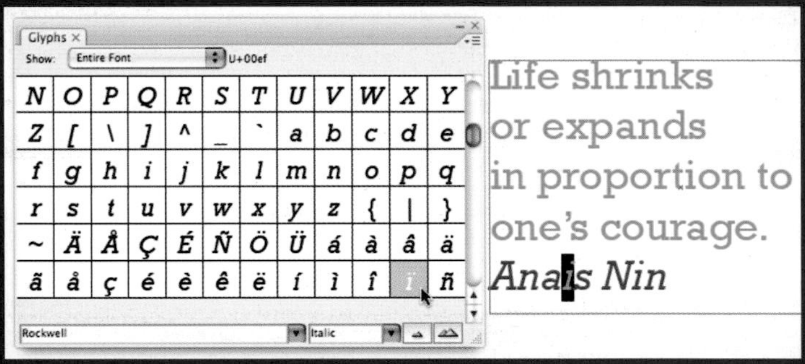

### 7 Double click on "ï" to change the symbol.

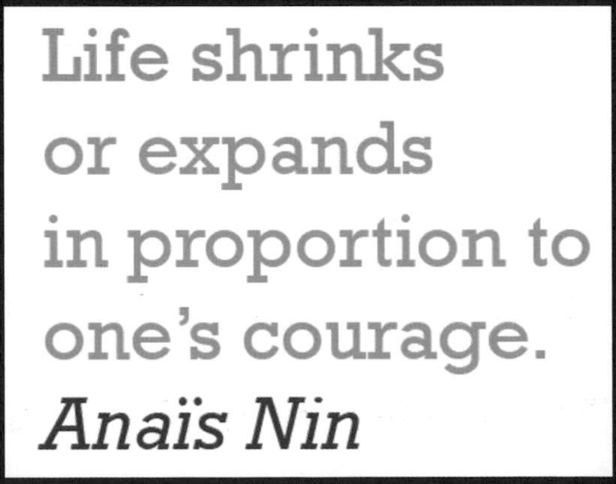

Life shrinks
or expands
in proportion to
one's courage.
*Anaïs Nin*

### 8 Click your cursor away from the blue box, to view your quote without the type frame.

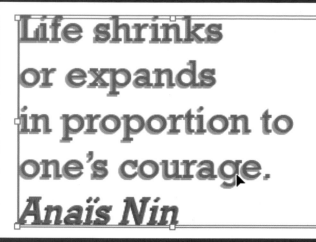

## 9 Design two more

Try alternative styles that enhance the message. Click on the text box with the black Selection tool. Press Command + C to copy, then press Command + V twice to paste two more type boxes. The second copy will paste directly over the first copy. Use the black Selection tool to move the duplicates away from each other on the page.

Select the type in the second box and set an alternative typeface, size, format, and color. To modify the proportions of the type box, use the black Selection tool. Click and hold a corner control button, then drag to adjust the size of the type box.

## 10 Modify the fonts

Highlight all of the text in the box, including the words you can't see, by pressing Command + A. The tiny red square in the lower right indicates there is more text than is visible. You can reduce the type size or increase the text-box size to accommodate your design.

Change the font, style, size, format, and color as in steps 3, 4, and 5. The versions below use Zapfino, 36 pts., left-aligned format, Futura, Light, 18 pts., centered format., and Gill Sans Ultra Bold, 16 pts., right-aligned format. Try your own font choices.

### Tip

Did you notice the unusual placement of the period in the example at bottom right? This technique, called hanging punctuation, is used by skilled designers to give blocks of text very clean vertical margins. You can achieve this in right-aligned text blocks by adding spaces at the ends of the first and third lines. Give it a try.

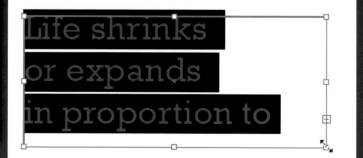

*Life*
shrinks or expands
in proportion to
one's courage.
Anaïs Nin

**Life shrinks or expands
in proportion to one's courage.**
**Anaïs Nin**

# 11 Printing

Well done. Now save your designs and print. Save and Print commands are on the File menu, or press Command + S to save, then Command + P to print.

**Tip**

Notice that the appearance of your designs on paper differs somewhat from their gorgeous appearance on the screen. Printed versions always appear a bit different. Use this knowledge to your advantage and preview your work in printed format before finalizing. Make adjustments to your quotation designs to refine the relationships, then save and reprint.

Life shrinks or expands in proportion to one's
c
o
u
r
a
g
e

● Anaïs Nin

# 12 Break the rules

On your own now—set this quote three more times, breaking the typographic rules to express the meaning of the words. These designs were created by students Brian Forte, Alex Moore, and William Loo.

**Tip**

The capital letters of the word LIFE (below) were adjusted with kerning. You can adjust the space between capital letters and punctuation by placing your cursor between a letter pair; then hold the Option key down, and press the left or right arrows on the keyboard to increase or decrease the spacing. Professionals will kern the letters in a logo or in an all-caps title, but we never kern lowercase letters because as the space between letters increases, identifying each word becomes more difficult.

# Design Project 1: Lyrical Layouts

Set the lyrics of a song or a poem to demonstrate a sophisticated understanding of typography and layout. Use 10–20 lines of text, the artist's name, and the title.

1— Select a poem or lyrics with 10–20 lines.
2— Identify a typeface that reflects the nature of the words for the title and another typeface that contrasts and has high legibility for the body of the text.
3— Set the text following the Type Tips and format guidelines.

These projects are by students Alessandra Epstein and Marc Hadjibay.

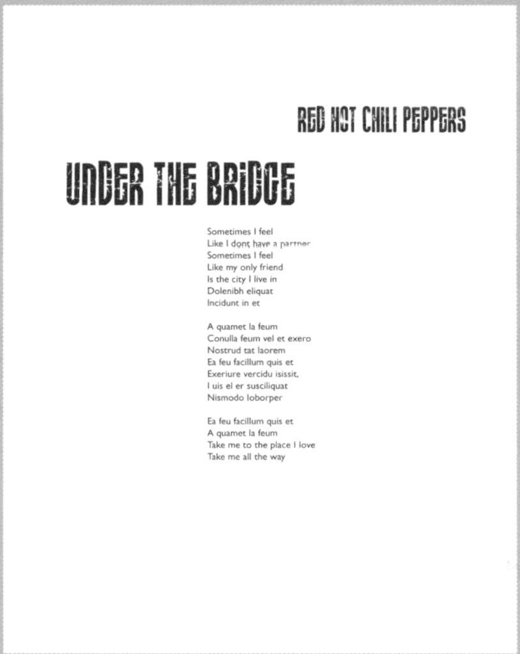

## Blow Blow Thou Winter Wind

**William Shakespeare**

Blow, blow, thou winter wind.
Thou art not so unkind
As man's ingratitude;
Thy tooth is not so keen
Because thou art not seen,
Although thy breath be rude.
Heigh-ho! sing heigh-ho! unto the green holly:
Most friendship is feigning, most loving mere folly:
Then, heigh-ho! the holly!
This life is most jolly.

Freeze, freeze, thou bitter sky,
Thou dost not bite so nigh
As benefits forgot:
Though thou the waters warp,
Thy sting is not so sharp
As friend remember'd not.
Heigh-ho! sing heigh-ho! unto the green holly:
Most friendship is feigning, most loving mere folly:
Then, heigh-ho! the holly!
This life is most jolly.

## RED HOT CHILI PEPPERS

### UNDER THE BRIDGE

Sometimes I feel
Like I don¡t have a partner
Sometimes I feel
Like my only friend
Is the city I live in
Dolenibh eliquat
Incidunt in et

A quamet la feum
Conulla feum vel et exero
Nostrud tat laorem
Ea feu facillum quis et
Exeriure vercidu isissit,
I uis el er suscibiquat
Nismodo loborper

Ea feu facillum quis et
A quamet la feum
Take me to the place I love
Take me all the way

# Design + Software Skills 3.2:
## Illustrator Shape and Type on a Path

## Objectives
Learn to use advanced type and drawing tools.

## To Do
Create a typographic target using the word "TARGET," a circle, and the Type on a Path tool.

### 1 Draw a circle
Open a new letter-size file using the File > New window. Select the Ellipse tool by clicking and holding your mouse over the Rectangle tool. Once the Ellipse tool is selected, take your finger off the mouse.

Draw a perfect circle by holding the Shift key as you click and drag the Ellipse tool on the page. Make the circle about 4 inches (10 cm) across.

Press Command + R to show rulers at the top of the file.

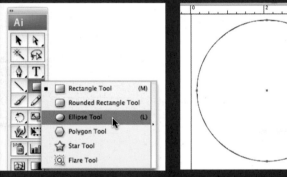

### 2 Type on the circle
Click and hold your mouse over the regular Type tool in the toolbox to select the Type on a Path tool.

Click the cursor at the top point in the circle.

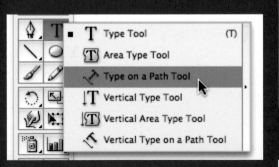

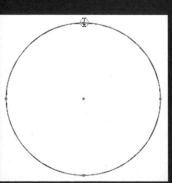

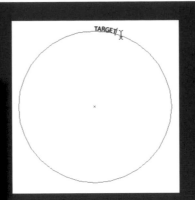

# 3

## Format the text

Type "TARGET." All capital letters will give your type design a more uniform edge.

Still using the Type tool, select the entire word. Then set the font to Myriad, style to bold, and size to 18 pts. If Myriad is not on your computer, choose another sans-serif font.

Change the color to red by clicking on the red square in the Swatch window.

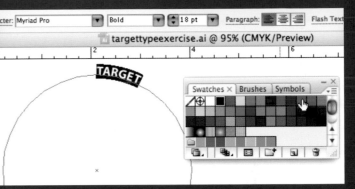

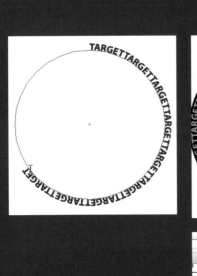

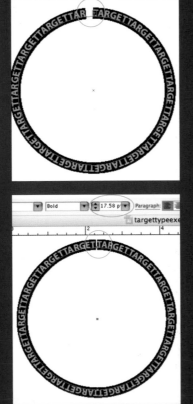

# 4

## Copy, paste, and adjust

Using your keyboard shortcuts, press Command + C and Command + V to copy and paste the word "TARGET" around the circle. Notice that the last paste doesn't fit perfectly. Adjust this by selecting the entire circle of text with the Type tool.

Modify the font point size so that the entire word fits. Typically the adjustment is only fractional but this minor modification makes for a better overall design (your point size will probably differ from the number shown here).

# 5 Copy a smaller circle

Choose the black Selection tool and click on the circle.

Then, place your cursor over the Scale tool (circled on the toolbox) and click twice to open the Scale window. Type "85%" in the Uniform Scale window and press the Copy button.

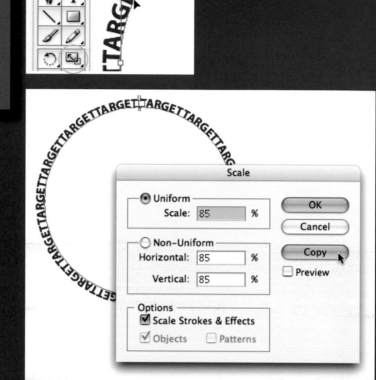

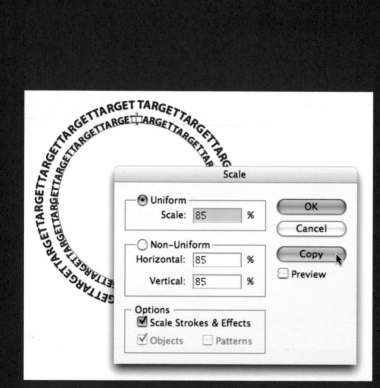

# 6 Build the target

Repeat the scale and copy process to create several circles. Double click on the Scale tool, keep the percentage at 85%, and press Copy for each circle.

Nice work.

# Design + Software Skills 3.3:
## Illustrator Pen and Area Type Tools

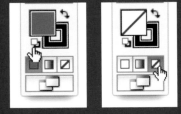

## Objectives
You will learn to draw with the Pen tool and fill shapes with text. You'll also learn new uses for the Rotate tool.

## To Do
Draw several triangles and rectangles using the Pen tool. Next, draw an arrow shape and use the Area Type tool to fill it with text. You will copy and rotate the arrow to create a new form.

### 1 Prepare to draw
Open a new file, letter size. Click on the default color squares, just below the fill and stroke colors in the toolbox. This puts the default colors, white and black, into the fill and stroke squares.

Click on the red diagonal-lined square, just below the large color squares, to modify the fill color to no fill color.

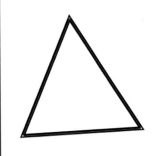

### 2 Draw a shape
Select the Pen tool to draw a triangle using three clicks of the mouse. Click once, take your finger off the mouse, and move the cursor to draw a diagonal line. Click again, take your finger off the mouse, and move the cursor to create the second line of a triangle. Click on the first point to complete a triangular shape.

## 3 Practice

Draw several triangles. Try drawing rectangles and polygons.

After you've filled the page with shapes, press Command + A to select all of the shapes in the file, then hit the Delete key to clear the workspace.

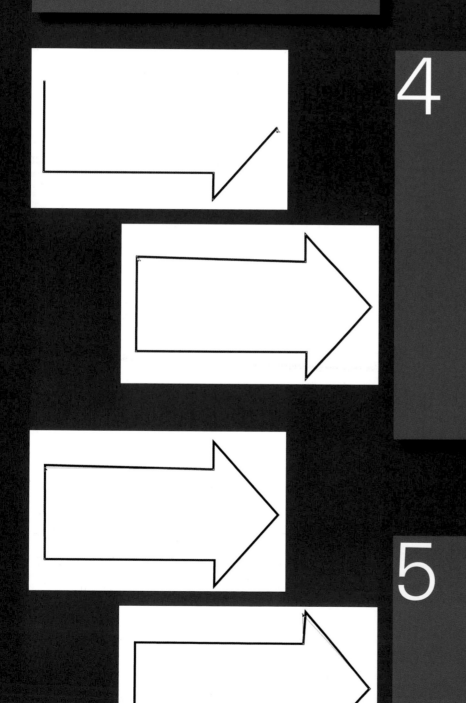

## 4 Draw an arrow

Draw an arrow shape with eight clicks of the mouse.
— a. On the left of the page, click once, move the mouse down about 2 inches (5 cm).
— b. Click and release, then move the mouse to the right about 4 inches (10 cm).
— c. Click and release, and move the mouse down a short distance.
— d. Click and release, and move the mouse diagonally up, to make the arrow point.
— e. Click and release, and move the mouse diagonally upward toward the left.
— f. Click and release, and move the mouse down a small amount.
— g. Click and release, and move the mouse to the left.
— h. Click on the beginning point to complete the arrow shape.

## 5 Adjustments

Once the entire shape is drawn, you can use the white Direct Selection tool to click on specific points and adjust the overall shape of the arrow.

### Tip

If you have trouble selecting a particular point with the Direct Selection tool, it's because the entire object is already selected. Click off the shape, then click exactly where you expect to find a point on the line.

# 6  Type the text

Select the Area Type tool. Click at the highest point on the shape. Type the phrase "Who else is gonna bring you a broken arrow?" (Tender lyrics from Robbie Robertson.)

| T | Type Tool | (T) |
| T | Area Type Tool | |
| T | Type on a Path Tool | |
| T | Vertical Type Tool | |
| T | Vertical Area Type Tool | |
| T | Vertical Type on a Path Tool | |

# 7  Format the text

Select the text and modify the font, size, and color. This example is Rosewood, 6 pts. Rosewood provides a dense texture. If it's not on your computer, try a bold serif font. Select the formatted text with the Type tool, and copy and paste to fill the shape.

Type   Select   Filter   Effect   View   Window   Help

Character: Rosewood Std   Fill   6 pt   Paragraph:

**WHO
ELSE IS
GONNA
BRING YOU A
BROKEN ARROW?**

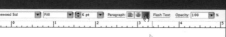

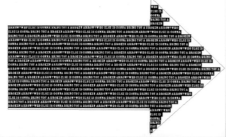

# 8  Change the alignment

While the Type tool is selected, press Command + A to select all of the text. Select right-aligned paragraph format. Notice how this fills the shape more distinctly on the right. Try the left format for comparison.

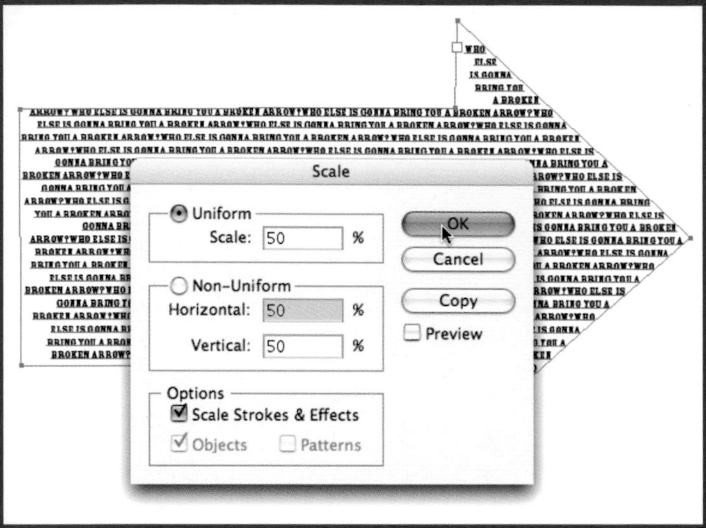

### Scale

Uniform
Scale: 50 %

Non-Uniform
Horizontal: 50 %
Vertical: 50 %

Options
☑ Scale Strokes & Effects
☑ Objects    ☐ Patterns

OK
Cancel
Copy
☐ Preview

## 9 Resize

Reduce the size of the arrow. Double click on the Scale tool, then type "50" into the Uniform Scale window. Confirm that the Option Scale Strokes & Effects is checked. Press OK.

## 10 Rotate and copy

Make a mirror copy of the arrow: click on the arrow with the Selection tool, then double click on the Rotate tool to bring up the rotate window. Type "180" into the Angle box, then press Copy (not the OK button).

Using the black Selection tool, click on the new arrow and move it so that it faces the first arrow.

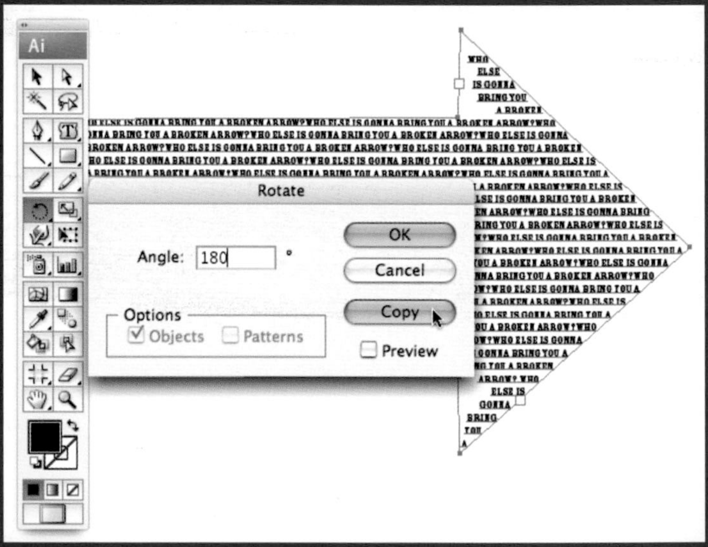

### Rotate

Angle: 180 °

Options
☑ Objects    ☐ Patterns

OK
Cancel
Copy
☐ Preview

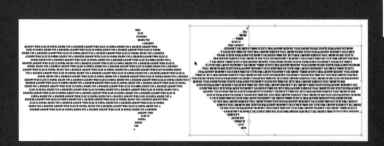

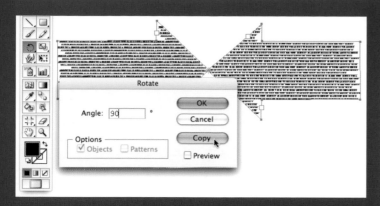

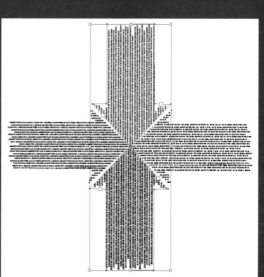

# 11 Rotate and copy

Hold the Shift key and select both arrows with the Selection tool. Double click on the Rotate tool. Type "90" into the Angle box, then press Copy (not the OK button). Move the two new arrows to construct a new shape.

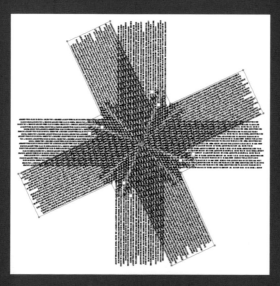

# 12 Finishing off

Hold the Shift key and click on all four arrows with the black Selection tool. Now click on the Rotate tool and move the cursor to freely rotate the entire shape.

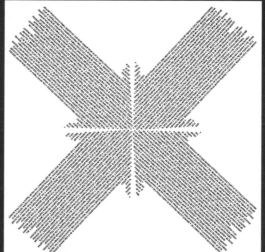

# Design + Software Skills 3.4:
## Illustrator Pen Tool, Curves, and Type on Paths

## Objectives
You will learn to draw curved lines using the Pen tool.

## To Do
Draw a wave using the Pen tool and use the Type on a Path tool to line it with "Mahalo," the Hawaiian word for thanks.

**1** ### Draw a curved line
Open a new file, letter size. As in exercise 3.3, set the Fill Color to None and Stroke Color to Black.

Select the Pen tool and draw a wavy line with four points. Click on the left of the page, then move the cursor about an inch (2.5 cm) to the right. Click and hold the mouse button as you drag to the lower right. A curved line will appear.

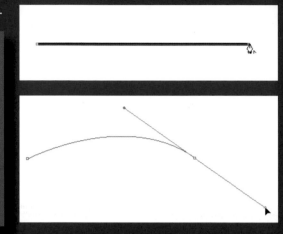

**2** Click again, about an inch (2.5 cm) to the right, and release the mouse button. This line's curve will mirror the previous curve.

Click again, and hold the mouse button as you make another point, dragging to the right to create the curve.

**3** Click again another inch (2.5 cm) away. You've drawn a wave. Don't expect perfection initially—you can undo (Command + Z) as many times as you like to practice your curved lines.

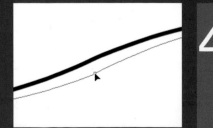

**4** ### Adjustments
Professionals fine-tune by clicking on points in the line to make minor adjustments. Select the Direct Selection tool. Click on the line to make it active so that you can see the control points. Click off, then click on one of the tiny blue squares and drag to adjust the position of the point in the line.

## 5 Adjustments

Notice the diagonal lines that run off the points on the line. These handles are used to adjust the depth of the curve. Click on the tiny blue square and drag right or left to make the curve shallower or deeper.

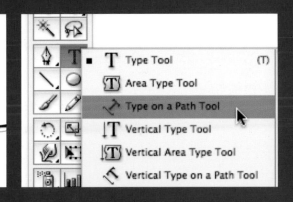

## 6 Add and format text

When you're satisfied with your wavy line, select the Type on a Path tool and click at the beginning of the line.

Type "Mahalo." Choose a typeface, size, and color. This example uses Zapfino, 12 pts.; make it blue. Zapfino has a casual elegance and lovely ascenders that create a varying height to the curve. If it's not on your computer, try another script.

## 7 Finishing off

Highlight the text, then copy and paste (Command + C; Command + V) to fill the line. Aloha.

# Design + Software Skills 3.5: Illustrator Convert Type to Shapes

Kick

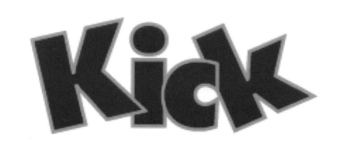

## Objectives

Convert type into shapes to expand their design possibilities as graphic elements.

## To Do

Type a word and make shapes from the text. Free rotate the letters and adjust their overlapping positions.

## 1 Add and format text

Open a new file, letter size.

Select the Type tool and type "Kick." Format the type; this is Futura, Extra Bold, 72 pts., Red Fill, Orange Stroke and Stroke is set to 2 pts. This typeface is big and dynamic. If it's not on your computer, try another bold sans-serif font.

Stroke: 2 pt
Character: Futura
Extra Bold
72 pt
Kick

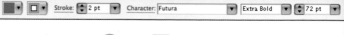

## 2 Convert the text to shapes

Click on the text box with the black Selection tool.

Choose Type > Create Outlines. After you've chosen this option, the letters cannot be edited as text.

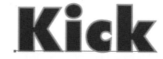

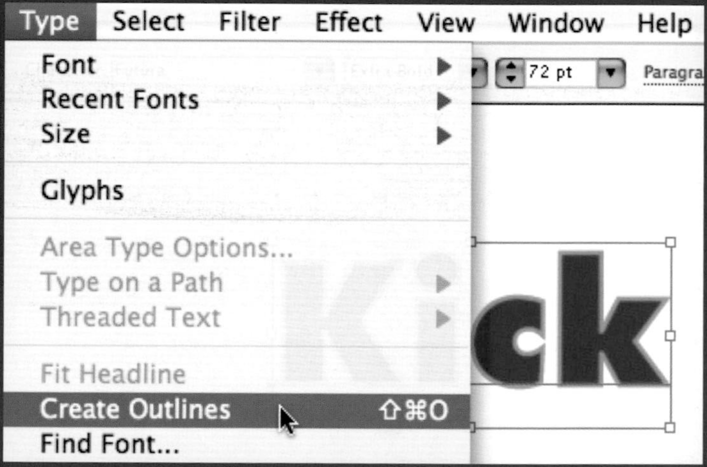

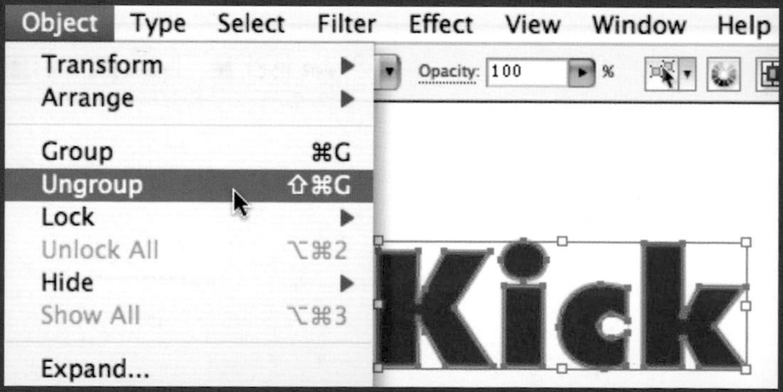

Type
Select
Filter
Effect
View
Window
Help
Font
Recent Fonts
Size
Glyphs
Area Type Options...
Type on a Path
Threaded Text
Fit Headline
Create Outlines
⇧⌘O
Find Font...
72 pt
ck

Object
Type
Select
Filter
Effect
View
Window
Help
Transform
Arrange
Group
⌘G
Ungroup
⇧⌘G
Lock
Unlock All
⌥⌘2
Hide
Show All
⌥⌘3
Expand...
Opacity: 100 %
Kick

## 3 Ungroup the shapes

While the box is still selected, choose Object > Ungroup.

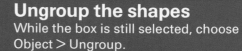

# 4  Rotate the shapes
Click off the entire word.

Select the Rotate tool, click on the K and drag your mouse to rotate the letter. Click on the other letters and slightly rotate them too.

| Object | Type | Select | Filter | Effect | View | Window |
|---|---|---|---|---|---|---|
| Transform | | ▶ | | | | |
| Arrange | | ▶ | | | | |
| Group | | ⌘G | | | | |
| Ungroup | | ⇧⌘G | | | | |
| Lock | | ▶ | | | | |
| Unlock All | | ⌥⌘2 | | | | |
| Hide | | ▶ | | | | |
| Show All | | ⌥⌘3 | | | | |
| Expand... | | | | | | |
| Expand Appearance | | | | | | |

Bring to Front    ⇧⌘]
Bring Forward    ⌘]
Send Backward    ⌘[
Send to Back    ⇧⌘[

Send to Current Layer

# 5  Adjustments
Make the K and the c appear in front of the other letters. Hold the Shift key down and click on the K and c to select both letters. Then choose Object > Arrange > Bring to Front.

Good work. Now try this with your name.

# Design Project 2:
# Slang Type

On your own now, use typeface and color to express the meaning of one of your favorite slang words. (Keep it clean!) These designs were done by students Kim Richardson, Haruka Sawano, Allie Weinberger, and Alex Cheng. Notice that no pictorial images or geometric shapes are needed for these expressive designs.

# Design Project 3:
# Lyrical Layouts

Create a second layout using the lyrics or poem from the earlier project (see p. 83). Experiment with type to express the meaning of the words. Using type forms as graphic elements has an inspiring history. Here is French poet Guillaume Apollinaire's "Il Pleut" ("It's Raining") from 1918. The letters sprinkle like rain down the page.

    For this project, use only type and other keyboard symbols, not images. Since you practiced the traditional type design guidelines in the first project, deviate from a few here if it helps to convey your feelings about the words. Use the type drawing techniques that you learned in exercises 3.2–3.5 to construct your design.

    Students Liz Kauff, Antonette Naclerio, and Kim Rescigno designed these projects.

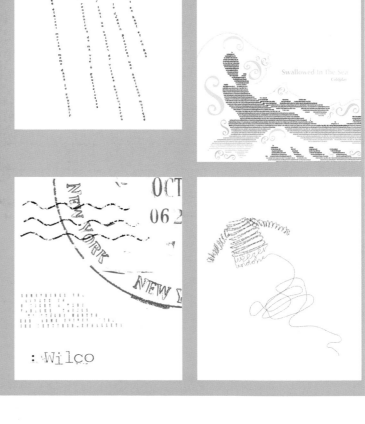

# Major Points Summary

— The language of typography includes many useful terms that are illustrated in the diagram at the beginning of this chapter (see page 66).
— The term "typeface" refers to the overall character set of a particular design. It is used to describe the design of the letters.
— "Font" refers to the complete set of characters in any given size and style, and the software version of a typeface.
— The major categories of typefaces are serifs, sans serifs, scripts, and novelty.
— Serifs are the little notches at the ends of letters.
— Serif typefaces have been in use for over 2,000 years. They are considered conservative in style and highly legible.
— Fonts designed by typographic groundbreakers such as Garamond, Baskerville, and Bodoni remain popular hundreds of years after they were created.
— Serif typeface categories include Old Style, Transitional, Modern, and Slab Serif.
— Designers often combine two typefaces on a page; avoid combining typefaces from the same category because they look too similar and their use can appear to be a mistake.
— Leading contemporary typographers such as Matthew Carter and the team at House Industries often design with computer displays in mind, but also use hand-drawn, traditional media in their designs.
— Mono-weight letters are more legible on screen displays.
— Novelty typefaces provide designs with immediate tone, but only use them for titles or small amounts of type because they can lack legibility.
— Type families provide variety for a typeface: roman or regular, italic, bold, and condensed are typical varieties. They can be combined effectively because they share characteristics such as x-heights.
— Justified type formats align on the left and right edges. This format has an orderly appearance and is highly readable.
— Left-aligned type format is also very easy to read. The edges align on the left and have a ragged right edge, minimizing hyphenation.
— Right-aligned type can be used for a few lines of type to balance a page. A complete paragraph or more would be unreadable, as the eye never knows where the next line begins.
— Centered type is a formal format. Take advantage of the pauses created by the line separations and make meaningful, or at least logical, line breaks.
— Asymmetrical type layouts really slow the eye down, so use them thoughtfully.
— Contour formats align to the edge of an image. Make the margin between the text and image consistent throughout.
— Type tips for fonts, contrast, and format are summarized (see page 77).

# Software Skills Summary

— Illustrator type and drawing skills.
— Keyboard shortcuts.
— Skills: text frames, type options bar, color swatch window, glyphs, kerning, type on paths, type in shapes, default colors, draw curves, convert type to outlines, ungroup images, hanging punctuation.
— Tools covered in depth: pen, direct selection, type, area type, path type, rotate, ellipse, scale.

# Recommended Readings

Once you've mastered these typography fundamentals, continue developing your knowledge by consulting other books on typography. I highly recommend *Type and Typography* by Phil Baines and Andrew Haslam, which reveals type-related gems from phonemes to font files. Robin Williams has written several charming books on type and layout for beginning designers. To read more about the history of graphic design, find anything written by Alston Purvis, in particular *Meggs' History of Graphic Design*. For even more detailed history on type, sprinkled with useful tips, read *Stop Stealing Sheep and Find Out How Type Works* by Erik Spiekermann and E.M. Ginger. For contemporary inspiration, check out Roger Fawcett-Tang's *New Typographic Design*.

# Images

4

**Milton Glaser**
**Bob Dylan poster**
**1967**

Throughout his fifty-year career, New York designer Milton Glaser explored new graphic techniques and influences. Consequently, his work never revealed a particular visual style. All of his designs were conceptually rich and often witty. In this iconic poster, Dylan's hair is inspired by Art Nouveau arabesques, the flat colors by Japanese prints, and the black outlines by comic books. The black profile is a bit of a tease—the details must be filled in by the viewer's imagination. You can thank Milton Glaser for the I ♥ NY logo and inspiring a vast number of variations.

**What makes you stop, look, then read a graphic design? My bet—the image grabbed you.**
**Designs use photographs and illustrations to get our attention, and it is only then, after we're hooked, that they can really provide information. A well-chosen image communicates a great deal: subject, mood, issue, humor, and/or information. An amalgamation of photos—old and new—illustration, icons, and text combine for a compelling image in this "Designed Diary."**

Great design relies on excellent images. Students have ready access to digital photographs, yet have few guidelines for their selection and use. This chapter will give tips on finding the *best* image for the job. You'll learn the meaning of those baffling file formats and you'll discover how to reproduce images at the best possible quality. Let's go beyond settling for the first image that matches our subject—let's get the ideal image for our design.

And, let's go beyond using photography exclusively. Illustrations can be produced in a variety of mediums: ink, pencil, collage, digital, paint, cut paper… the list goes on. The handmade quality of illustrations can be advantageous with many subjects.

# Illustration

When are illustrations more beneficial to a design than photography? Illustrators can *eliminate details*. Due to the minimal background and clothing, this image can be interpreted in many ways, perhaps allowing more viewers to relate their own experiences to the characters shown.

This page Original sketches showing front, side and rear views of Prada's sculptural-style shoes.    Opposite, top Two views of a black leather peep-toe court shoe with decorative looped wedge and an eye-catching slit in Brazilian hardwood heel. bottom Two views of a black and aubergine-coloured leather court shoe featuring the designer's signature slit in heel made from stacked Brazilian hardwoods. The upper also features a contrasting sculptural leather detail.

Many subjects and processes cannot be photographed. Medical illustrators produce images that are essential to the health care industry—their work shows details of body parts, functions, and chemical processes. Keith Kasnot is a medical illustrator who works with software and traditional media to produce gorgeous images that visualize things we can't actually see. This anatomically correct 3D model was created with Maya animation software—the heart actually beats. A still image was captured from the animation and Keith added details in Photoshop.

On the other hand, illustration can be used to enhance details. Notice how the complex leather structure of these glamorous shoes is more apparent in the drawings than the photos in Sue Huey and Rebecca Proctor's book *New Shoes*.

Illustrations can have a timeless quality. Photographs of people may look dated quickly because of changes in fashion. It's not just clothing—hairstyles, makeup, even mustaches—can date an image. If your product is supposed to have a long shelf life, consider using illustration. This street scene looks trendy, yet the details do not date the image.

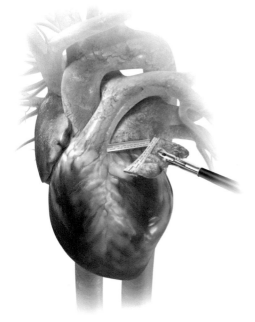

For dealing with life in the urban (and suburban) wild, we offer these funky tops and jackets. Lightweight but warm, they're perfect for smoothing things out when the weather gets rough. They're part of the Levi's' World's Finest' collection — tops featuring designs and styles from around the globe. And there's only one place to find them in the U.S.: your Original Levi's Store.

Button up, baby! Available only at your Original Levi's Store.

ORIGINAL JEANS FOR ORIGINAL PEOPLE

SPICY ORANGE UTILITY JACKET  When the temperature drops, turn up the color. One part parka and two parts groovy auto mechanic, this red jacket looks cool shaken or stirred.

ZIP POLO SHIRT  Whether you wear it out with your friends or in with your folks, this comfortable pullover is the ultimate in casual-guy cool. Available in any color...so long as it's black.

FLAT-KNIT SHERPA SWEATER  Since faux fur is all the rage, this groovy little cotton sweater features a fleecy sherpa collar— so you'll look hot no matter how low the temperature gets.

ZIP CARDIGAN  A hip take on the classic cardigan. Slim fitting and snuggly warm, this zippy sweater is perfect for navigating rugged hills or jam-packed malls.

Photography is now so ubiquitous that the mere use of illustration attracts attention. You can use it to provide your designs with a fresh look. Notice how handwritten text complements rustic figures in Robert Maganck's Folk Festival poster. This not only adds texture—the integration of the copy with the image engages and informs the audience.

Steve Snider's book cover design for *The Preservationist* has an antique look. Titled *The Flood* in the UK, David Maine's novel is about the goings-on in Noah's ark as told by his family. The two-part cover reveals animals beneath surging waters. This design was honored with the Victoria and Albert Museum Illustration award. The artist, Bill Sanderson, used scraperboard technique, which mimics wood engraving.

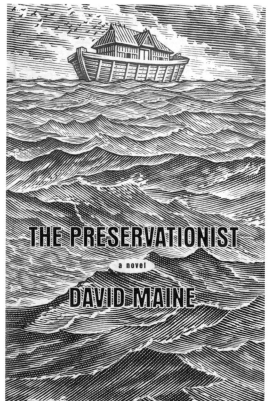

Fantasy images are made possible by the use of illustration. Styles vary with the themes, from photorealistic science fiction to gouache cartoons. Here illustrator Dean Gorrisen's charmingly improbable scene makes an appealing poster announcing Krispy Kreme doughnuts' arrival in Australia.

The handmade quality of images is often used to provide notes of authenticity, humor, and character. This illustration serves as the website menu for illustrator Jennifer Taylor's Paper Dog Studio. As the dog-cursor moves, rooms light up and labels reveal the menu items.

**Herbert Matter**
**Swiss tourism poster**
**1934**

Herbert Matter was a lucky young man. He studied painting in Paris under Fernand Léger and later worked on posters with A.M. Cassandre. At age twenty-five he returned home and worked for the Swiss National Tourist Office where he applied photomontage and Modernist techniques to poster design. Matter pioneered the use of collages with dynamic scale changes and integration of type and image. Notice all of the ways this poster shows a sense of movement and evokes the Swiss locale: Swiss crosses overlap multiple planes, skiers speed over diagonal white lines that cover the mountains, even the type is slanted for downward movement. This poster shows Matter's innovative integration of areas of color into black and white photography. Matter's new approach explored reducing photographs to visual symbols, then combining images and words in surprising ways.

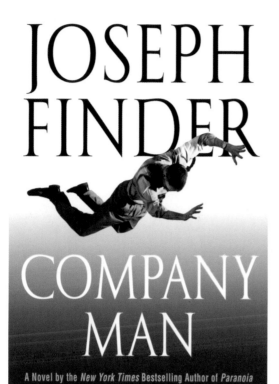

JOSEPH
FINDER

COMPANY
MAN

A Novel by the *New York Times* Bestselling Author of *Paranoia*

# Photography

Have you ever found yourself examining an image, wondering whether it is an illustration or a photograph? How about the poor fellow on this book cover, or this building image? Look closely at this page from a Miami architecture magazine. What initially appears to be photos are computer illustrations of apartments yet to be built. The line between illustration and photography has blurred with the capabilities and widespread use of digital photo editing software.

Until just the last decade, there was a long-standing trust in photography. Most people believed that photographs could not lie—they were considered factual records. Police departments, for instance, employ professional photographers who record crime-scene evidence as fact for use during trials. Now, digital technology has changed the reputation of photography as truth.

Readers were outraged several years ago when a revered international magazine modified a photo of the Giza pyramids so that they appeared closer together—simply to fit the format of the cover. That's messing with one of the greatest architectural feats on earth to suit the needs of a magazine cover! We can make the sky over a resort appear bluer. Is that an ethical choice when the locale is typically rainy? Be thoughtful with your choices and cognizant of the role of photography-as-truth when using this powerful software.

**M.E.:** One of my inspirations – I can't say if Revuelta thought about it or not – were the local two and three story garden apartments. The MiMo type buildings with long balconies. They reflect a certain climate in the city that I wanted my building to reflect as well.

We ended up splitting the core of the building to make sure even the middle units run front to back, giving this building that feel but on a larger scale.

**H.M.:** *What's the end result of that split?*

**M.E.:** Well, we have two large 1800 square foot plus flats on either end.

**H.M.:** *Is this flow-through style also a reference to those garden apartments from the 50s and 60s where you could open the front and back windows and have a breeze blow through the house?*

**M.E.:** Yes, and here, the old "cat walk" becomes a service corridor, because another thing the split accomplished was to allow us private elevator lobbies within each apartment. That cat walk balcony can now also become a social connecting point… where two neighbors might meet each other.

I hate interior corridors, and with this building I've pretty much done away with them. I've been able to achieve a sort of "single-family-living" in a high-rise.

**H.M.:** *How many types of units are there at Cielo?*

**M.E.:** There are only two types. One we call Marina flats which are each 1880 square feet. The other is our townhouse unit, which have two floors. These have wonderful master baths with Roman tub and a shower with an enormous window. So you are bathing with a view of the Bay.

**H.M.:** *That's a fantastic idea. Looking at the plans, the balconies seem awfully generous as well.*

**M.E.:** Well, I wanted to create outdoor rooms, really. Places where friends could

"ONE OF MY INSPIRATIONS – I CAN'T SAY IF REVUELTA THOUGHT ABOUT IT OR NOT – WERE THE LOCAL TWO AND THREE STORY GARDEN APARTMENTS. THE MiMo TYPE BUILDINGS WITH LONG BALCONIES. THEY REFLECT A CERTAIN CLIMATE IN THE CITY THAT I WANTED MY BUILDING TO REFLECT AS WELL."

**HOME** MIAMI

17

# Resolution: High, Low, Good, Bad

Have you ever sat at the computer waiting, waiting, and waiting for images to appear on a website? The probable reason for the delay is the image file size is too large. As digital image resolution increases, image quality improves, but file size grows too. As this happens, software processing time increases. This has an effect on our work as we create designs and on how well the image is displayed in the final product.

The typical resolution values you'll see are 72 dpi and 300 dpi. Dpi, an abbreviation of dots per inch, refers to the number of dots of ink on printed paper. When printing, more dots of ink per inch create sharper images: there are typically 300 dots of ink per inch. Resolution refers to the dpi number and indicates the sharpness of the photo. We call 72 dpi low-res (low resolution) and 300 dpi hi-res (high resolution).

These numbers, 72 and 300, also correspond to ppi, or pixels per inch. Pixels are tiny squares of light emitting from your computer screen. There are 72 pixels across each inch of a typical computer screen.

Low-res images aren't always bad. Since most computers display images at a resolution of 72 ppi, these images look fine on computer screens. But the same image would look fuzzy when printed on a 300 dpi printer.

In general, digital images will be 72 dpi for screen displays and 300 dpi for printed publications. As you enter professional studios, these typical numbers may be modified depending on the media being produced. The dog on the left is 300 dpi; the photo on the right was saved at 72 dpi. Take a look and see where the image quality differs.

To have consistently high-quality image reproduction, print designers typically work with 300 dpi images. In professional situations, some images will be scanned at higher resolutions such as 1,200 or 2,400 dpi for the final printing. Even in this situation, the designer may create the layout using the 300 dpi image because it is a more reasonable file size while working in the software. When it is ready for press, a higher resolution version is linked to the file. You'll see that as our projects become more complex, the software will take longer to process the commands with large file sizes.

# TIFF, EPS, JPEG, GIF, PNG, and PDF File Formats

You've seen these terms—but *come on*, does anyone really know what they mean? Yes, good designers know these terms and understand how to use them to create better designs. You can too.

### High Quality (printing)
*TIFF (Tagged Image File Format)*
TIFFs are used for high-quality images that are to be printed. TIFFs are large files, they are often uncompressed. The term "uncompressed" means that none of the original image data is eliminated to make the file smaller when it is saved in this format. Consequently, TIFFs maintain high image resolution. All of the designs in this book were saved as 300 dpi TIFFs.

*EPS (Encapsulated Post Script)*
Similar to TIFFs, EPS files are uncompressed, high-quality images. Currently, they are used less commonly than TIFFs.

### Compression Formats (screen display)
*JPEG (Joint Photographic Experts Group)*
JPEGs are used for photographs and complex illustrations intended for screen displays. This is the most common compression file format. File compression results in smaller file sizes, but it eliminates some details. JPEG files can be saved with low, medium, and high quality. High-quality JPEG files will eliminate less information, but the file size will be bigger. After you save an image as a JPEG, you can't restore the original quality, so keep a copy of the original file; the file extension is often shortened to .jpg. All of the images of student projects on my website are saved as JPEGs.

*GIF (Graphics Interchange Format)*
This is a low-res, compressed file type for screen display only. GIFs are used for text, logos, and charts on websites. GIF compression eliminates variations of colors to reduce file size. GIFs are great for graphics that have few colors. All of the menu buttons on my website are saved as GIFs. Don't save photographs as GIFs because the compression will reduce smooth gradients to bands of colors.

*PNG (Portable Networks Graphics)*
PNGs can be used when you need transparency around a graphic. This is a compression file format.

*PDF (Portable Document Format—the Glorious Hybrid)*
PDF files accurately display all the characteristics of a design, even unique typefaces, without requiring the original software or fonts to be on the recipient's computer. They are used for sending designs via email, for large graphic and text documents that are available on websites, and also for cost-effective printing. PDFs can be compressed with low, medium, or high quality for screen or print; they are created and viewed using Adobe Acrobat software.

# Acquiring Digital Images

If you have a digital camera, you can capture your own digital images and import them into your computer with programs like iPhoto or Bridge. You can then export images as JPEGs or TIFFs for use in design software. Additionally, designers can retrieve images from the Internet in several ways or you can scan printed material. Here are suggestions for getting the best-quality images from these sources.

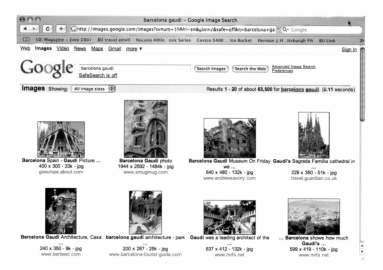

### Internet Images
By now you've probably used Google to search for images. For professional design purposes, the quality of images retrieved from Google can be mixed. Let's refine your search strategy to find better-quality images.

The first step in choosing high-quality images from Google is to look at the file-size information listed just below each thumbnail photo. You'll see several numbers below the image title. Let's focus on the second image in the top row: 1944 x 2592—1484k—jpg. The most important number is just before the file format—this is the file size: 1484k is 1.4 MB. This is a large file, which implies very good image quality. The other numbers are the image dimensions in pixels. A 300 dpi file has 300 pixels per inch. So, divide the dimensions by 300 and you'll learn that this example's dimensions are 6.48 x 8.64 inches (16.46 x 21.95 cm). Just by looking at the numbers we immediately know this image has good reproduction quality for print.

Many file sizes will be much smaller, especially when they're saved at 72 dpi, and therefore only suitable for screen display. The third image in the top row is labeled 640 x 480—132k—jpg. The clue to the 72 dpi resolution is the number 132k, much smaller than the previous example.

# Design + Software Skills 4.1:
## Image Banks and Photoshop Good Crop, Bad Crop

## Objectives
You will search an image bank for a photo and build Photoshop skills for modifying images. There are over a thousand image banks on the Internet. In this exercise, we'll use Masterfile, one of the largest independent stock image agencies in the world.

## To Do
Find the best photo that fits one of the descriptions on the right. Crop the image so that the content is enhanced, and try also to crop it so that the content is misleading. Why a bad crop? This is a quick and fun way to remind you to avoid cropping an image just so that it fits a format in a layout. Cropping can strengthen or weaken the impact of an image in your design.

## Choose one of these topics
— Time passing
— Couples in love
— Couples fighting
— Ugly animal
— Athletes in action

To acquire images in this exercise, use www.masterfile.com to search for photos. All Internet image banks use very similar search techniques.

**1**
### Search for photos
Go to www.masterfile.com. Type your search keywords into the window. Use keywords that narrow your search to find the best image for your topic.

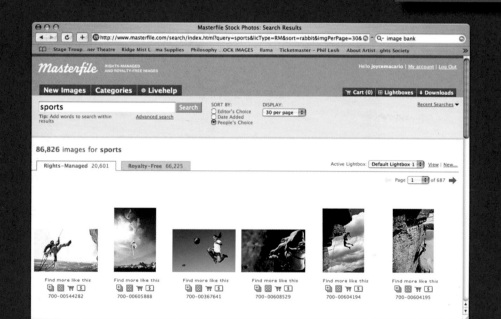

**2**
### Selecting
Browse through the thumbnails of matched images. If you don't see any you like, change your keyword selection. For example, I got more specific results from the phrase "sports extreme" than "sports."

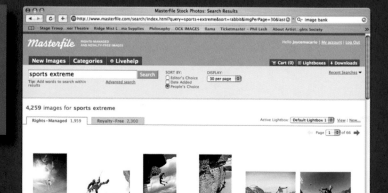

# 3 Previewing

Once you find a great image, click on it to enlarge your view. It opens in a preview window that provides prices, files sizes and rights information. Click on Prices to determine the cost to use the photograph for a specific purpose.

# 4 Pricing

Notice that just below the photo number is the term "rights-managed." This means that the price is determined using a calculation based on the photo's intended use. This includes the media in which it will appear, the client industry, the distribution, and duration of use. I used information about this book to determine the price that is shown in this screen.

## Tip

Image-bank photos are protected from illegal use with a logo watermark imposed on the image. When you register with Masterfile, you may use a watermark-free image for comping, as you see here. You can use a download of a low-res image from the websites to mock-up a design. A fee must be paid (typically by the client) for any commercial or non-educational use beyond the classroom.

## 5 Copy

Click on the enlarged photo, hold your mouse button down, and drag it to your desktop. Then open the file in Photoshop.

## 6 Crop

Now we'll do a Good Crop/Bad Crop exercise. First try the bad one. Crop your image so that the visual message is impaired. Choose the Crop tool from the toolbox. Drag the cursor over the image. A box appears over your photo and a gray outside border darkens the area that will be deleted.

Adjust the selection by pulling the control boxes on each edge of the image.

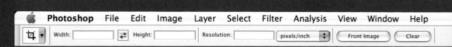

## 7 Crop

When satisfied, hit the Return key. The image has been permanently cropped to your selection. With this bad crop, the photo is less dramatic, the centered placement of the skier draws attention away from the majestic mountains.

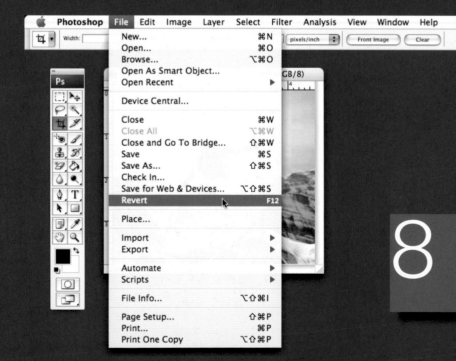

## 8 Revert

To go back to the last saved version of your image, choose File > Revert. Photoshop will bring back the original photo.

## 9 Crop

Now create a good crop to enhance the photo's message. You want a balanced image with the most compelling content to tell the story. Choose the Crop tool from the toolbox. Drag the cursor over the image. A box appears over your photo and a gray outside border darkens the area that will be deleted. Adjust the selection by pulling the control boxes on each edge of the image. When satisfied, hit the Return key. The image has been permanently cropped to your selection. When final, press Command + S to save your edited image.

## 10 Rule of Thirds

A traditional photography composition strategy is called the "Rule of Thirds." This proposes that you envision three columns and three rows across a photo. Place major horizontal and vertical features into the columns and the focal point near an intersection of the lines. In this photo, notice how the mountains fill the bottom row and the position of the skier on the grid. Expertly situated, the yellow skis and orange parka "pop" against the cool blue sky and mountains.

# Design + Software Skills 4.2:
# Photoshop Image Size

## Objectives
Learn how to use the Image Size window to evaluate image-size information and to resize a photo proportionately.

## To Do
Proportionately reduce the size of a stock photo.

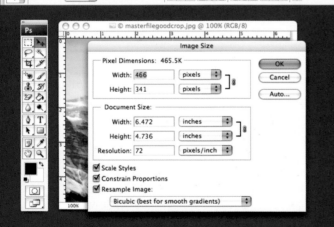

## 1 Image Size

For this exercise, use your recently cropped image or search for another photo from the topic list: Time passing | Couples in love | Couples fighting | Ugly animal | Athletes in action. If using a new image, choose the best image from your search results, click to see a larger version, and drag this low-res comp to the desktop. Open the image in Photoshop.

Then, choose Image > Image Size.

## 2 Image Size window

Look at the Image Size window to determine the dimensions of your comp. The top line lists the file memory size. A typical low-resolution comp will be 200 KB to 1 MB. This one is 465.5 K.

The next two lines list Pixel Dimensions, which are valuable for new-media designs such as websites that are measured in pixels. Document Size displays width and height in your choice of measurements used for print designs, such as inches and centimeters. Below these windows is the file Resolution. The Resolution for comps is usually 72 dpi, because it is for screen display and mock-up purposes. When a free comp is provided, its low resolution is another form of copyright protection. You would not prepare a professionally printed design with a 72 dpi resolution photo, the image quality would be too fuzzy. When you do acquire a hi-res image, the resolution will typically be 300 dpi and the file size listed at the top of this window will be many many megabytes.

### Tip
Some image banks, such as Masterfile, will provide hi-res files of photos to regular clients for comping purposes.

# Layout

## Think small.

Our little car isn't so much of a novelty any more.

A couple of dozen college kids don't try to squeeze inside it.

The guy at the gas station doesn't ask where the gas goes.

Nobody even stares at our shape.

In fact, some people who drive our little flivver don't even think 32 miles to the gallon is going any great guns.

Or using five pints of oil instead of five quarts.

Or never needing anti-freeze.

Or racking up 40,000 miles on a set of tires.

That's because once you get used to some of our economies, you don't even think about them any more.

Except when you squeeze into a small parking spot. Or renew your small insurance. Or pay a small repair bill. Or trade in your old VW for a new one.

Think it over.

© 1962 VOLKSWAGEN OF AMERICA, INC.

**Helmut Krone
and Julian Koenig
Volkswagen
advertisement
1960**

The NYC advertising agency Doyle Dane Bernbach broke all the norms of advertising. Instead of elaborate images and overbearing exclamations, they used white space and clever copy to get the reader's attention. Inspired by his work with designer Paul Rand, Bill Bernbach paired each copywriter with an art director, so design became integral with the creation of the message. Before this copy/art pairing, the writer wrote the copy and then sent it to the design department to do their best with it. These groundbreaking VW advertisements were developed in the new collaborative setting. In the days of large luxury cars as status symbols, the ads attracted attention not just with their clever headlines, but also with their vast areas of white space that emphasized the unusually small size of the original Beetle.

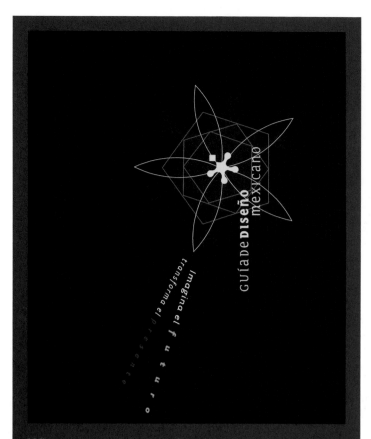

**Where do your eyes go first in this poster? Where do they go next? And then? An effective path layout leads our eyes through an entire design (even when we don't know the language). In this Mexican design poster we start at the yellow asterisk—the brightest object on the page is the focal point—before the position and colors of the text lead us through the rest of the path layout.**

Effective layouts grab the audience's attention and hold it until they've read through the entire design. Layouts are tools designers use to communicate a lot of information cohesively and aid the enjoyment and comprehension of publications. We'll explore two different layout strategies that create effective graphic design: the path and the grid.

# Path Layouts

A good path layout may look like an effortless, spontaneous solution. But it's not. In a path layout, the designer skillfully arranges the objects on the page so that the audience's eyes are brought through all of its contents in a meaningful sequence. This is a particularly effective approach for single-page designs such as print advertising and posters.

A good path starts with a focal point. This is the area of the page where the eyes go first: it attracts attention and encourages the viewer to look further. Let's face it, people are inundated with visual information. How do we get noticed without using nudity in every design?

Modernista!, a Boston-based agency, created the bottled-water advertisement below using path-layout strategies. There is a lot of movement in the photo; the unique vantage point of the swimmer intrigues us—she and the water look powerful. This could be visually overwhelming, but the activity is balanced by the calming white space on the right. The red shirt "pops" against the cool blue water, creating an effective focal point, then the product logo in the same red pulls our eye to the right. The tag line is integrated with the logo so we're more likely to read the copy. Finally, we notice the unusual placement of the web address. Our eyes are led through all of the information on the page, ensuring that the client's message is quickly and thoroughly communicated.

closer.

GAP

gap.com

Shop Gap three ways: go to gap.com, call 1.800.GAP.STYLE, or stop by any Gap store in the US.

## Focal Points

The focal point establishes an emphasis in the design that becomes an appealing entry to the path layout. To establish a focal point you can use contrast to:

— Make an object a bright color (as you see in the preceding example)
— Make the object dark, and everything around it light
— Emphasize a compelling image or word
— Make one object sharp and all other elements softly focused
— Give the object a different texture or gloss
— Make the object color and the rest black and white
— Change the value of an object to create contrast with the background
— Place an object in an unusual direction or position on the page (also used here)
— Isolate the object on the page

This last tip is interesting; areas of white space have worked wonders, as we saw in the classic VW Beetle advertisements. In this Modernista!-designed Gap ad, nearly half the page is empty. This becomes an effective focal point—a large blank area in print is so unusual that it tweaks our curiosity. We search the page for the rationale and find intriguing copy, then we see the image—by now we're hooked. So we move through the rest of the layout and read the supporting copy. Now that we're informed and have seen the product, we're more likely to shop for it. A successful path effectively communicates information for your clients.

### Integrating Type and Image

Place your headline near the focal point, or along the path, to integrate the text with the image and ensure that the audience will read your copy.

In another ad by Modernista!, the focal point is a skier whose ski tips lead us directly into the headline. The supporting copy is placed at the end of the main text, where our eyes are coaxed to linger by three more ski tips.

There are many ways to establish a good focal point, but remember, it's part of a whole. If it's too strong, the reader will stop there and miss the rest of the design's content. On the other hand, if you don't establish a focal point, you'll end up with a confusing design; the audience won't know where to focus their attention and will move on. The goal is to begin the eyes on a path and then lead them through all of the elements of the design. Accents, such as supporting images and text, can be placed to lead the eye through the page. Repetition of colors, shapes, and textures also creates flow.

Visual hierarchy refers to the relative importance of the elements on the page. Notice the variation in sizes and colors of text in this ad. The headline is largest and brightest; yellow against the blue snow draws you in. The logo is small and tucked in a corner, but, in white, it's noticed. The supporting copy is smaller, yet still readable. Then, finally, we see the small, dark, barely legible copyright information at bottom left. Your audience will follow the path, understanding each object's significance based on its size, color, and placement in the layout.

## Design Analysis: Path Layout

| Objective | Analyze the effectiveness of path layouts, recognize focal points and visual hierarchy. |
|---|---|
| To do | Sketch the focal point and path of an existing print advertisement. |

**Tip**
Analyze the visual hierarchy; describe how the elements are arranged. Is this arrangement based on their relative importance to the message? Here's an example "sketched" in Illustrator by student Lisa Hayward. Go through magazines and tear out good examples, then draw the path directly on the printed version.

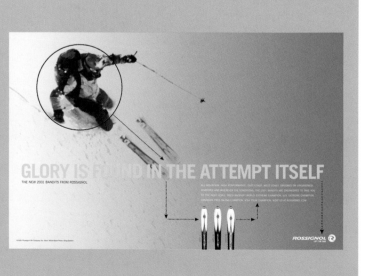

# Introduction to Adobe InDesign

Adobe InDesign is primarily used for multiple-page layouts. Oh, but it is so much more. It is excellent for organizing images and for the preparation of files for professional printers (prepress). It has many of the capabilities that you'll use in Illustrator. Yet the best thing about InDesign is that it was developed to support graphic designers' work processes. Nearly everything we want to do in multiple-page layouts has been thoughtfully included in the software. You will use Photoshop to optimize your photographs and Illustrator to create logos and drawings, but InDesign is essential software for multiple-page, text-heavy publications and prepress organization.

## The InDesign Toolbox

You'll notice the toolbox looks like Illustrator's. The tools are similar, yet their capabilities are specialized for text and linked-image needs. One new tool is the most essential: Frames. Frames provide structure for the placement of images and text. Sure, you can simply place images and text into a document, but when position is key, frames are important, and when document layouts are used repeatedly, frames are fabulous—copy and photos can be changed in the frames and the layout stays the same. When you press and hold on the Rectangle Frame tool, you'll see it also provides elliptical and polygonal options.

Another thoughtful addition to the InDesign toolbox is just below the Fill and Stroke Colors. Notice the tiny box and the tiny T. Click on one or the other to apply new colors to either the frame shape or the text.

An important distinction arises with Frames and Selection tools in InDesign. Use the black Selection tool to adjust the Frame (size, position, etc.). Use the white Direct Selection tool to adjust the photo (size, crop, etc.) inside the frame.

InDesign will link your images to the indd file, so when using images, always create a folder that contains the indd file and the image files that will be placed in the design.

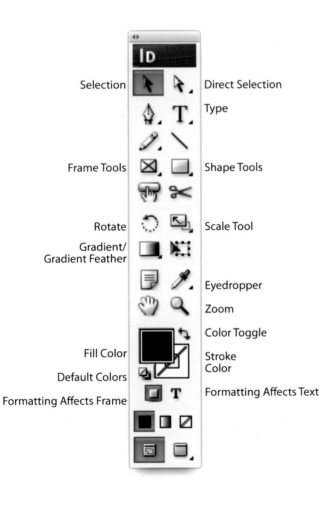

## General Shortcut Keystrokes

**Hide Frames**
Command + Ctrl + H

**Hide Guides**
Command + ;

**Select all text in Frame**
Command + A

**Spell Check**
Command + Option + L

**Switch to Type tool**
Press T

**Switch to Selection tool**
Press V

**Switch to Direct Selection tool**
Press A

**Show Rulers**
Command + R

# Design + Software Skills 5.1:
## InDesign Place Image and Path Layout

## Objective
Introduction to InDesign. Use Frames, place images and format copy to create a path layout advertisement.

## To Do
Place a photograph into InDesign and add text to create an effective path layout. The advertisement we'll recreate here was designed by student Kori Mausner with a photograph by Mitch Weiss.

**Tip**
This photo treatment is called full-bleed. It means that the image goes to all four edges of the page. Bleed refers to the ink that extends beyond the borders of the design, and the edges must be trimmed after printing to produce these pages. Designs that are not full-bleed are often cost-saving devices because they can be produced without trimming the edges, reducing paper and production expenses.

Swedish Sashimi*

*Food served soft and chewy.

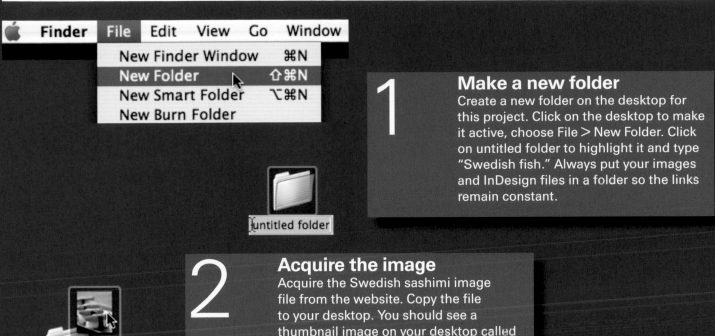

# 1 Make a new folder

Create a new folder on the desktop for this project. Click on the desktop to make it active, choose File > New Folder. Click on untitled folder to highlight it and type "Swedish fish." Always put your images and InDesign files in a folder so the links remain constant.

# 2 Acquire the image

Acquire the Swedish sashimi image file from the website. Copy the file to your desktop. You should see a thumbnail image on your desktop called "Swedishsashimi."

Click and drag "Swedishsashimi" over the "Swedish fish" icon to put it in the folder.

Swedish fish

# 3 Create a document

Open a new document. Choose File > New > Document.

In the New Document window, click off Facing Pages (this setting is useful for double-page spread projects such as magazines). Make it letter size, one column (the default settings).

Change the margins at the bottom of the window to zero. Put your cursor in the top margins box, change the number to 0, then press Tab. All of the margins automatically change to zero. Press OK.

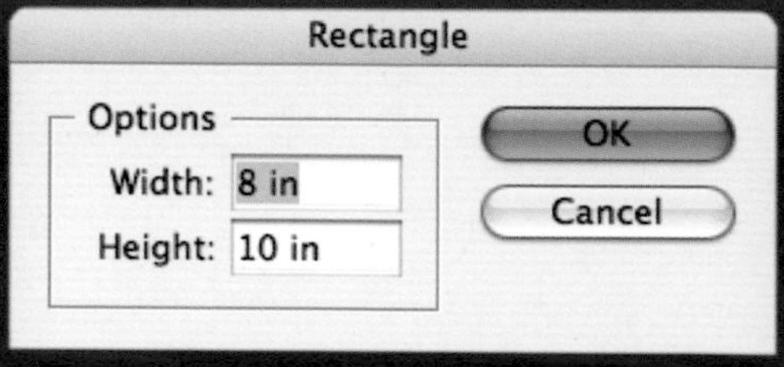

## Rectangle

Options

Width: 8 in

Height: 10 in

OK

Cancel

# 4 Draw a frame

Select the Rectangle Frame tool. You can draw frames freehand, but to be exact, just click once in the file window. Type 8 inches (20.32 cm) and 10 inches (25.40 cm) in the Frame window width and height boxes. These are common magazine advertisement dimensions and allow you to trim off a white margin for the full-bleed presentation.

Choose the black Selection tool to click and move the frame into the center of the page.

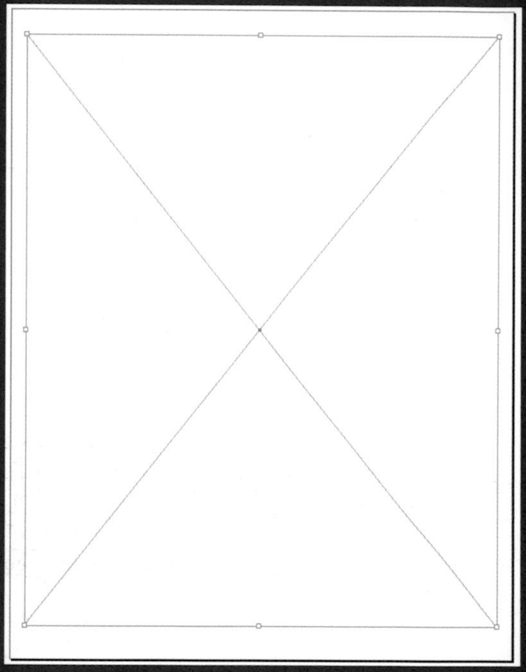

# 5 Place the image

Choose File > Place and select the Desktop "Swedish fish" folder, then "Swedishsashimi" from the file listing. Press Open.

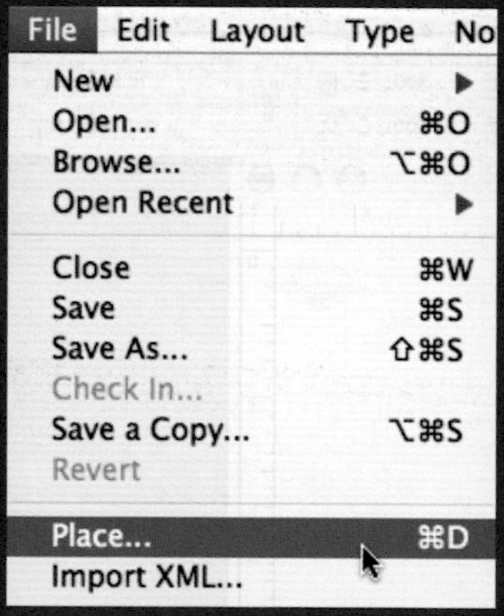

| File | Edit | Layout | Type | No |
|------|------|--------|------|-----|
| New | | | | ▶ |
| Open... | | | | ⌘O |
| Browse... | | | | ⌥⌘O |
| Open Recent | | | | ▶ |
| Close | | | | ⌘W |
| Save | | | | ⌘S |
| Save As... | | | | ⇧⌘S |
| Check In... | | | | |
| Save a Copy... | | | | ⌥⌘S |
| Revert | | | | |
| Place... | | | | ⌘D |
| Import XML... | | | | |

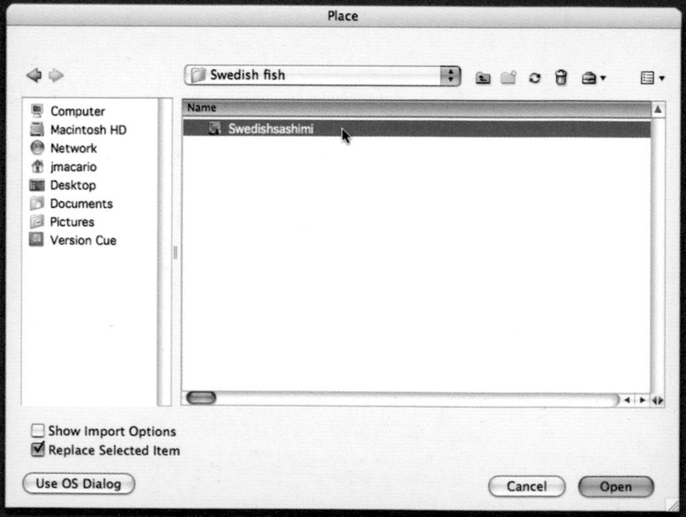

## Place

Swedish fish

Computer
Macintosh HD
Network
jmacario
Desktop
Documents
Pictures
Version Cue

Name
    Swedishsashimi

☐ Show Import Options
☑ Replace Selected Item

Use OS Dialog          Cancel    Open

# 6 Move the image

You'll see the photo appear in the frame.

Now choose the white Direct Selection tool to click on and adjust the position of the photo in the frame. Notice the control box is now red. This indicates you are adjusting the image, not the frame.

Nudge the photo over (using keyboard arrow keys if you like) so that the sashimi are well situated in the frame.

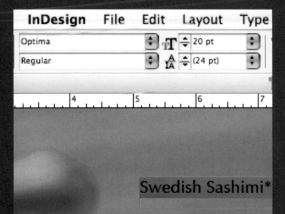

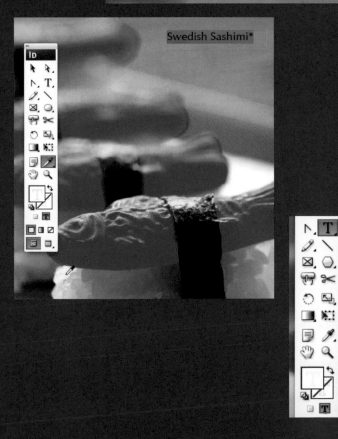

# 7 Add the headline

Choose the Type tool and click and drag a text box into the upper-right area of the page. Type "Swedish Sashimi*." In the Control Bar, modify the font and size. This example is Optima, 20 pts., Regular. Optima is an elegant but unusual typeface: it is primarily sans serif, but non-mono-weight and is accented with a few serif gestures. If Optima is not on your computer, choose another elegant typeface.

While the text is selected, choose the Eyedropper tool and position it over the rice in the foreground. Click on a warm white. The Eyedropper tool will select a color from the image. This technique integrates your text color with the photo. Rather than use a stark white, we've chosen a softer off-white.

When the Type tool and text is selected, the color in the fill box appears as a T and the tiny Affects Text indicator is on.

## 8 Positioning and locking

Use the Selection tool and click on the Text box to adjust its position on the page.

> **Tip**
> Sometimes, another frame gets selected and we unintentionally move another object. If this happens, press Command + Z to undo the unwanted move, then lock the background image into place.

Click on the background image (you know it's selected if the blue box is around it) and choose Object > Lock Position.

You can go back and Unlock the object at any time using the same menu—choose Unlock Position.

*Food served soft and chewy.

## 9 Finishing off

Add supporting copy to the lower-left corner. For good visual hierarchy, we'll use the same font as your headline in a smaller point size. Choose the Type tool, drag a text box, and type "*Food served soft and chewy." Select the text, choose the Eyedropper tool, and click on the "Swedish Sashimi*" text. Your lower text will be formatted with the headline text box settings. When used with text, the Eyedropper tool copies the typeface attributes to the selected copy. In the Control Bar, simply adjust the size of the lower copy to 12 pts.

Toggle off the appearance of the blue text boxes by pressing Command + Control + H.

Press Command + S to save your work into the "Swedish fish" folder.

Press Command + P to print. Use a straight edge and X-acto knife to trim the page margins to create the full-bleed appearance.

Nice job.

Swedish Sashimi*

*Food served soft and chewy.

## Unity

The graphic design principle of unity means that all the elements on a page look like they go together. Achieving unity becomes more challenging as the number of elements increases. The best approach is to ensure that each object has a relationship with another object on the page. You can do this with alignment, or create visual connections using color, line quality, direction, size, shape, texture, and/or value. The layout itself, whether using a path or grid, can create unity.

Everything on this book cover is in a shade of blue or white. Notice the position of the title and blurb in white text: both align on the same right-hand edge. Additionally, all of the text is in one typeface, with variations in size, case, and color to help establish effective visual hierarchy for the copy.

The Plug nightclub poster plays on the unifying theme of wires; the image and the type reinforce the name. The letters of the font are in one continuous cord and their colors are reflected in the vivid undulating wires swirling around the dancer. Notice how the title runs from edge to edge and its centered placement adds stability to the undulating image.

# Design Project 4:
# Path Layout Advertisement

Create your own candy advertisement for the college demographic. What sweet product can you reintroduce to the college crowd using a strong image and succinct copy? For this project, find or take a photograph that has an effective focal point. Come up with a one- to three-word headline. Place the text so that it is integrated with the focal point but not simply on top of it. Add the product website and place these along the path layout.

Students Betsy Brand and Liz Kauff designed these two projects.

## Symmetrical Layout | Asymmetrical Layout

Centered layouts are symmetrical; all of the elements are arranged equally on either side of the center. Imagine a line down the center of this book cover design. The photo is half on one side, half on the other, with the type balanced symmetrically along the central axis. Placing the author's name and title behind the blood vial creates depth and visual interest. Owing to their symmetry, centered layouts are not always as visually engaging as this.

In asymmetrical layouts, designers place dissimilar elements unevenly—yet still achieve balanced results. Though the image may be more on one side of the page and the headline and supporting copy on the other side, the design has an overall balance. This approach is more challenging than the symmetrical layout, but it is also more visually compelling and therefore more likely to capture and hold your audience's attention.

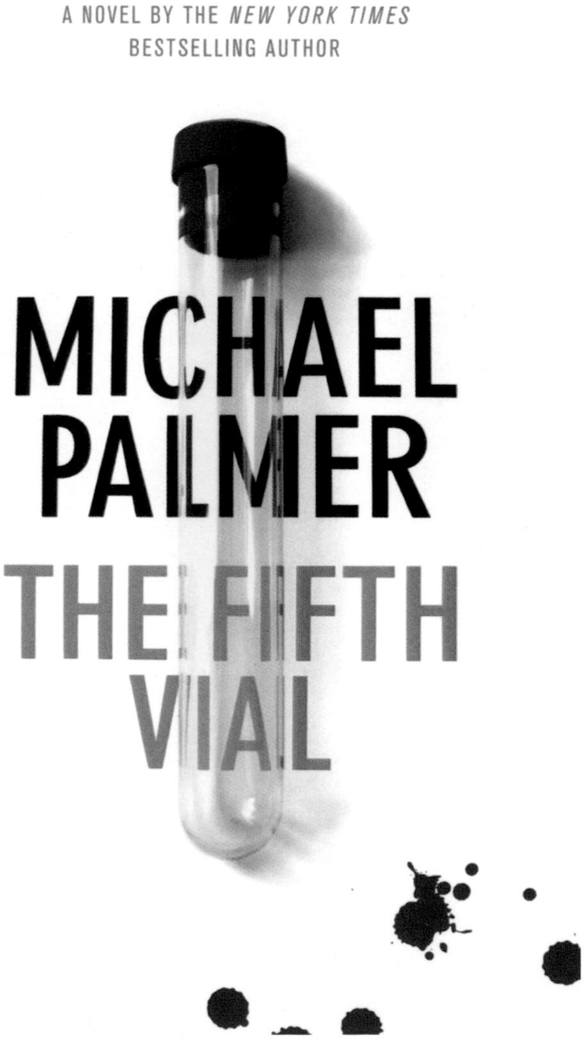

A NOVEL BY THE *NEW YORK TIMES* BESTSELLING AUTHOR

MICHAEL PALMER THE FIFTH VIAL

Gorgeous color and abstract shapes suggest the smart but casual appeal of the band Nickel Creek. Vermont's JDK Design screenprinted the posters for two concerts in limited editions. To further enhance its rare appeal, they used blue ink for the first night and green for the second night concert.

Brazilian Clarissa Tossin's poster for Gossamer achieves asymmetrical elegance. Inspired by thermographic charts, her imagery flows from top right to fill the bottom where it surrounds the electronic minimalist band's name. In smaller, simpler fonts, the record label logo and additional information are placed in the negative space on the left to balance the layout.

To achieve asymmetrical balance, consider every position, weight, size, value, color, shape, and texture of a mark. A balanced design seems to hold together and feel natural. An unbalanced design makes the viewer uncomfortable. Think about the relative visual weight of all of the elements on the page. The position on the page will affect an object's visual weight. What position might make an object appear bigger or more powerful? What position on the page lessens an object's visual strength? This thoughtful approach can be a powerful tool for emphasizing particular aspects of a design.

When creating a layout, place all of the elements on the page in such a way as to achieve a relationship based on visual hierarchy and balance. Even if you manage to live well with messy closets, overstuffed drawers, and black-hole backpacks (like me), make it a goal to organize your designs using layout strategies.

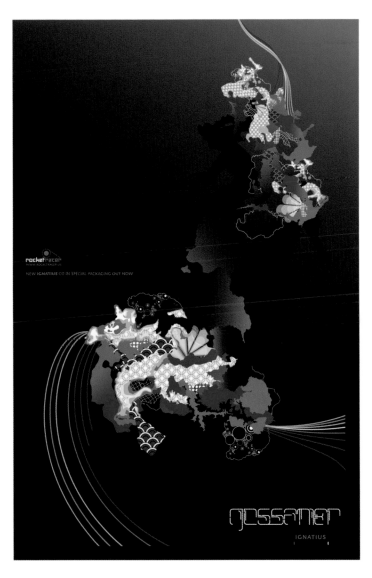

**Herbert Bayer**
**Kandinsky exhibition**
**poster**
**1926**

Herbert Bayer graduated from the Bauhaus and was immediately hired to start a new printing and advertising workshop. Walter Gropius, the Bauhaus director, commissioned Bayer to design a universal typeface for all the school's printed materials. This poster for Kandinsky's sixtieth birthday exhibition expresses, in typographic terms, Gropius's belief that form follows function and exemplifies Bauhaus design principles. Bayer used sans-serif fonts, and after careful analysis of the copy, set extreme contrasts of sizes and weights to establish clear visual hierarchy; bars and rules subdivide the space, lead the eye through the content, and draw attention to important details. An implied grid provides horizontal and vertical alignments and then the entire design is rotated on a diagonal, so it achieves a dynamic yet balanced result. These Bauhaus principles will serve you well with your own designs.

# Grid Layout

From magazines to websites, many graphic designs are multiple-page. Such projects use grid layouts to unify the whole. Turn the pages or click menu items to reveal the grid layout. Grids are also used for single-page designs. The grid is the underlying structure that allows the designer to create complex layouts with consistency throughout the entire publication. They aid reading, understanding, and enjoyment of a publication. Have you ever noticed clever placement of titles or page numbers? That's part of the grid layout.

The word "grid" sounds rigid, yet it does not necessarily constrain the design; rather it allows for many possibilities and experimentation. Its typically invisible structure is used as a guide for the placement of images and type on the pages.

Here are three versions of one page from a catalogue designed by BlackCoffee; the published version is on the left. The center image shows the alignment of images and text to the grid. The empty grid on the right displays the consistent proportions underlying each position. Notice that the text aligns with the left-hand edges of the photos. The top brown bar ends at exactly the same position on the grid as the right-hand edge of the photos. Where has the designer used the dimensions of a shape as the dimensions of negative space? The repetition of shapes and negative spaces brings order to the overall design.

At the bottom of the page, one grid is used for two different issues of the *Home Miami* magazine contents page. Notice the consistent placement of the top two feature-article photos and the same positions for the masthead and list of contributors. Where has the designer introduced some variation?

When selecting images for a grid layout, choose images that work together as a whole. The images should have a collectively similar style or palette to be visually consistent throughout a design.

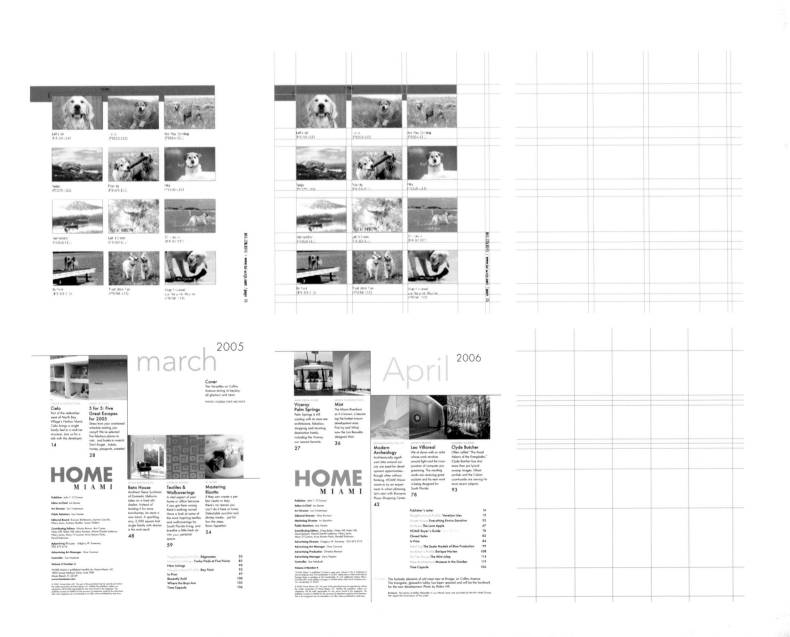

This is a three-panel brochure by Dickinson Associates for a building management company. Notice that the center page is a simple two-image grid; this is a pleasing break from complexity. The left- and right-hand pages are based on the same four-column layout. This is one of the ways the designer achieves unity in a complex document. Can you find others? Subtitle bars span two columns and the medium-sized photos fit in one. Did you see the unique placement of the numbers? These are the street addresses of the properties in the pictures (that's the Dickinson group in the top left).

Grid structures are based on the overall page format and an ideal column width of 50–70 characters. The character-width guideline is based on the area of a page that readers can see at a typical reading distance without moving their head or getting eyestrain. Three- and two-column layouts adhere to this guideline; these are then separated into six or four columns for variation. Many tried and true formats exist for standard paper sizes. Three/six- and two/four-column grid structures are the most common because of their appropriate text-to-column width measurement. Be wary of text columns that are too narrow. It can be difficult to format the text, or even read.

When choosing a grid, consider the copy. How long is it? How many inserts, subheadings, and lists does it have? How many photographs or illustrations? Does your publication have more pictures than text or more text than images? In a publication that is mostly text, a simple grid will work well. In a publication with many images or charts, a more complex grid allows for greater variation. But as grids become too complicated, unity and rhythm are harder to see. Keep in mind that the smaller the squares in the grid, the more choices are needed about placement.

Grid inconsistency can lead to lack of visual organization and create confusion. Be consistent throughout the publication or you risk losing your audience. Monotony is another risk with a grid structure. That's the reason for a common graphic design phrase: breaking the grid.

## Divine Proportions

Grids have a significant history in graphic design that predates text in many parts of the world. Egyptian books of the dead (papyrus scrolls) used grids to organize rows of hieroglyphics. Much more recently, in the mid-20th century, designers used this approach to influence international business.

After the Second World War, organizations became more active internationally, so designers developed styles that no longer appeared to be from a particular place or culture. Called the International Typographic Style, practitioners simplified type and imagery and used grid-based layouts.

Josef Müller-Brockmann was one of the most influential developers of the Swiss International Style. He designed the poster "der Film" ("The Film") in 1960. Its proportions are based on the golden ratio, also called divine proportion. Müller-Brockmann and countless other designers have used the golden ratio to their advantage in graphic designs.

The golden ratio is illustrated with the diagram below right. Notice the relationship of the rectangle to the square—it remains the same at every size. This is the divine proportion. This principle was developed by the ancient Greeks and was considered the most beautifully proportioned rectangle based on universal mathematical truths. The Greeks based their architecture on this—the best-known example is the Parthenon.

Using the divinely proportioned rectangle, the "der Film" poster is divided into three columns and five rows. Of the fifteen total rectangles, the top nine approximate a square (the divine proportion). The title fills one of the lower rows, "Film" fills exactly two units of this row. The secondary information on the poster aligns with the "F" of "Film" along the left-hand edge of the second column.

The design grew out of functional communication needs. The large white title against the black background projects clearly at great distances. Remarkably, although this poster contains only type, there is an underlying conceptual basis for the text overlap, which suggests the cinematic editing technique of scenes dissolving into one another.

Müller-Brockmann had a huge influence on the field of graphic design. He believed that copy, images, and logos are all subservient to the underlying grid structure in a well-crafted design. In his manifesto *Grid Systems in Graphic Design*, Müller-Brockmann asserts: "The grid system implies the will to systematize, to clarify… the will to cultivate objectivity rather than subjectivity."

Image Now design studio and gallery in Dublin recently exhibited forty-eight Müller-Brockmann posters. Their website is organized on a gray grid based on the golden rectangle. Featured on this page is one of their poster designs for a recent film screening in Dublin, clear evidence of the contemporary appeal of the grid.

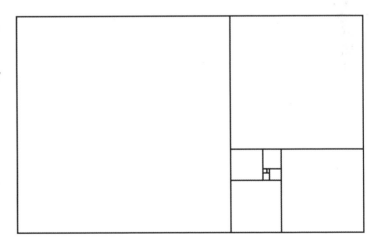

wim crouwel   helvetica

image now
consultants

sweetalk 24 poster
wim crouwel presentation
helvetica a documentary film
irish premier screening

image now
17a new bride street
dublin 8
ireland

+ 353 1 411 3290
post@imagenow.ie

# Design + Software Skills 5.2: InDesign Grid Layout

**Type Tips**

| TYPEFACE | Use a serif font for body text, sans serif for titles, or vice-a-versa. |
| | Don't use novelty typefaces for body copy. |
| | Use Italics within body text only for emphasis. |
| | Never use all capital letters. PEOPLE WILL THINK YOU ARE YELLING. |
| | Limit the number of fonts to two per page. |
| | Limit the number of different font sizes to three per page. |
| | Simplify. |
| CONTRAST | Add visual interest to your page by contrasting titles with body copy. |
| | Achieve contrast with size, weight, font style, separation or color differences. |
| | Produce the best legibility with high contrasting black text on white paper. |
| | Reduce legibility with low contrasting black text on red or dark paper. |
| | Simplify. |
| FORMAT | Keep the space between words and letters consistent. |
| | Separate paragraphs with a line space or indents, but not both. |
| | Limit text to 50 - 70 characters per line. |
| | Use the Auto Leading setting as a good standard. |
| | Leading is vertical line spacing (pronounce leading as led-ing). |
| | Auto Leading is approximately 2 pts more than the font size for body text. |
| | Place every element on the page with the edge of another element. |
| | Leave plenty of white space around the edges. |
| | Make your document balance, from top to bottom, left to right. |
| | Stand back and view your page as a whole. |
| | Simplify. |

## Objectives

Create a grid layout and place text from a Word file into a frame. This project also reinforces the type tips from Chapter 3 and provides an opportunity to create an asymmetrical layout.

## To Do

Create a grid layout for the Type Tips text.

### Tip

InDesign allows us to place very large Microsoft Word text documents into a file. When the amount of copy is more than one frame or column, hold the Shift key down and the copy will automatically thread or flow through as many frames as needed. For this exercise, we'll use three frames for the heading, subheads, and copy, so no threading is required.

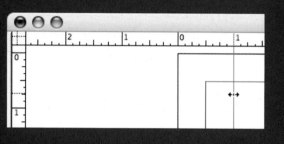

InDesGridExercise.indd @ 89%

## 1 Make the grid

Open a new document in InDesign. Make it letter size, one column and 0.5 inch (1.27 cm) margins all around.

Draw the grid. Press Command + R to make rulers appear at the top and left of the file. Place your cursor in the left ruler, click and drag a vertical guide to the 1 inch (2.54 cm) mark. Then draw three more vertical guides at the 2.75 inch (6.99 cm), 3 inch (7.62 cm), and 7.5 inch (19.05 cm) points on the page.

Place your cursor in the top ruler, click and drag to place horizontal guides at the 1.5 inch (3.81 cm), 2 inch (5.08 cm), 2.75 inch (6.99 cm), and 9 inch (22.86 cm) points. You've drawn the grid.

## 2 Add frames

Draw three frames for the copy. Select the Frame tool. Click your cursor at the first intersection of the top two lines. Drag it to the next intersection of lines. This will frame your title. The three x-ed boxes on the right show the frame positions.

For your subtitles column, draw a frame that fills the area between 1 inch (2.54 cm) and 2.75 inches (6.99 cm) horizontally, and between 2.75 inches (6.99 cm) and 9 inches (22.86 cm) vertically.

For the Type Tips copy, draw a frame that starts at the 3 inch (7.62 cm) point and ends at the 7.5 inch (19.05 cm) point horizontally, and 2.75 inches (6.99 cm) to 9 inches (22.86 cm) vertically.

## 3 Add copy

Add the copy. Select the Type tool, click in the top left frame and write "Type Tips." Format the text. This example is Impact, 30 pts., right-aligned. Impact is strong yet narrow. If it's not on your computer, try another bold, condensed sans-serif font.

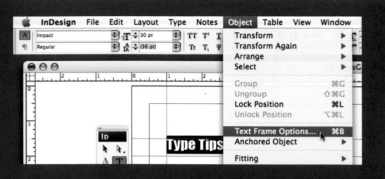

## 4 Adjust the alignment

Modify the position of the words in the frame. Currently, they are aligning with the top of the frame. We want the grid to be apparent, so we'll change the position to bottom.

Choose Objects > Text Frame Options. In the Vertical Justification section, change the Align setting to Bottom. Now your title sits at the lower edge of the frame.

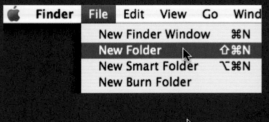

## 5 Make a new folder

Create a new folder on the desktop for this project. Click on the desktop to make it active and choose File > New Folder. Click on Untitled Folder and type "Grid."

## 6 Acquire the text file

To acquire the copy, go to the website and download "typetips.doc" onto your desktop. You should see a thumbnail image on your desktop called "typetips.doc."

Click and drag "typetips.doc" over the Grid icon to put it in the folder. Although InDesign will not create a link to the Word doc, it's a good way to keep track of your files.

M

| File | Edit | Layout | Type | Notes | Object | Table | View | Windo |

New ▶
Open... ⌘O
Browse... ⌥⌘O
Open Recent ▶

Close ⌘W
Save ⌘S
Save As... ⇧⌘S
Check In...
Save a Copy... ⌥⌘S
Revert

Place... ⌘D
Import XML...

Adobe PDF Presets ▶
Export... ⌘E
Cross-media Export ▶

## Type Tips

Use a serif font for body text, sans serif for titles, or vice-a-versa.
Don't use novelty typefaces for body copy.
Use Italics within body text only for emphasis.
Never use all capital letters.
PEOPLE WILL THINK YOU ARE YELLING.
Limit the number of fonts to two per page.
Limit the number of different font sizes to three per page.
Simplify.

Add visual interest to your page by contrasting titles with body copy.
Achieve contrast with size, weight, font style, separation or color differences.
Produce the best legibility with high contrasting black text on white paper.
Reduce legibility with low contrasting black text on red or dark paper.
Simplify.

Keep the space between words and letters consistent.
Separate paragraphs with a line space or indents, but not both.
Limit text to 50 - 70 characters per line.
Use the Auto Leading setting as a good standard.
Leading is vertical line spacing (pronounce leading as led-ing).
Auto Leading is approximately 2 pts more than the font size for body text.
Place every element on the page with the edge of another element.
Leave plenty of white space around the edges.
Make your document balance, from top to bottom, left to right.
Stand back and view your page as a whole.
Simplify.

Use a serif font for body text, sans serif for titles, or vice-a-versa.
Don't use novelty typefaces for body copy.
Use Italics within body text only for emphasis.
Never use all capital letters.
PEOPLE WILL THINK YOU ARE YELLING.
Limit the number of fonts to two per page.
Limit the number of different font sizes to three per page.
Simplify.

Add visual interest to your page by contrasting titles with body copy.
Achieve contrast with size, weight, font style, separation or color differences.
Produce the best legibility with high contrasting black text on white paper.
Reduce legibility with low contrasting black text on red or dark paper.
Simplify.

Keep the space between words and letters consistent.
Separate paragraphs with a line space or indents, but not both.
Limit text to 50 - 70 characters per line.
Use the Auto Leading setting as a good standard.
Leading is vertical line spacing (pronounce leading as led-ing).
Auto Leading is approximately 2 pts more than the font size for body text.
Place every element on the page with the edge of another element.
Leave plenty of white space around the edges.
Make your document balance, from top to bottom, left to right.
Stand back and view your page as a whole.
Simplify.

**Place**

Grid

Name
typetips.doc

Computer
Macintosh HD
Network
jmacario
Desktop
Documents
Pictures
Version Cue

☐ Show Import Options
☑ Replace Selected Item

Use OS Dialog          Cancel    Open

## 7 Place the text

Select the Type tool and click in the largest frame. Choose File > Place and choose the desktop Grid folder, then "typetips.doc" from the file listing. Press Open. The text is placed in the frame.

## 8 Format the copy

Select all of the copy and format. While the Type tool is selected and positioned in the large frame, press Command + A to select all. Use the Control Bar to format your text. This selection is Cochin, 11 pts., Regular, left-aligned. Cochin is a serif typeface. If it is not on your computer, try another serif font that contrasts with your title.

Notice that some of the tips wrap one word to a second line. One word of copy on a line is considered poor design. Fix this by clicking on the frame's right control button and drag it open to the 8 inch (20.32 cm) margin line.

**Tip**
A line of type should be at least six words wide—this applies to websites too.

# Logo Design

6

an Eye for perception, insight, vision.
e Bee for industriousness, dedication, perseverance.
an "M" for motivation, merit, moral strength.

A somewhat unusual perspective of the familiar
IBM logotype, and a light reminder of some of the funda
mental qualities that have come to characterize
the outstanding men and women who have built, and who
continue to build, the success of the IBM company.

**Paul Rand**
**Eye Bee M poster**
**1981**

When Paul Rand created this poster for a company event, it was temporarily banned at IBM for fear that employees would take liberties with the logo. The IBM logo is based on the City Medium font; horizontal lines were added later to unify the letters and evoke the lines on a computer screen. This poster is a rebus of the logo, where two letters are replaced with pictures for their sounds. This is typical of Rand's playful approach to design. His ability to develop innovative concepts and reduce the message to its symbolic essence made him influential while still in his twenties. Later, his work with Bill Bernbach became the inspiration for the copy/art team that was adopted by the advertising industry. Rand taught several generations of designers at Yale, including some of my professors (I seem to recall one professor admitting that Rand's critiques made him cry).

# Design + Software Skills 6: Illustrator Convert Type to Outlines, Redraw Letters and Symbols

## Objectives
Develop Illustrator type and drawing skills while learning how to customize letters.

## To Do
Create outlines from text and customize letters. Draw swoosh symbols.

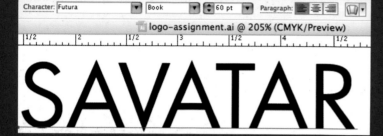

### 1 Format the name
Start Illustrator. Open a new file, make it 7 inches by 5 inches (17.78 by 12.70 cm). Type "SAVATAR," make it Futura, Book, 60 pts. Futura has distinctive pointy apexes. If it's not on your computer, try another sharp-edged sans-serif font.

### 2 Create outlines
Convert the text to shapes. Select the name with the black Selection tool. Choose Type > Create Outlines.

### 3 Ungroup the letters
Choose Object > UnGroup.

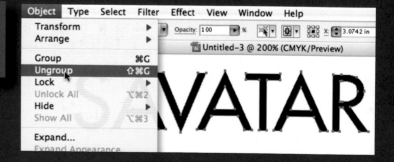

**4** ## Customize the As

There are several ways to proceed. Let's take the approach that leads to the highest-quality shape. So the next step is to trace part of the letter A.

Select just the letter A, then lock it. From the Object menu, choose Lock > Selection.

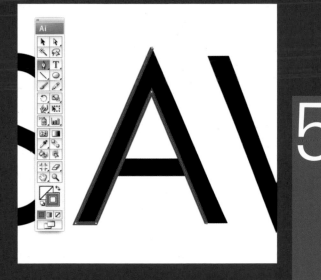

**5** ## Draw the new A

Select the Pen tool, change the settings to No Fill. Click on the Stroke color box and set it to a vivid color so you can watch as you trace.

Using the Pen tool, trace the letter. Click at the top of the A, then click at the bottom to draw the diagonal, click to the left, and then again to the top of the inside of the letter. Continue around the letter, completing the shape by clicking on the beginning point at the top of the A.

**6** ## Make it black

Make the new "A" black. Click the Toggle arrow to make the shape Filled, then click on Black in the color window.

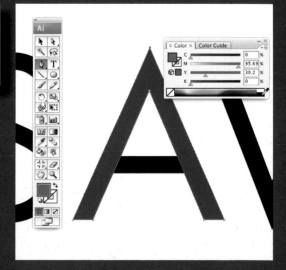

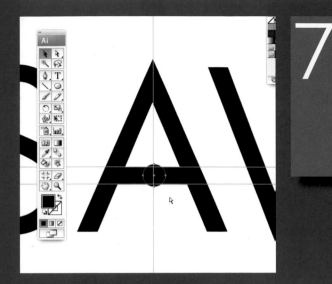

## 7 Draw the dot

Draw the center circle over the existing crossbar. First, draw guides to show the position of the center of the A and the crossbar.

Choose the Ellipse tool. Hold the Shift and Option keys down and draw a circle starting at the intersection of the guides.

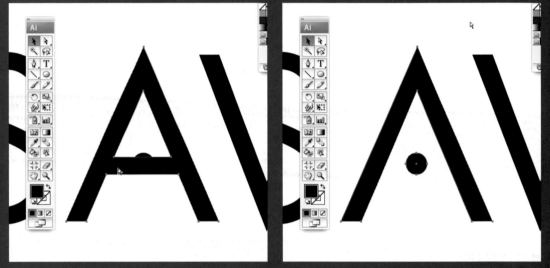

## 8 Remove the old A

Choose Object > Unlock. Click on the old A and press Delete.

## 9 Make two more As

Hold the Shift key down and click on the new A and circle. Copy and paste the new A (Command + C, then Command + V).

Click on the new A, copy and move it over the second A. Once it's in position, click on the old A and press Delete. Repeat for the third A.

# SAVATAR

**10**   Gorgeous!

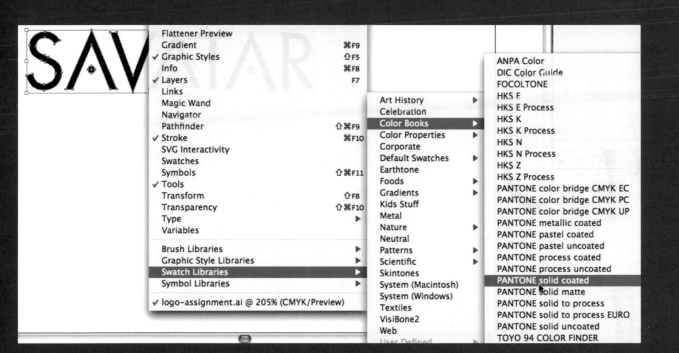

**11**   **Select a Pantone color**
Change the logo color to PMS 447 C.
Select the entire logo (Command + A).

Open the Pantone Swatch window.
Choose Window > Swatch Libraries >
Color Books > Pantone solid coated.

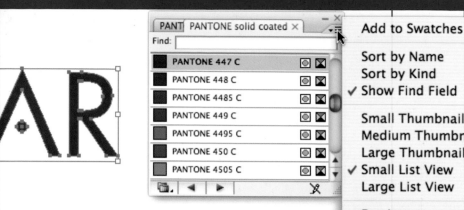

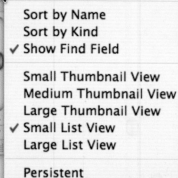

## 12 Choose the color

From the right-hand pull-down menu, choose Show Find Field and Small List View.

Type "447" in the window and click on the color. This will change the color of the logo to PMS 447 C and it will place the color in your file's Color Swatch window.

## 13 Draw the swoosh symbols

Choose the Ellipse tool and draw an oval over the name to create a template for the swooshes.

## 14 Make a template

Choose the Rotate tool. Click on the oval and rotate it.

Choose Object > Lock Selection to lock the oval so you can trace over it.

## 15   Draw the curve

Choose the Pen tool. Click on the oval. Then reposition your cursor at the other side of the curve, then click and drag so that the curve matches the oval shape. It may take a couple of tries to match the curve.

## 16

Click on the second point. Then position your cursor over the first point and click and drag the curve to create a thickening shape for the swoosh.

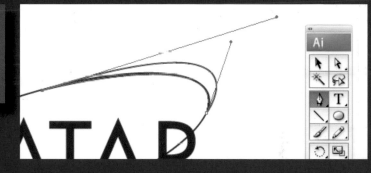

## 17   Make the swoosh black

Choose the black Selection tool and click on your new shape. Click the color Toggle arrow to make the swoosh filled, no stroke color.

## 18   Copy the top swoosh

While the swoosh is still selected, double click on the Rotate tool and type "180" into the Angle box. Click Copy (not the OK button).

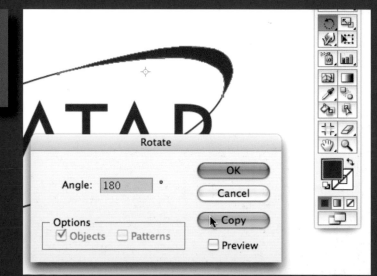

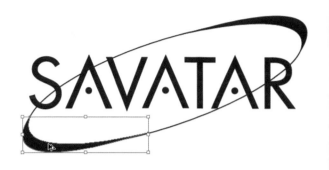

## 19 Place the lower swoosh
Choose the black Selection tool and move the second swoosh to the bottom left. It should mimic the lower curve of the oval template.

| Object | Type | Select | Filter |
|---|---|---|---|
| Transform | | | ▶ |
| Arrange | | | ▶ |
| Group | | | ⌘G |
| Ungroup | | | ⇧⌘G |
| Lock | | | ▶ |
| Unlock All | | | ⌥⌘2 |
| Hide | | | ▶ |
| Show All | | | ⌥⌘3 |

## 20 Delete the template
Choose Object > UnLock All. Press Delete and the oval template will be erased.

| | | |
|---|---|---|
| Gradient | ⌘F9 | |
| ✓ Graphic Styles | ⇧F5 | |
| Info | ⌘F8 | |
| ✓ Layers | F7 | |
| Links | | |
| Magic Wand | | |
| Navigator | | |
| Pathfinder | ⇧⌘F9 | |
| ✓ Stroke | ⌘F10 | |
| SVG Interactivity | | |
| Swatches | | |
| Symbols | ⇧⌘F11 | |
| ✓ Tools | | |
| Transform | ⇧F8 | |
| Transparency | ⇧⌘F10 | |
| Type | ▶ | |
| Variables | | |
| Brush Libraries | ▶ | |
| Graphic Style Libraries | ▶ | |
| Swatch Libraries | ▶ | |
| Symbol Libraries | ▶ | |
| ✓ logo–assignment.ai @ 205% (CMYK/Preview) | | |

| | |
|---|---|
| Art History | ▶ |
| Celebration | |
| Color Books | ▶ |
| Color Properties | ▶ |
| Corporate | |
| Default Swatches | ▶ |
| Earthtone | |
| Foods | ▶ |
| Gradients | ▶ |
| Kids Stuff | |
| Metal | |
| Nature | ▶ |
| Neutral | |
| Patterns | ▶ |
| Scientific | ▶ |
| Skintones | |
| System (Macintosh) | |
| System (Windows) | |
| Textiles | |
| VisiBone2 | |

| |
|---|
| ANPA Color |
| DIC Color Guide |
| FOCOLTONE |
| HKS E |
| HKS E Process |
| HKS K |
| HKS K Process |
| HKS N |
| HKS N Process |
| HKS Z |
| HKS Z Process |
| PANTONE color bridge CMYK EC |
| PANTONE color bridge CMYK PC |
| PANTONE color bridge CMYK UP |
| PANTONE metallic coated |
| PANTONE pastel coated |
| PANTONE pastel uncoated |
| PANTONE process coated |
| PANTONE process uncoated |
| PANTONE solid coated |
| PANTONE solid matte |
| PANTONE solid to process |
| PANTONE solid to process EURO |

## 21 Show Pantone swatches
Make the swooshes PMS 875 C, a metallic copper-colored ink for coated paper.

Hold the Shift key down and select both swooshes.

Choose Window > Swatch Libraries > Color Books > Pantone metallic coated.

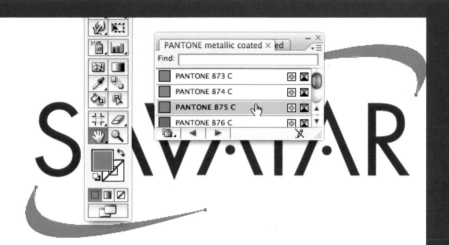

## 22   Choose the color

Type "875" into the window and click on the color. This will make the swooshes an approximate metallic copper color and it will place the color in the Swatch window for your file.

## 23

Phew. Now you can use these software skills to create your own logo design.

# Design Project 5:
# Logo Design

Design a logo. Use only two colors and add a tag line.

Choose one from this list of fictitious companies:

**Lux—a wireless service.**
Tag line: Where you are

**Memo—a paper store.**
Tag line: get.it.write

**Tint—a sunglasses shop.**
Tag line: Look Out

**Bom Dia—a Brazilian bakery**
(from the Portuguese this translates as "good day")
Tag line: Brazilian Bakery

These logos were created by students (from the top left to bottom right): Lux: Kristin Kruger, Liz Austin; Memo: Melanie Morris, Evan Silverberg, Ashleigh Bateman, Antonios Baskinis; Tint: Kyley Tucker, Shi-Min Chin; Bom Dia: Nicholas Nikic, Jessica Darke.

**Tip**
Follow the creative process to generate unique ideas for your logo.

1 — Restate the project in your own words, then do some research on the industry for the company you've chosen.

2 — Analyze existing logos that you see.

3 — Have a brainstorming session. Identify a few good ideas.

4 — Do some thumbnail sketches, work quickly, and let the ideas develop.

5 — Once a sketch reveals a possible solution, go to the computer to produce it in Illustrator. Check the fonts that are already in your computer: look for typefaces that suggest the personality of the brand. Remember to explore upper- and lowercase for each letter. You can expand your search to online font websites and purchase them or find free fonts. If developing a symbol, remember to sketch while looking at photos of the subject. You can even draw over a photo that is placed and locked in Illustrator.

6 — You've already learned all the basics to produce a logo using Illustrator. This will develop your software skills as you create the mark. Step back and evaluate your work; make revisions if necessary.

7 — Think about how you'd present your logo to the client or the class. Briefly explain why you chose the font, colors, and other design decisions.

8 — Good luck and enjoy the process.

# Major Points Summary

— Logos convey a lot of information immediately: quality, style, value, and origin.
— Logo designs must be simple to enhance recognition, and ease recall and reproduction.
— Logos need to have a black and white version for faxes, copies, and newspapers.
— Logotypes are defined as the name of the company or product in unique typography.
— When developing a logo, look closely at the characteristics of letters and choose a typeface that evokes the personality of the organization.
— Abstract symbols are commonly used in logos because they don't emphasize one particular area of a diverse organization.
— Abstract symbols that somehow suggest the nature of the business are called allusive symbols.
— Pictorial symbols look like the product or service they represent.
— Associative pictorial symbols don't look like the product but have an association with the business.
— Pictorial symbols should be simplified. Choose one or two elements of a subject to emphasize in the icon (to help convey the brand dynamics).
— The creative process is a series of steps taken to successfully tackle and complete a design project. Most creative professionals develop a unique, individualized process.
— The steps suggested for beginning designers are:
  1. Understand the problem. 2. Get inspired. 3. Brainstorm.
  4. Sketch. 5. Produce (and revise).

# Software Skills Summary

— Illustrator Advanced.
— Develop advanced skills: type options, create outlines for type, ungroup objects, lock selection, pen tool, draw/trace closed straight-edged shapes, ellipse tool, Pantone swatches, color swatch window, draw closed curved shapes, rotate window, unlock.

# Recommended Readings

Read the very informative book *Logo* by Michael Evamy for a comprehensive exploration of marks from around the world. For additional inspiration by designers who shared their work for this book, check out *The Best of Business Card Design 6*, edited by Mark Gallagher and Laura Savard of BlackCoffee Branding, and *Logo Savvy*, edited by Perry Chua and Dann Ilicic.

# Visual Themes

7

**Saul Bass
The Man with
the Golden Arm
1955**

The movie *The Man with the Golden Arm* marked the first time a comprehensive design program unified print and media graphics for a film. Saul Bass designed the logo, theater posters, print advertisements, and a groundbreaking movie title animation. The title animation begins with a single white vertical bar on a black screen; three more bars then join it, jaggedly moving to a staccato jazz soundtrack. Names of the actors interact with the jazzy bars which then rotate horizontally to interact with the title and rotate again for the production names. The music gets louder and more intense, the lines run vertically and then converge to form the jagged arm you see in the poster. With this film, Bass pioneered a new approach to film title design where forms appear, disintegrate, reappear and transform through space and time. This Otto Preminger movie is about a heroin addict. As with all of his designs, Bass was able to reduce his message to a single dominant image. He used freely drawn or cut paper so the images appear casual, yet still powerful.

**The Wow! logo appears in many places with an array of edgy finishes. How does this branding company maintain its identity from walls to cards, doors to brochures? Establishing visual themes maintains consistency when designs occur in many different situations or across many pages. Vancouver's Wow! Branding uses die-cutting, laser-cutting, etching, and embossing, yet all of the collateral works as a group. What elements are used in all four pieces to create the visual themes throughout?**

Ah, the last chapter. Now you'll bring together all of the design skills you've acquired and create multiple-page designs. Websites, magazines, annual reports, even packaging are examples in which visual themes unify the overall look of these publications. Unlike a poster or advertisement, which can be understood with a glance at one page, in multiple-page publications the entire design strategy is only revealed as the reader goes through the pages. Without visual themes—consistent use of typefaces, colors, image style, and layout—the audience can get confused. As a result, designs are less capable of communicating ideas.

Create the visual theme with repetition of typefaces, number and width of columns, leading, alignment, image style, and color palette. Paper choices and printing techniques such as die-cutting and varnishes can establish distinctive tactile textures. All of these design elements are used to establish visual consistency throughout a publication; repetition and variation of these are the keys to successful visual themes.

Typeface choices are important for consistency throughout a publication. Typically, one typeface is selected for the titles, another for the body text. These two are used throughout and variations are introduced with contrasting size, color, style, and position.

In the Dragonfly CD book, the monochromatic layouts use two typefaces, with a few size and placement modifications to make each page-turn interesting. Notice how the lyrics are similarly set, left-aligned on white columns. The gray-screened titles are so large they bleed off the page. One title is so big and loud it even loses a letter on the bottom right.

Color choices establish an appropriate palette for a design. Choose enough colors for interest, but not too many, since this could dilute the overall impression. Color can be used to establish the visual hierarchy of titles and subtitles throughout the publication, adding visual interest to the page and giving the reader clues about the content.

The style of images within a visual theme should be consistent—their content provides the variety. If the image style is very distinctive it is difficult to introduce another without disrupting the overall tone. For four twelve-inch single covers, Nordic woodland creatures are collaged using paper that was printed with various wood grains. The illustrations represent the origins of Norwegian producers Lindstrom & Prins Thomas.

Dee Clothing promotion cards share a vibrant color scheme, simultaneously maintaining the brand and marking the season. Notice the image styling. It's unusual to see rumpled clothing in marketing, yet each item group is similarly scrunched. These photos feature fabrics and colors: some items are closely cropped, others leave plenty of negative space. The different intensities of the crops provide variation within this unique style.

Using a simple, consistent color palette, each track on this CD has been interpreted as an image and produced as a die-cut sticker. CD packages that have unique design features provide an additional incentive to purchase albums—an effective way to compete with the ease and economy of online music purchases.

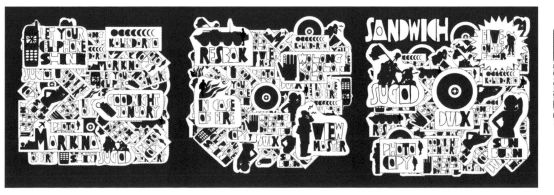

**Jamie Reid**
**God Save the Queen**
**poster**
**1977**

Jamie Reid's designs for the Sex Pistol's albums, posters, and T-shirts helped turn the London punk scene into an international movement. His graphics became punk icons. Punks rejected the values of the establishment: their torn clothing was adapted as coarsely handcrafted graphics: cut-out printed words—ransom note-style—trash the Queen's portrait. This single was released to coincide with the Queen's Jubilee. The song was so shocking it was banned from the airwaves, which of course made it number one on the record charts. Some say this design, which was also used as the cover for the single, had as much to do with the success of the band as their music.

# Design + Software Skills 7: InDesign Advanced Images, Type and Page Layout, Photoshop Burn Tool

## Objectives

Use all of the design strategies and skills you've gathered throughout the book to create this package. Establish and carry out visual themes. Expand your InDesign skills to multi-page designs. Edit linked images. Use Photoshop to burn an image so that overlying type can be more legible.

## To Do

Create a four-page CD package layout. Place images and text that establish effective visual themes.

### Tip

In this exercise, we'll produce a CD mix of music for walking the dog called *Tail Waggers*. Bear with me—you can create your own mix very shortly! The visual theme includes full-color, full-bleed photographs of Archie sniffing around sidewalks; the two fonts are Geometric 231 and Geometric Slab 703, in white outline and white fill. Titles and song list numbers are right-aligned and the song titles are left-aligned. Variations in the visual themes are the photo contents and the size of the titles; on the spines the titles are white fill.

## 1 Put the images in a folder

Make a new desktop folder called CD Design. To acquire the images for the CD, go to the website and copy all four Archie photos to your desktop.

You should see four thumbnail images on your desktop called "ArchieFront," "ArchieInside," "ArchieDisc," and "ArchieBack." Click and drag all four over the CD Design folder icon to put them inside. With all of the images in the folder, the links will stay constant.

ArchieFront

ArchieInside     CD Design

ArchieDisc

ArchieBack

### New Document

| | |
|---|---|
| Document Preset: [Custom] | OK |
| Number of Pages: 4 ☑ Facing Pages ☐ Master Text Frame | Cancel |
| Page Size: Compact Disc | Save Preset... |
| Width: 4.7222 in  Orientation: | More Options |
| Height: 4.75 in | |

**Columns**
Number: 1     Gutter: 0.1667 in

**Margins**
Top: 0 in     Inside: 0 in
Bottom: 0 in     Outside: 0 in

## 2 Create a four-page document

Open InDesign. Choose File > New > Document window. Make it four pages and confirm that Facing Pages is checked. With facing pages, we can see the inside cover next to the disc.

Choose Compact Disc from the Page Size pull-down menu and set the margins to zero.

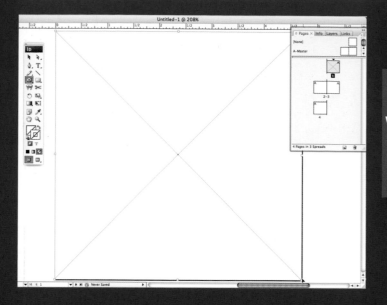

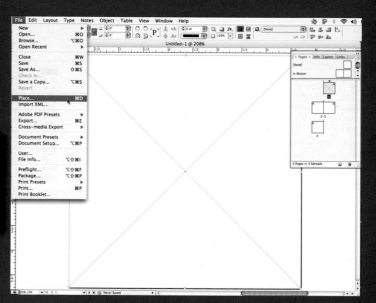

## 3 Draw a frame

Open the Pages Window by choosing Window > Pages. Double click in the top rectangle to make the first page active. Then select the Frame tool and drag a frame from top left to bottom right to fill the page.

## 4 Place the photo

Place a photo on the front cover by selecting File > Place. Choose "ArchieFront" from the CD Design folder and press Open.

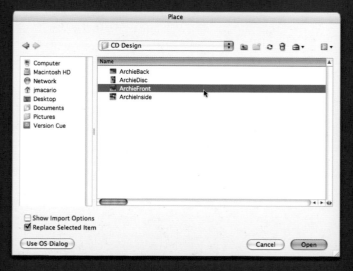

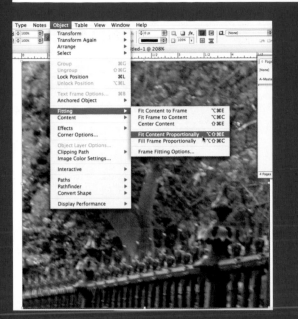

## 5 Resize

Resize the photo proportionately to fit the cover. Choose Object > Fitting > Fit Content Proportionately.

### Tip
InDesign displays images at low resolution for faster processing times. Your high-quality photos and vector images may appear bitmapped but will print out fine. To view images in high resolution, click on the photo and choose Object > Display Performance > High Quality Display.

## 6 Add the titles

Select the Type tool, click and drag a text box, add the title and format it. Tail Waggers is Geometric Slab 703 Extra Bold, 30 pts., right-aligned; the subtitle is Geometric 231, Regular, 11 pts., right-aligned. The text boxes are right-aligned. These fonts are available free from the Internet. Or select another Slab Serif font for the title and a sans-serif font for the subtitle.

To make the title appear white, open the Swatches Window and click on Paper. This means that when the project is printed, the paper will show through (white ink is not used to produce the text).

Like Illustrator, InDesign has the wonderful Change Case menu. Choose Type > Change Case to view the title variations; make the most effective case choice for your font.

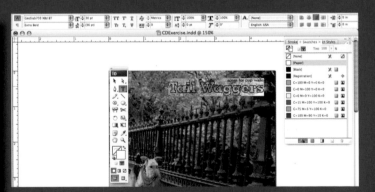

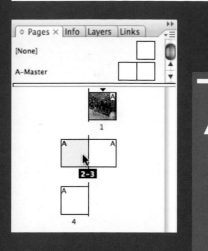

## 7 Make the inside cover

Double click on the second rectangle in the Pages Window to make the inside cover page active. Just as you did in step 3, select the Rectangle Frame tool, and click and drag a frame to fill the page. Use a short-cut command to place the image. Press Command + D and choose "ArchieInside" from the CD Design folder.

Resize the image to fit into the frame. Choose Object > Fitting > Fit Content Proportionately.

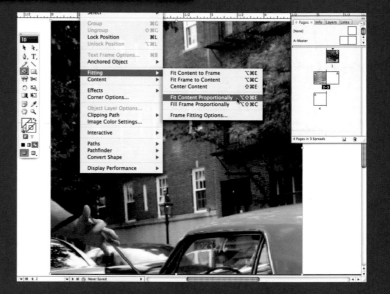

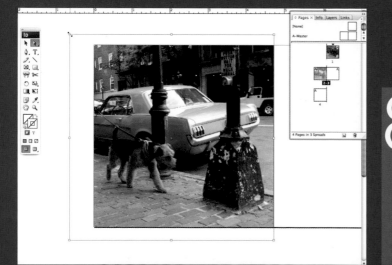

## 8 Adjust the photo

Select the white Direct Selection tool and click on the image to make specific adjustments to the photo. To resize proportionately, always hold the Shift key down, and click and drag on a corner control button to make it fit the frame vertically. You can also use the Arrow keys on your keyboard to adjust its position within the frame.

# 9   Design the disc

Double click on the third rectangle in the Pages Window to begin the disc design. Press and hold your cursor over the Rectangle Frame tool to choose the Ellipse Frame tool.

With the Ellipse tool, click once in page three and type "4.63" (11.76 cm) in the width and height boxes. Use the black Selection tool to move the frame into the center of the page.

# 10   Place and adjust the photo

Press Command + D and choose "ArchieDisc" from the CD Design folder. Choose Objects > Fitting > Fit Content Proportionately to resize the image to fit the disc format.

Select the white Direct Selection tool to adjust the image so that it works well within the circle format. Keep in mind that there will be a hole in the middle! When resizing, always hold the Shift key down and use a corner control point so that you resize proportionately.

## 11 Draw the center hole

Draw a black circle to indicate the center hole. First make the blue frame edges show by pressing Command + Cntl + H. Now draw two guides that intersect the center control points of the frame.

Select the Ellipse tool (press and hold the Rectangle Shape tool).

Position your cursor at the intersection in the center of the circle.

Hold the Option and Shift keys down and drag to draw a 0.60 inch (1.52 cm) circle. The Option key ensures the circle draws from the center point, the Shift key ensures that the ellipse is circular. Use the toolbox fill color to make it black.

## 12 Add the title to the disc

First, copy the front cover formatted copy. Double click on the front cover thumbnail in the Pages Window. Using the black Selection tool, hold the Shift key down and click on the two title boxes to select them. Press Command + C to copy.

Then double click on the page three thumbnail in the Pages Window to bring you back to the disc page. Press Command + V to paste the title onto the disc.

Modify the size and placement to better suit the round format. This text is now the same style, but 18 pts. and 8 pts.

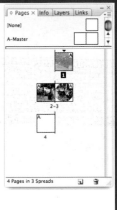

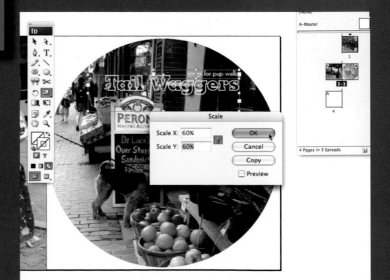

## 13 Make the back cover

Double click on the fourth page in the Pages Window to make the back cover active.

Brace yourself—we're going to change the entire file format to accommodate the wider back cover and spines (this will not affect the frames you've already completed).

Choose File > Document Setup. Change the Width to 5.88 inches (14.94 cm) and press OK.

## 14 Draw guides for the spines

The spines are 0.25 inches (0.64 cm) wide and will print with the back cover. They are then folded so they appear in the sides of the CD case. Click in the left ruler and drag a guide to indicate the spine at 0.25 inches (0.64 cm).

Reposition the zero point on the right-hand edge of the rectangle and drag another guide to 0.25 inches (0.64 cm) away from the right side. To reposition the ruler zero point, click in the top-left-hand corner of the rulers and drag the zero point to the right-hand edge of the document.

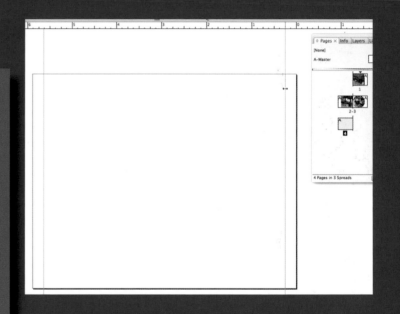

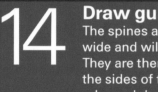

## 15 Design the back cover

Draw a Rectangle Frame that is 5.88 inches (14.94 cm) wide and 4.75 inches (12.07 cm) high. Press Command + D and choose "ArchieBack" to place the photo on the back cover. Then choose Object > Fitting > Fit Object Proportionately.

Use your white Direct Selection tool to adjust the position of the image in the frame.

## 16 Add the copy

Add a text box and song titles. You can get the song title list from the website. Copy "songlist.doc" onto your desktop and move it into your CD Design folder.

Press Command + D to place the "songlist.doc" into the text frame on the back cover.

Format the back copy with one of the typefaces you've already used. This is Geometric 231, Roman, 9pts. This listing has two text boxes. The songs are left-aligned, and the numbers are in a narrow box with right-aligned format.

## 17 Add titles for the spines

Add another narrow type box for the spine titles. Highlight the text and use the Eyedropper tool to copy the back cover formatting to the spines copy. You can then modify the spine copy. The spine title format was changed to Geometric Slab for the main title and Geometric 231 for the subtitle; both are 9 pts.

## 18 Place the spine titles

Once you've formatted the spine titles, rotate and place them in the spine areas. Click on the spine title text box, choose the Rotate tool, click on the file to open the Rotate window and type "90" in the Angle box. Press OK. Use your black Selection tool to move it into position on the left.

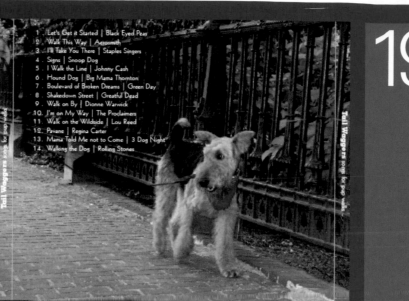

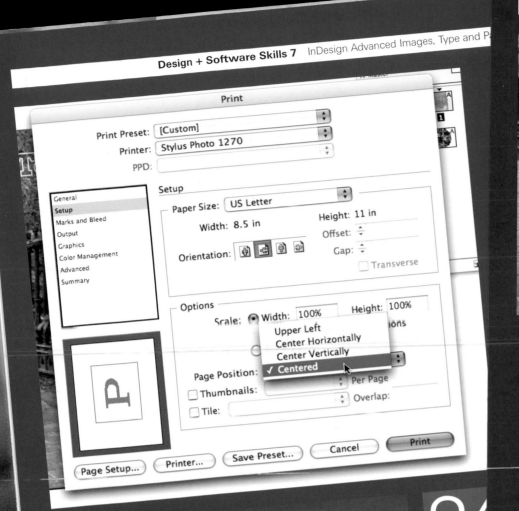

24

**Print**

Print Preset: [Custom]

Printer: Stylus Photo 1270

PPD:

**Setup**

Paper Size: US Letter

Width: 8.5 in          Height: 11 in

Offset:

Orientation:          Gap:

□ Transverse

General
**Setup**
Marks and Bleed
Output
Graphics
Color Management
Advanced
Summary

**Options**

Scale: ● Width: 100%      Height: 100%

Upper Left
Center Horizontally
Center Vertically
✓ Centered

Page Position:          Per Page

□ Thumbnails:          Overlap:

□ Tile:

( Page Setup... )  ( Printer... )  ( Save Preset... )  ( Cancel )  ( Print )

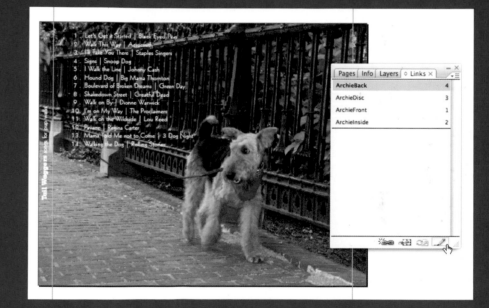

## 19 Position the spine titles

After it's positioned sideways, make the title centered on the spine. Use the Selection tool to pull the text frame as long as the cover height. Then choose the Type tool, click in the frame, and use the Control Bar to set the format to Align Center.

Copy the title to the other spine. Choose the Rotate tool again, change the angle value to 180, and press Copy (rather than OK). Move this text box to the right-hand margin.

Press Command + S to save your fantastic work.

## 20 Edit the photo

Now you can modify the image in Photoshop to burn (slightly darken) the area behind the text so that it is more legible. Click on the Links tab in the Pages window. Click on "ArchieBack" in the window so the line highlights blue. Click on the Edit Original button in the lower right of the window. This will open the file in Photoshop.

### Tip

All of your placed images are listed in the Links window. If you move a file or rename a file or folder, InDesign will prompt you to fix the link. Relink automatically using the bottom left-hand button.

21

## 22 Update the photo

Go back to InDesign and update the photo on page four. Notice the exclamation mark next to "ArchieBack" in the Link window—this indicates the image has been edited. Simply click the Update Link button at the bottom of the window to update the image in your InDesign file.

---

For Olivia and Lauren Alvarez, Elspeth White, Johanna Edwardsen

First published in Great Britain 2001 by
Kyle Cathie Limited
122 Arlington Road
London NW1 7HP
www.kylecathie.co.uk
general.enquiries@kyle-cathie.com

Published in paperback 2006

ISBN (10-digit) 1 85626 658 3
ISBN (13-digit) 978 1 85626
658 1

Text © 2001 Alison Price
Photographs © 2001 Tim Winter
except for those listed on page 176

Senior Editor: Helen Woodhall
Editorial Assistants: Andrie Morris &
 Esme West
Copy editor: Gillian Haslam
Stylist: Pippin Britz
Designer: Paul Welti
Production: Sha Huxtable & Alice
 Holloway
Index: Helen Snaith

Alison Price is hereby identified as the author of this work in accordance with Section 77 of the Copyright, Designs and Patents Act 1988.

A Cataloguing In Publication record for this title is available from the British Library.

Colour separations by Colourscan

Printed by Tien Wah Press, Singapore

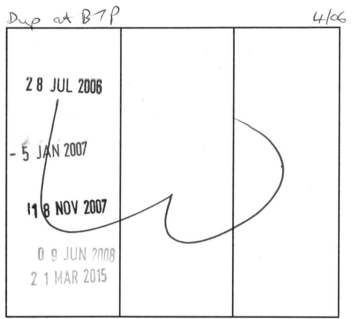 

# contents

# introduction

Something old, something new, something borrowed, something blue – the centuries-old chant for a bride on her wedding day. The tradition of the wedding predates pagan times, when the bride wore a simple white dress as a sign of purity, perhaps with flowers in her hair, and exchanged wedding rings made from straw or crude bands of metal with her betrothed. Although the ritual and meaning of the wedding ceremony has its roots firmly in the past, marriage in the twenty-first century is still just as important as it was in ancient times.

We started our wedding planning business over twenty years ago and I have lost count of how many weddings we have organised. As a company, we have had the opportunity to travel far and wide and feel very lucky to be involved. Some brides allowed up to a year to plan their day, while others gave us as little as ten days! Each celebration is totally different, from the grand dinner and dance to a simple family lunch.

Yet whatever the scale of the celebration, one thing remains constant – above all, the occasion is very personal. To be able to create a day that is so special that it will remain in people's memories for the rest of their lives is certainly a great responsibility and honour. Watching as the bride appears for the first time is quite magical, as is observing the just-wed couple arriving from the ceremony so happy they rarely stop smiling. It is a privilege to hear wonderful speeches and to understand that we have played a major part in creating a very happy and memorable day.

And when it is over, I arrive home after all the months of planning, knowing every detail has been perfect. That we have helped to make a dream come true gives me a great sense of personal satisfaction. We have taken time to get to know the families and understand exactly how they would like the wedding to be. Not that it has necessarily been plain sailing all the way. There have been hours spent planning

with the bride, making decisions on invitations, flowers, music, menus and drinks, the site, the style of dress and the number of attendants – the attention to detail all pays off on the day.

The advice I have given over the years is first of all to set a realistic budget and stick to it. Plan very carefully, taking into consideration the smallest detail, but do not become stressed over details you cannot change. This should be a happy time, so try not to become bogged down in the fact that you cannot have the car you wanted because it is already booked. The amount of decision making, attention to detail and sheer effort that is required can be quite daunting. Do make sure to discuss with your fiancé what you both want. It is very important not to make him and his family feel they are not included in the arrangements. There will be many times you may have to be the diplomat, so be ready to play that part.

No other celebration surpasses the importance of a wedding. Marriage is a rite of passage, and is celebrated in different ways throughout the world. Although it will probably be the most important day of your life, remember that your wedding is also a day to be enjoyed by all. Arriving at that point requires great planning. This is not too difficult to do, just pay lots of attention to detail. You have probably never had to arrange a wedding before, but by the time your wedding arrives you will be an expert planner. This book contains years of experience; it is full of valuable advice and ideas on styles, drinks and menus, flowers and entertainment. I hope it will give you the enthusiasm you need to plan your very special day, and to enjoy the whole experience.

*Alison Price*

# first steps

So, the question has been popped, the champagne too, and now it's time to come back down to earth and

start organising. It may seem that there are a million and one things to do before the day, and the truth is,

there are. But by taking it step by step and keeping track along the way, you'll achieve your dream day.

# the engagement

The traditional length of an engagement is six months, and during this period of time all the activities of planning the wedding will take place, but this is not to say you cannot be engaged for a shorter (or, indeed, longer) period of time.

## ANNOUNCING YOUR ENGAGEMENT

Even in these modern days it is still appropriate for the man to 'pop the question'. However terrifying this must be, there comes a time in most relationships when this is the natural step. The tradition is for the man to ask the father of his fiancée for her hand in marriage, and I feel this custom is very charming and correct. Once this formality has taken place, he will then inform his parents. But in modern times, the couple will announce their intentions together.

Whatever you decide to do, there are some details and courtesies that are often followed. The groom's parents should write to the future in-laws expressing how delighted and thrilled they are. If the parents have not met, then an invitation from the groom's parents is usually extended for lunch or dinner. When families have been informed, start to tell other family members and friends. You may wish to announce your engagement in the forthcoming marriages section of your local or a national newspaper. The bride's family normally pays for this. Each family must be consulted, and parental divorce, remarriage and widowhood dictate the wording. Write a letter or send a fax confirming the details of the announcement. If you are unsure of the correct wording, your chosen publication will be able to guide you. Do take advice as it would be very embarrassing to make a mistake and unintentionally upset someone.

Here are some examples of typical engagement announcements.

---

*Mr R.A. Graeme and Miss E.M. Garden*

*The engagement is announced between*
*Robin, elder son of Dr and Mrs Nicolas Graeme*
*of Crosbies, Hampshire, and Emily, third daughter*
*of Mr and Mrs John Garden*
*of Georgetown, Suffolk.*

---

If the parents of the bride or groom (or both) have been widowed, the announcement may be along these lines:

---

*Mr R.A. Graeme and Miss E.M. Garden*

*The engagement is announced between Robin,*
*the elder son of the late Dr and Mrs Nicolas Graeme*
*of Crosbies, Hampshire, and Emily, third daughter*
*of the late Mr and Mrs John Garden*
*of Georgetown, Suffolk.*

---

Where parents are separated the announcement might read as follows:

---

*Mr R.A. Graeme and Miss E.M. Garden*

*The engagement is announced between*
*Robin, elder son of Dr Nicolas Graeme of Kensington,*
*London, and Mrs Julia Graeme of Crosbies,*
*Hampshire, and Emily, third daughter*
*of Mr John Garden of Georgetown,*
*Suffolk, and Mrs Mary Garden of*
*Knightsbridge, London.*

---

If the groom's parents are separated, and those of the bride remarried, the wording may be like this:

> *Mr R.A. Graeme and Miss E.M. Garden*
>
> *The engagement is announced between Robin,*
> *elder son of Dr Nicolas Graeme of Kensington, London,*
> *and Mrs Julia Graeme of Crosbies, Hampshire,*
> *and Emily, third daughter of Mr John Garden*
> *of Camp Street, Edinburgh, and*
> *Mrs Mary Hunt of Seatons,*
> *Devon.*

If both mothers have remarried after divorce, the announcement could read as below.

> *Mr R.A. Graeme and Miss E.M. Garden*
>
> *The engagement is announced between Robin,*
> *elder son of Dr Nicolas Graeme of Kensington, London,*
> *and Mrs Albert Hall of Hotpot, Lancashire, and Emily,*
> *third daughter of Mr John Garden of Camp Street,*
> *Edinburgh, and Mrs Mary Hunt of Seatons,*
> *Devon.*

The bride may have been married and widowed, in which case she may be referred to by her married name:

> *Mr R.A. Graeme and Mrs Emily Gage*
>
> *The engagement is announced between Robin,*
> *elder son of Dr and Mrs Nicolas Graeme of Crosbies,*
> *Hampshire, and Emily, third daughter of Mr and*
> *Mrs John Garden of Georgetown, Suffolk,*
> *and widow of the late Mr John Gage.*

## CHOOSING THE RING

When a friend of mine proposed to his wife, he hedged his bets by selecting three rings for his bride-to-be. Luckily for him she chose the first ring she was shown and the remaining rings were returned to the jewellers. I still think of that moment when she opened the velvet box to find the most beautiful emerald and diamond ring. A few years later we discussed this rather unusual approach by her husband. She said there was no way she would have wanted any other ring – as far as she was concerned that was the one and only.

I'm happy to admit I am rather old-fashioned in this respect and I still love the thought of the man down on one knee, slipping the ring on his fiancée's finger. It has been selected out of love and will be cherished for the rest of their lives together. However, on a practical note, most grooms should consult their bride as to the style of ring they prefer, because it will be worn almost every day.

So where do you start, with so many styles now available? You may be lucky and receive a ring that has been in a family for generations. The ring given to one of our brides had been in the groom's family for three or four generations. When her husband proposed he slipped the ring on her finger, only to discover it was far too big. However, it took her at least two years to have the ring altered, and this was only after a few panic-struck moments thinking she had lost the ring because it kept slipping off. If you are given a family ring, please make sure that you have it altered to fit by a reputable jeweller. This applies to all

engagement rings. Remember that on hot days your hands swell and on cold days your hands shrink. Rings purchased in an auction house or antique shops are very good value for money. The important rule is to go to somewhere reputable. Choose carefully, as years of wear can weaken the settings. Do not let this put you off – simply take the ring to a trustworthy jeweller for any repairs and cleaning.

One of my oldest friends selected the most wonderful solitaire diamond for his bride's engagement ring and they then chose the setting together. Some brides are lucky enough to commission a design of their own choosing and select the stones for the setting. For most people, however, the choice will be a new ring or an antique from a retail shop, antique shop or even an antique market.

The first point to consider is to select a stone that will sparkle and catch the eye. Diamonds are the logical choice, representing purity and eternity. There are certain rules to follow when selecting diamonds. The value is determined by the four Cs: cut, clarity, carat and colour. The cut determines whether the stone is sparkling or lifeless. Clarity is the absence of any flaws. Carat is the weight of the stone and colour is rated on a scale from D to Z, with D representing the most perfect colour and also the most expensive.

Not everyone's choice will be a diamond. Some may prefer a coloured stone; my personal favourite is a sapphire. As with diamonds, the colour of the stones is very important to the value. Sapphires should be almost a cornflower blue, emeralds a deep green, rubies crimson. Although the most popular choice is a brilliant-cut solitaire diamond ring, if your choice is a coloured stone surrounded by diamonds, think about the shape of the coloured stone and setting. Remember the centre stone is the focal point of the ring, so the side stones should not detract.

Retail jewellers have vast selection of designs and stones. This is relatively good value because mass production of rings can keep costs low. Also remember that if you set your heart on platinum or white gold for the setting, this must complement the wedding ring as they are nearly always worn together. Some styles of engagement rings may be difficult to wear with a wedding ring, so take all these points into consideration.

*'did you know that in ancient Rome, parents as well as the betrothed would exchange rings?'*

One point to remember is styles go in and out of fashion. My advice is to select a style that will not date. You will always want to wear the ring you chose together. A further alternative to consider is a ring that doubles as an engagement and wedding ring. This is usually a simple band set with diamonds or other stones placed at intervals, or two bands connected with diamonds.

You may consider having your birthstone incorporated into your engagement ring. It is said to bring luck. Here is a list of stones and their meanings.

| | |
|---|---|
| JANUARY | – Garnet – *Truth* |
| FEBRUARY | – Amethyst – *Sincerity* |
| MARCH | – Aquamarine – *Courage* |
| APRIL | – Diamond – *Purity* |
| MAY | – Emerald – *Harmony* |
| JUNE | – Pearl – *Wisdom* |
| JULY | – Ruby – *Love* |
| AUGUST | – Peridot – *Contentment* |
| SEPTEMBER | – Sapphire – *Wisdom* |
| OCTOBER | – Opal – *Good fortune* |
| NOVEMBER | – Topaz – *Intelligence* |
| DECEMBER | – Turquoise – *Success* |

## AN ENGAGEMENT PARTY

The announcement of your engagement is the start of celebrations with family and friends. As a couple you will be the centre of attention during the months leading to your wedding day. If you wish to arrange a party to celebrate your engagement, it can take any form you wish, from a small dinner party at home to a drinks party, usually hosted by the bride's parents with an informal speech given by the girl's father. Or, as the couple, you can host your own party and make an informal speech. Engagement parties are by nature small gatherings of friends and family, they are not meant to be large affairs. That will be your wedding.

# getting started

Now you are engaged and things have calmed down, start discussing and making decisions on the date, budget and style of wedding you both would like. Most couples have limitations, mainly concerning the budget, but also over where and when the wedding will be held. Whatever you decide, you must be flexible and prepared to make compromises to achieve your wedding dreams.

Choosing the date of your wedding concerns not just you and your fiancé. It involves both sets of parents and the availability of your chosen professionals and venues. Diaries will have to be co-ordinated, taking into consideration the day of the week. Have alternative dates in mind, not only for the place of the ceremony, but also the honeymoon destination, the venue for the reception and the services of the floral decorator, marquee company, band, photographer, car hire and reception venue.

Choosing the time of year will make a difference to your options. If your choice is to marry at a traditional time of year or away from home, this will probably limit the number of guests who are able to attend. Most people think only of marrying in the spring and summer months, but do consider the autumn or winter months. You know that the weather may not be wonderful, so you can stop worrying about it. You will probably be able to have first choice on the time of day for your service and chosen venue. Most of your guests will be able to attend. Hotels for the honeymoon are also cheaper out of the high season. When planning the time and place you wish to marry, consider the guests who will have to travel a long way – do not expect your guests to arrive bright-eyed for an early morning wedding.

Discuss together the style of wedding you would both like and start working out your budget. Write a list of your wishes, trying to be practical and taking the not-so-obvious things into consideration. Everything you decide upon will affect the outcome of the next

decision to be made, so you must understand fully the implications of all your choices before they are set into motion. For example, there is no point having your wedding at five or six o'clock in the evening when your budget will not allow you to have a large reception and dinner. If your budget is restricted and you would like a large number of guests, plan an early or mid-afternoon wedding followed by a reception serving canapés or afternoon tea.

Decide on your priorities. If flowers and music are what really matter to you, then allocate a larger proportion of your budget to these items. If sitting down to an amazing lunch or dinner with fine wines is your dream, then cut back in other areas. Keep priorities in perspective. If you are planning a large reception, remember you will not be able to spend time with your guests – a short hello will be the only few words you are able to exchange. Don't expect to do more than that as it's simply not achievable.

Another point to consider is not to plan a wedding that is outside your normal entertaining style. Weddings are a way for you to express your personalities. By tradition, a wedding involves many social and financial backgrounds, as well as ages. You are not there to shock and your guests must feel comfortable. Every wedding we have planned and catered for has always reflected the personality and style of the couple's families.

Investigate all these things before confirming the date. Most brides who contact us have alternative dates; they want to have the reception venue in place before they confirm the place of service because it is becoming increasingly difficult to secure popular venues and services. Bringing all the elements together can almost feel like a military operation. Keep your options open, be very practical. If the venue for your reception is not available until midwinter and you have set your heart on a summer wedding, it will need a little more research and compromise. When you have nearly all the elements in place, you can confirm the date. Do not even think of doing this before as you could be disappointed and you will probably have to start the hard work all over again.

# the wedding planner

Planning a wedding can be a very complex affair, but this planner will prove to be invaluable. Tick off each item when it has been organised

## SIX MONTHS OR MORE AHEAD

If your families have not met, arrange an informal get-together.
Place an announcement in a newspaper of your choice.

CHOOSE THE DATE  Decide on what style of wedding you would like. If you are planning your wedding during the busy season, discuss alternative dates and try to be flexible as you may not be able to have your first choice of date. Arrange to see your minister, priest, rabbi or registrar to arrange the ceremony.

DRAW UP THE GUEST LIST  When you have worked out how many guests you want to invite, plan your budget. Reserve accommodation at local hotels for your guests from out-of-town.

PLAN YOUR BUDGET AND YOUR PRIORITIES  Now you can plan what style of wedding and reception you would like, within the budget you have set. Your dream may be to have the most amazing flowers, or food may be your passion, so decide now which elements are the most important.

ARRANGE THE RECEPTION  Visit venues and hotels. If you are planning your reception in a marquee, arrange for at least three estimates from reputable marquee companies.

CHOOSE A CATERER  The cost of the food and drinks served will depend entirely on the budget you have set. If you are using a hotel or civil venue, they may have deals that include pre-lunch or dinner drinks, canapés, three-course dinner, wines, soft drinks, wedding cake, a toast-master and sometimes music. Most caterers will provide sample menus. Ask them to include all the elements — food, service, hire of equipment, drinks, ice, etc. Don't forget to give timings. A good caterer will arrange for a tasting; this is usually held at their offices. Decide whether the caterer or florist will provide flowers for the tables.

CHOOSING YOUR FLOWERS  Arrange to see florists who will understand the style you like. When you make your choice, confirm immediately in writing as good floral decorators are in great demand.

BOOK YOUR PHOTOGRAPHER  Discuss with your photographer the style you would like. Ask what the price includes and the cost of prints. This also applies if you wish to have your wedding videoed. Check that the minister or registrar will allow photos to be taken or a video recorded during the ceremony.

THE WEDDING DRESS  Order your dress, shoes, gloves, veil and accessories. Start to think about any special lingerie, stockings or other hair accessories that your dress design will require.

BRIDESMAIDS AND PAGEBOYS  Start to think about who you would like.

HAIR AND MAKE-UP  Book your hairdresser and make-up artist.

ENTERTAINMENT  Arrange to see any bands or musicians you would like and book them as soon as you have made your choice.

HONEYMOON  Plan and book your honeymoon. If you are marrying in the height of the holiday season, have some alternative destinations.

## FOUR TO SIX MONTHS AHEAD

THE CEREMONY  If you are marrying in a church or synagogue, arrange to see the minister to discuss the service, music and readings.

INVITATIONS AND SERVICE SHEETS  Visit printers to choose your style of invitations. If you wish to have the invitations specially designed, start planning now. Also order place cards, seating cards, menus, service sheets and favours.

WEDDING GIFT LIST  Make your lists and register with your chosen outlets.

WEDDING CAKE  Choose the style and flavour of cake and place your order.

TRANSPORT  Arrange any necessary transportation.

WEDDING RINGS  Order or purchase wedding rings.

WEDDING NIGHT  If you plan to stay in a local hotel for your wedding night, now is the time to make your choice and book the room.

GROOM'S AND GOING-AWAY OUTFITS  Purchase or reserve the groom's outfit.

and always confirm all your arrangements in writing, keeping copies of the letters for your own file. Check that you are keeping to your budget. If you have less than six months to plan your wedding, don't panic. Just start as soon as possible.

Arrange hire of best man's outfit and other male members of the bridal party. Start looking for the bride's going-away outfit.

ATTENDANTS' GIFTS Choose thank-you gifts for your attendants and best man.

NAME CHANGES If you are changing your name, remember to allow plenty of time for a new passport. Notify your bank and building society.

## TWO TO THREE MONTHS AHEAD

INVITATIONS Send out invitations at least eight weeks before the day. Make a list of acceptances, refusals and any special requests. Confirm any hotel arrangements for guests who require accommodation.

HAIR AND MAKE-UP Make a separate appointment with your chosen hairdresser and beautician to discuss your requirements.

GIFTS FOR THE BRIDE AND GROOM Choose presents for each other and for parents of both parties.

## ONE MONTH AHEAD

PRESENTS Start sending thank-you notes as gifts arrive.

WEDDING ANNOUNCEMENT Send wedding announcement to your chosen paper.

MARRIAGE LICENCE Obtain the licence.

## TWO WEEKS AHEAD

SEATING PLAN This is probably one of the most difficult things to arrange, so start to think about it. Write seating plan and place cards.

WEDDING DRESS AND SHOES Arrange for final fitting. Most brides lose weight before the wedding day, so if you feel that you may lose a few more pounds, tell your designer or fitter. Start to break in the shoes at home.

SPEECHES AND TOASTS Start to write speeches.

CATERER Confirm final numbers.

BEAUTY TREATMENTS Have a facial and massage to relax, have a trial run with your headdress and make-up.

## ONE WEEK AHEAD

WEDDING DRESS Pick up your dress or have it delivered. Try on your entire outfit including headdress, underwear and shoes, but don't forget to leave one item off – it's considered unlucky to try on the whole outfit before the day.

HONEYMOON Start packing for your honeymoon.

## THE DAY BEFORE

REHEARSAL Have a rehearsal if possible.

BEAUTY Have a manicure and pedicure.

## ON THE DAY

PRESENTS Give presents to your parents and bridal party with a note of thanks for their help and support.

BEAUTY Have a relaxing massage if possible.

FOOD Arrange to have a light snack and just one glass of champagne. It's important that you have something to eat before the wedding.

TIMING Allow at least two hours for hair and make-up, thirty to forty-five minutes for dressing and thirty minutes for photos at home.

# setting the style

Most young girls have dreamed of what style of wedding they would like. The childhood fantasy often takes the shape of a fairytale princess in the most beautiful dress holding a bouquet of garden roses, surrounded by her friends and family, followed by dancing to romantic music under the stars with her groom. I think it has become increasingly difficult to define the traditional wedding as there are now so many styles and many more considerations apply, such as interfaith and interracial marriages, second and third marriages and marriage between couples who have lived together for a long time. What style of dress applies to a second or third marriage? Some brides remarry in white, others in cream or soft colours. Who is to say what is right or wrong? Only you can determine the style for your day.

Most of the couples whose weddings we have planned have definite ideas for their special day, but reality has to come into play. Our first question is always budget. Once this is determined, then you can plan the style you would like. Start by making a list of the priorities. Discuss in detail what you both would like. Take into consideration the time of year. Most couples think of early or late summer for their nuptials. Charlotte Barford, who works with us, married in February. She planned a winter wonderland style, her dress trimmed with white fur, the church decorated with frosted branches complete with icicles! And to complete the fairytale, during the afternoon reception, as guests gazed out of the windows, it snowed.

For a wedding we arranged in the autumn, we created a suitably seasonal style. The bride carried a beautiful bouquet of berries and foliage, and the lunch tables were decorated with sweet chestnuts still in their prickly shells, pears, dark purple grapes, walnuts, squashes and pumpkins.

During the spring and summer, on Saturdays I hardly pass a church without seeing signs of a wedding. Spring brings forth such wonderful flowers and fresh colours. Bouquets of snowdrops, white hyacinths and paper whites tied with simple garden twine. On dining

'for most people, planning the
reception at home can bring a new
vitality to the house and garden'

tables, a collection of small glass containers holding snowdrops and grape hyacinths complete the picture of spring. Marrying in summer means that with the wealth of flowers available you can create the most romantic style, choosing soft sweetpea colours for bridesmaids' dresses and for the bride, a bouquet of peonies. Dining tables can be draped in cloths the colours of sweetpeas and decorated containers filled with garden roses and peonies.

I know that not everyone's budgets will be able to accommodate some of the ideas presented here, but this does not prevent you from scaling down. Home – be it a large house or small flat – offers the most personal of all sites for the celebrations. It has its own warmth and character simply from being lived in, creating a feeling of comfort and familiarity for all, making it suitable for an intimate lunch for close family and friends, afternoon cocktail reception, barbecue or marquee in the garden for dinner followed by dancing. Decorations can take their cue from the style of the home. Some may dream of creating a style from the eighteenth century, but this won't work if the house is very modern. Some houses are just made for a wedding, with large flat lawns for marquees, wonderful gardens just right for photographs. Another house may require serious efforts to achieve this. But for most people, planning the reception at home can bring a new vitality to the house and garden through repairing, painting and replanting the garden with flowers that will be at their peak on the day. At one wedding where we provided the catering, the mother

of the bride planted a bed of white cosmos. On the day they were perfect, the tall, delicate plants swaying in the afternoon breeze, looking so soft and romantic.

# spring is in the air

On a spring evening our reception takes place in a conservatory. Pre-dinner drinks and snacks are served in the garden. Inspired by the conservatory, the tables are decorated with hand-painted pots of variegated thyme. As the evening progresses the scent of thyme fills the air. Place cards are plant labels tucked into pots for guests to take away and plant in their herb garden or window box as a memento of the happy day. Placed on the plates are small favours filled with Provençal herbs for cooking. A cream cloth reflects the pots while green runners complement the natural colours of the herbs and also serve to mark the place settings. As the light fades, the tables are illuminated from above by simple glass lanterns, the chains on which they hang entwined with beautiful stephanotis. Blossoms are scattered around the base of the candles, adding to the scented air. Around the ledge small candles flicker. Herb-flavoured breads are baked in small terracotta pots and herb butter moulded into small wooden bowls. All these elements harmonise with the conservatory and the garden beyond to create a feeling of serenity.

**(Left) Natural colours and materials – growing herbs, wooden bowls and terracotta pots – combine to create a calming and gentle scene. (Right) Herbs grown in pots make an interesting change from the more usual arrangements of flowers and can be taken home by guests at the end of the day.**

(Left) Stephanotis petals scattered in the lanterns add the finishing touch.

(Right) Placing fabric runners horizontally across the table divides the table naturally into place settings.

(Below) The garden theme started by the growing herbs is continued in the plant markers, each inscribed with a guest's name.

# twilight by a lake

This romantic setting by a lake is just perfect for an evening reception at twilight on warm summer's evening. Simple white linen covers the tables. In the centre of the tables, candles float in tall glass cylinders reflecting the light on the water and the wine glasses. Single Old English garden roses, musk mallow and miniature artichokes set in single tiny vases are the only flowers required to add to the cool romantic feeling. Clear glass lanterns hang from the trees and from shepherds' crooks. As night falls, the bridge is illuminated with candles. The atmosphere is one of mystery and the romance of candlelight, the setting cool and relaxing. When the dinner is over, the path back to the house is scattered with rose petals and marked with tall hurricane lanterns filled with water and floating candles.

**Make the most of a natural setting such as this by using a simple colour scheme and flowers in keeping with the country setting.**

NfB
*Twenty Seventh July 2002*

Tony Mascolo

(Left) Linen napkins and beautiful glassware add a touch of luxury to the simple colour scheme. (Below) Frosted glass salt and pepper pots are used with matching bone spoons.

(Left) Even the bridge is co-opted into the wedding picture by placing candles all along its handrails. (Right) Spiky artichokes provide a contrast to the soft fullness of the roses. (Below) Groups of candles of differing heights look more inviting than a single candle placed in the middle of the table.

# autumn bounty

Most of us think of weddings in the spring or summer, with soft colours and warm days. We tend to forget the wonderful Indian summers which continue until early autumn. Flowers and foliage are the bright jewels of autumn. The colours are magnificent – shades of cream, yellow, rust, orange, red, bronze and brown are all stunning. Our autumn wedding is designed to use all these colours. The tables are dressed with light brown top cloths, elegantly edged with a double satin ribbon. Pumpkins and squashes act as vases to hold flowers. Little squashes have been hollowed out and carved with hearts to become nightlight holders. The place card holders are golden and red pears with a green leaf attached with a dainty ribbon. Each place setting has a tiny vase of flowers. Napkins secured with ribbon complement the edge of the tablecloth. The light reflecting through the squashes and the warmth of the colours create a friendly atmosphere.

**Make the most of natural seasonal produce when planning your theme. It will make a lasting impression on you and your guests who will be reminded of your special day every year when autumn arrives.**

# winter wonderland

Our winter wonderland reflects the season of Christmas. The inviting warmth seen through the doors welcomes guests. To make the entrance romantic, hearts made from white roses frame the doors; they are linked with a sage-coloured grosgrain ribbon. The box balls are wrapped with tiny lights.

As guests enter the house they are offered a welcome glass of mulled wine. The scent of spices pervades the air. An old mophead bay has been given new life as a favour tree. Sprayed silver, bunches are decorated with miniature stockings filled with mulling spices for guests to take home as a reminder of the celebrations. To solve the problem of constantly keeping logs burning, candles fill the hearth and give a warm glow, twinkling in the silver ornaments decorating the mantel. The tables sparkle with silver and candles; each guest has a posy of white roses to which their place card is attached. Silver bowls filled with white amaryllis complete the chosen theme of silver, sage and white. Silver hearts, crystal drops and lights decorate the tree. All these elements will remind the happy couple of their wedding day each year as December approaches.

**A cool colour scheme of whites and silvers is given a warming and welcoming feel by the use of candlelight.**

(This page) White candles
used en masse make a
stunning focal point.
(Opposite) Rose hearts frame
the doorway and lead the way
to the party.

# who does what?

When planning a wedding – no matter how large or small – you will need supporters. This is the time to start making decisions together, learning to make compromises and to be tactful and diplomatic. Choose family or friends who will be a great source of strength, wisdom and good advice and who can be very practical. Choose carefully – you want to have the people who mean the most to you. There is no point in choosing someone who can only be there on the day as you will be working as a team. Sit down and discuss in detail whom you both would like as the chief bridesmaid and best man. Make your choices from friends and family you know you can trust. It's a good idea to have at least one person on your team who is married and can offer advice from personal experience.

## THE BRIDE

As the bride you are the focal point, and your duty is to make yourself look wonderful. You make the choice of your dress, shoes, flowers, hairdresser and beautician, not only for yourself, but also for your bridesmaids, pages and attendants. Plan your trousseau and going- away outfit. Choose the flowers at the church and reception, your bouquet and the attendants' flowers. Organise the music for the service. Select a wedding present for your husband-to-be.

## THE GROOM

As the groom, you appoint your best man and ushers, after discussion with your fiancée. You organise and pay for your wedding outfit, and pay for the wedding ring or rings. You are also traditionally expected to pay for your bride's bouquet and for those of the bridesmaids, plus buttonholes for yourself, best man and ushers.

The groom pays for all the church expenses, excluding the flowers and music. As well as selecting a wedding-day gift for your bride, you also give presents to the bridesmaids and pageboys. Although it is not traditional for the groom to give a present to the best man, I think it is rather unkind not to recognise all the hard work, kindness and effort he has contributed to make the day as seamless as possible not only for you but also the bride's family and guests.

So show your appreciation by giving a thoughtful gift with a letter of heartfelt thanks. The groom also pays for the hire of his car to the church or place of service and the car for leaving the reception, as well as organising and paying for the honeymoon.

## THE BRIDE'S PARENTS

The bride's parents traditionally bear most of the responsibility and cost of the wedding. In consultation with the groom's parents and the engaged couple, they compile the guest list and pay for announcements in the press. The parents organise the wording, printing and posting of the invitations and the printing of the service sheets. The transport for the bridal party and flowers and music for the service are also their responsibilities.

The bride's dress and her going-away outfit are traditionally paid for by her parents. There is also a debate concerning who pays for the bridesmaids' and pageboys' outfits. They used to pay for their own outfits, but these costs now seem to be borne by the bride's parents. The mother of the bride has the wonderful task of selecting her outfit and sharing the hairdresser and make-up artist with the bride. The father of bride selects his outfit for the day, arranges a haircut and, as with the groom and best man, makes sure there is no polish left on his shoes, just in case he steps on the bride's dress.

## THE GROOM'S PARENTS

They assume very few duties. They supply a list of guests and arrive on the day looking wonderful and are charming to all. One word of advice is not to upstage the parents of the bride, so try to ascertain the style and colour of the bride's mother's outfit well in advance. If the bride's parents live abroad or are deceased, I feel the groom's parents should take over the responsibilities of the bride's parents in helping the couple with the arrangements. If you feel the situation is appropriate, offer to help with the costs of the wedding.

## THE BEST MAN

The best man is extremely important and being asked to take on the role is a great honour. The best man plays a major role in all arrangements and should be a very close friend or family member who can be completely relied upon. Traditionally he is a bachelor, but these days I feel this is of little importance, so long as he is very organised and can deliver an excellent and witty speech (after all, his speech is nearly always the highlight of the reception). He must be kept informed of all the arrangements, such as who is coming to the wedding and the chosen ushers, bridesmaids and attendants.

He must also be very presentable. He has to make sure that all aspects of the groom's requirements are cared for, such as his wedding outfit, haircut and grooming, so he looks just as well groomed as the bride. On the day, he is responsible for looking after the groom's going-away outfit, as well as the honeymoon suitcase and bags, including passport and tickets.

He will also be in charge of organising the stag night and making sure the groom makes no payment for the evening. If the wedding is taking place away from the groom's home town, he books accommodation and arranges a dinner the night before the wedding, making sure the groom doesn't stay up until the small hours. He is responsible for making sure the groom has everything he requires for the wedding day and the night before. If the wedding is in the afternoon, he organises a lunch for the groom and ushers.

A few days before the wedding, the best man checks the service sheets have arrived and makes final checks on the transport

The bride's parents make all the arrangements for the reception. This includes food and drink, flowers, photographer, music, toastmaster, wedding cake and calligraphy for menus, place cards and seating cards.

Weddings can be extremely expensive affairs and I see nothing wrong in asking for contributions from the bride, the groom and his family. No one should put himself or herself under any unnecessary financial burden.

arrangements for the groom and himself and the going-away cars. He should check the ushers have a seating plan for the bride and groom's families at the service. In consultation with the bride's parents, he plans the timings of speeches and cake-cutting at the reception and knows the time of departure of the bride and groom. He may also act as toast-master.

On the wedding day, the best man prepares the groom's clothes and keeps the groom calm. He collects the buttonholes for himself, the groom and the ushers and double-checks he has the wedding rings. The best man accompanies the groom to the church and waits with him until the bride arrives, standing on his right-hand side. At the church, he ensures all relevant fees are paid and accompanies the chief bridesmaid to the signing of the register.

## THE CHIEF BRIDESMAID

The chief bridesmaid is usually about the same age as the bride. She can be married, but these days I think it sounds so very dull to be called the matron of honour. She helps the bride choose her dress or outfit and those of the other bridesmaids and pageboys, selecting colours, veils, shoes and even the style of the bouquets, and arranging for any necessary fittings. The chief bridesmaid checks the bride has all she requires for her honeymoon including the correct visas and

inoculations if necessary. She arranges the hen night or bridal shower. She is literally the bride's 'maid' – there to help and support in all matters pertaining to her day.

On the wedding day, the chief bridesmaid prepares the bride's clothes and ensures her suitcase and going-away clothes are at the reception. She checks that the bridal flowers arrive and generally helps to keep the bride calm and insists she has a snack before dressing. At the church, she waits for the bride to arrive for the ceremony, checking that everything is correct. During the service she looks after the bridal bouquet and takes care of the smaller bridesmaids and pageboys.

## BRIDESMAIDS AND PAGEBOYS

Once you have decided on the chief bridesmaid, think how many more bridesmaids you would like. Be practical about your numbers and choice. You really do not want an army. A chief bridesmaid and two others, not including pageboys, is a sensible number. If the groom has a sister then it is kind to include her. If you would like your bridesmaids to be children, make your choice from family or children of very close friends or your godchildren. Always ask the parents' permission before speaking to the child. Try not to choose children who are too young or over-excitable as they could be very disruptive during the ceremony. Think of the sizes too, as they will have to process down the aisle side by side and carry the train, so they should 'match' in height if possible. The bride is responsible for the attendants' outfits and they must follow what she would like to the letter. Bridesmaids carry posies of flowers, younger children baskets of flowers or petals.

## USHERS

Choose the ushers from both sides of the family and from friends of the bride and groom. This is important as they will be able to identify guests from both parties. The ushers are the best man's 'army', and as with all the main players they must be well groomed and charming. Their main duty is to welcome guests on the day and hand out the service sheets. Allow one usher per forty

guests, but you can never have too many. It is advisable for the ushers to have an informal evening with the groom and best man, running through their duties on the day. On the wedding day, the best man usually arranges for the ushers to have lunch with the groom. On the day, ushers should arrive at the church at least forty minutes before the start of the service to check all of the final details.

They should also welcome the guests, directing them to either the bride's or groom's side of the church. Family members, in particular the bride's mother, and all unaccompanied female guests should be escorted by the ushers to their seats. After the service, the ushers must ensure that all guests have transport to the reception.

# the guests

When thinking of your wedding, do you dream of a small gathering of close family and friends sharing an intimate lunch or dinner, where you are able to spend time with your guests? If a large party is what you have always longed for, you will probably only be able to have a brief time with your guests. If you have your heart set on a particular style and location, this will determine the numbers. The number of guests you wish to invite will be determined by the budget, so give yourself a maximum number. There are always different styles of receptions that will allow your budget to go further. An afternoon wedding followed by a reception of canapés and afternoon tea will make the budget go further, as will a buffet lunch or dinner. You may wish to have only close family and friends for the service, followed by a reception for the remaining members of your family and friends.

So you both have to sit down and start to draw up your lists, from friends and work and business colleagues. Parents of the bride and groom make their lists from family, friends, work and business colleagues. When the bride's parents are paying for the wedding, they are allowed to invite more guests; the same holds true if the groom's parents are paying. If you are paying for your own wedding and your budget becomes tight, I feel it's reasonable to ask parents for some financial help, particularly if their friends are on the guest list. If your parents are divorced and have remarried, then there will be more family and friends to invite.

Another thorny problem is those friends who think they are going to be invited and are not included in the guest list for reasons of your own. Be honest and say that you are having a small wedding and your budget is limited, as dealing with the problem honestly will head off any resentment. It is a courtesy to send invitations to the vicar and his wife, priest or rabbi and his wife or the officiant. It's also courteous to invite people you know will not be able to attend due to great distance or illness. The parents of the groom, best man, bridesmaids and ushers also receive invitations.

What remains most important is that you have the people you want to share your day with. So do not put yourselves under any more emotional pressure by feeling you are compelled to invite certain people, such as your boss or recent partners of your friends. Also consider whether you want so many business colleagues as this may make the occasion feel more like a corporate party than your wedding. You will have to consider some business and work colleagues, but the number is up to you, the budget and the space available.

Handling difficult situations such as recently separated or divorced couples if their ex-partners are invited calls for tact and diplomacy. My advice is to send each person an invitation. It's up to them to make up their minds whether they are going to attend. Don't do it for them by excluding one person, as this could cause bitterness and hurt.

You must set some limits – not only yourselves but also your parents. When you have compiled your guest list, if it is large, now is the time to edit. Within each family relationships are different, and both of you must be prepared to compromise. All sides must give and take when it comes to reducing the list. A good idea is to make an A and a B list. For example, there may be many courtesy invitations to families and friends who you know will not be able to attend. When you start to receive regrets, start sending invitations from the B list. However, do not do these weeks after the first invitations have been sent as they will definitely be perceived as an afterthought.

One problem that comes up time and again is whether or not to invite children to a wedding. This can be a delicate problem. All you can do is make a decision and stick to it. Once you have decided not to invite children, you must not make any exceptions. If you do, this is likely to cause offence to other guests. If, on the other hand, you decide that you will invite children, it's a good idea to arrange for child-minders and some form of entertainment. Make these arrangements clear on the invitation.

People love weddings. You can allow at least an 80 per cent acceptance rate. If the wedding is abroad, still send invitations and you may be surprised how many guests will attend. After all, it's a great excuse to have a holiday as well.

(Left) An etched glass
invitation is a luxurious
memento of the day.
(Below) Enclosing fresh rose
petals with each invitation
gets the celebrations off to a
romantic start.

*'the most important
point to remember
is that it is your day –
invite people you will
be happy to share
it with'*

## SENDING THE INVITATIONS

Plan to send your invitations not less than six weeks before the wedding (I recommend ten to twelve weeks). The style of the invitation should reflect the family and couple. Any further information such as local hotels, maps and where the wedding list is held can be included. If your guests are from out of town and you are providing transport, coaches or cars, include these details as well. If you have chosen evening dress, this must be included on the invitation, otherwise there is no reference to dress. Make dress known by word of mouth.

If you are planning other celebrations, such as a dinner the night before the wedding or a lunch on the day after, these invitations are also enclosed. Some people like to enclose an RSVP card. All the enclosures should be printed on paper, apart from the reply card. The paper and card must match the colour of the invitation. The guest's name is always written by hand in ink in the top left-hand corner of the invitation. Some people like to employ the services of a calligrapher. They will need the correct names and titles of the guests. Decorations and prefixes are not included on the invitation, but are on the envelopes which are written in black ink.

Wedding invitations have retained their traditional form over the years. If you intend to change from the traditional style, it is important that etiquette is followed.

Traditional-style invitations are usually printed on heavy white or cream card with copperplate engraved script. This style of printing can be quite expensive. Another printing choice is thermography which resembles copperplate but you do lose the subtlety. It is a cheaper, quicker way of printing. Black is the preferred colour of ink.

You may wish to have your invitations designed to suit your style of wedding and both your personalities. I have known couples who have made their own invitations, purchasing paper and cards from specialist suppliers, creating something unique. When you have found your printer, you will need to discuss in detail the style and how many you require. It is important to ask how long it will take to print. Some printers quote six to eight weeks. While you are discussing the invitations, you may wish to include service sheets and thank-you cards. Ask to see samples of cards and textures of papers.

Find out precisely what costs are involved. If you are not collecting the invitations from the printer, you will need to know the cost of postage or courier, plus any taxes such as VAT or sales tax. Always ask for a written quote. The printer will supply you with proofs. You must check every detail carefully as mistakes cannot be rectified later. It will be very costly to reprint and cause a delay. Confirm your approval or changes in writing. Ask the printer for the envelopes before the invitations are ready, so you can start addressing them. You must remember the busy times of year – if your wedding is in the popular season, allow plenty of time for the printing.

The choice of wording is governed by the hosts of the nuptials and their relationship with the bride. Let us start with the parents who are still married. The wording is as follows:

*Mr and Mrs William Smith*
*request the pleasure of your company*
*at the marriage of their daughter*
*Lauren*
*to*
*Mr John Brown*

*at Holy Saviour Church*
*Chelsea*
*on Tuesday 21 October*
*at 4.00 o'clock*
*Afterwards at*
*The Dorchester*

*RSVP*
*The Manor*
*Little Manor Farm*
*Manorshire*

If the bride's parents are divorced and the mother has remarried the wording is as follows:

> *Mr William Smith*
> *and*
> *Mrs Helene Bailey*
> *request the pleasure of your company*
> *at the marriage of their daughter*
> *Lauren*
> *to*
> *Mr John Brown*
> *etc.*

If the bride's father is deceased:

> *Mrs William Smith*
> *requests the pleasure of your company*
> *at the marriage of her daughter*
> *Lauren*
> *to*
> *Mr John Brown*
> *etc.*

Bride's parents who are separated or divorced but still share the same surname:

> *Mr William Smith*
> *and*
> *Mrs Helene Smith*
> *request the pleasure of your company*
> *at the marriage of their daughter*
> *Lauren*
> *etc.*

For divorced couples who are having a blessing in church, the invitation should read:

> Mrs Sophia White and Mr Patrick Churchill
> request the pleasure of your company
> at a service of blessing, following their marriage
> etc.

If the bride is hosting her own wedding, the invitation should read:

> Miss Lauren Elliott
> requests the pleasure of your company
> at her marriage
> to
> Mr John Brown
> etc.

The church may not be large enough to accommodate all the guests so invitations may be for the reception or a dance only.

> Mr and Mrs William Smith
> request the pleasure of your company
> at a reception following the marriage
> of their daughter Lauren
> to Mr John Brown
> on Tuesday 21 October
> at The Dorchester
> 6.00pm
>
> RSVP
> The Manor
> Little Manor Farm
> Manorshire

'ask the printer for the envelopes before the invitations are ready, so that you can start addressing them'

# wedding presents

Are you having problems deciding whether or not to have a wedding list? I fall into the category of a guest who likes to know the present I am giving is something the couple have chosen. It makes it a lot easier for me and for the couple. My advice is always to have a list. Do you really want presents that you will probably dislike and leave in a drawer or cupboard? Or receive ten lamps?

The list you plan must be in proportion to the number of guests you are inviting. Remember to think carefully about the price range so the list will suit all your guests. The details of where your wedding list is held must be ready to send with your invitations.

If your wedding is at a popular time of year, remember that the bridal registry of a department store or a specialist wedding list shop will also be busy so start planning early. It can be a real pleasure to sit down and put together ideas and styles you like. This will take time so do not try and achieve all this in one evening or a day. The gifts are to help you establish your new home together. If you already have a home, then look at upgrading items you already have. Check that what you are choosing is not about to be discontinued as you will not be able to replace items. Think about how practical certain items will be. Do you really have the time to hand-wash very delicate glassware?

The most practical way of starting is to visit several large department stores and perhaps a specialist wedding list shop. Take time to walk around the stores and get a feel for what you would like. When you have some ideas, talk to the store's bridal registry consultant. Some stores like you to make an appointment, while at others you can just turn up, so make a phone call before to check. If you do have to make an appointment, remember they are usually very booked up, so allow for alternative dates and times. Large department stores will give you a workbook. Write down the description and price of the items. Labels can be quite complicated so ask sales assistants

for guidance. If possible, visit the store during quieter times. You must be very focused: most shoppers tend to browse and this does waste a lot of time. Make it easy: give yourself a time limit and then stop, perhaps for lunch so you can discuss what you have chosen.

When planning your dining table, a good place to start is with your china, cutlery and glassware, as these items will guide your choice of linen and other accessories. Concentrate on the most essential items, only later adding those luxuries. Think about what you will use every day. These will probably chip or crack so add extra to the numbers you require. Also look to the future. You may not want certain items now, but in a few years' time this could change – ask friends and relatives which items they have found invaluable. When you are planning bed linen, allow four sets for the master bedroom and two sets for guest bedrooms. For bathroom linen, allow as for bed linen. If you select hand-painted or hand-made items, bear in mind that they may not be immediately available. On the other hand, if you choose items from what I would call a high fashion store, remember that they may not be able to supply the same articles in six months' time as the stock can change rapidly.

There are small specialist wedding shops that offer a very personal service. They can be a lot more flexible when it comes to making appointments outside working hours. This way of choosing your list is easy as it eliminates trawling around large busy stores. Large or small bridal registry shops or stores will spend more time getting to know you and your style. They will be in contact weekly, keeping you informed. And about two days before your wedding expect a phone call to wish you good luck and happiness.

When you have completed your list, the store will probably take up to ten days to register the items. As presents are bought, the store will update you weekly and this is a good prompt to send thank-you notes. Stores will send the gifts to the address you have given on the forms you have completed. Some stores do this before the wedding while others wait until the couple has arrived home from honeymoon. As you have so much to think of before your wedding, it can be nicer to arrive home from your honeymoon and receive your guests' presents then.

# the honeymoon

If asked my ideal honeymoon destination, the place that would come to mind is a lovely cottage on the banks of the Essequibo river in Guyana. On the edge of a tropical rain forest, it has everything required for a honeymoon: tranquillity, an exciting location, warmth, surrounded by the most beautiful flowers, birds and views. The only transport is by boat. The nearest town is seven miles away and the closest neighbours two miles up river. Total peace and quiet.

A honeymoon is extremely important for the newly married couple. After all the months of planning, tension and hard work, it's time for you both to have a complete rest. Planning the honeymoon has always been the responsibility of the groom and by tradition the destination should be a surprise for the bride. Even if you do not want to tell your bride her final destination, I feel it's fair she should have some idea of when and where as she will want to know what to pack.

As unromantic as it sounds, honeymoons must be planned within your budget and other considerations, such as the time you can reasonably take away from your professional life. A century ago the honeymoon often lasted a month to give the couple time to get to know each other. Today times have changed. As much as you would like to take a month, few couples are lucky enough to be able to.

You will feel ecstatic on your wedding day, but at the end of the day and after months of planning you will probably both be exhausted, so plan a restful time. Consider spending your first night in a hotel and then travelling the following afternoon. If you want an active honeymoon, take a few days' rest at the beginning and again at the end. If you have only a short time, don't take a long journey by plane as jet lag is debilitating and will add to your exhaustion. Plan for time that you can spend together in peace. Don't forget to allow for time at home when you return, before starting back at work.

Booking the airline tickets in your married name may become a problem with the bride's passport. You can either book the tickets in her maiden name or take the marriage certificate with you for identification. You will definitely require this for airport security.

If you are travelling to countries that require visas, these need to be applied for as soon as you have confirmed your destination. If you require inoculations, most doctors or airlines will be able to advise you what is required and the timing. Don't leave this until the last moment as some inoculations have side effects. Travel and medical insurance cover must be taken when travelling abroad. If you are travelling within your own country, some home insurance policies cover you for loss of baggage and personal effects. This will need to be confirmed with your insurance company.

If for some unfortunate reason you have to claim on your insurance, most companies will expect you to pay the cost. You retain all the bills and invoices and are then reimbursed when you make your claim on return to your home country. About a month before your wedding, order any foreign currencies and traveller's cheques. Credit cards are now used world-wide, but it is wise to make enquiries about which card is most widely accepted at your destination.

Where do you start to plan your perfect honeymoon? You will probably have some ideas on where you would like to go. Take time to visit a bookshop that specialises in travel or a bookstore with a good travel section and make notes. Remember seasons and weather patterns. If you are planning your own honeymoon, find a very reliable travel agent that can tailor your requirements specifically for you. Finding the right one for you will take as much planning as some elements of your wedding. When you have confirmation of all your arrangements, don't forget to check the tickets and hotel bookings. Make sure you have any vouchers required for hotels, car hire or other trips planned and paid for.

When you have found your ideal destination, you will need to plan the clothes you require. Start to do this as soon as you have made your confirmation. Try and travel as light as possible. That's almost impossible for me. I always take hand baggage when flying. In the bag I carry a wash bag, a change of underwear and a change of clothes, so if my luggage is lost or delayed I have something with me to change into. Bear in mind that you may arrive in a completely different climate to the one you have left behind at home.

Plan the books you would like to take with you, not only for the flight but also for reading on your honeymoon, including the guidebooks. If you are planning a beach holiday, take your sunscreen and a sun hat with you; also cream or gel for any sunburn. Also pack a small first-aid kit which should include plasters, pain relief, antihistamine creams and tablets, medicine for stomach upsets and mosquito repellent. Buy travel-size toiletries. If you take medication, check you have a sufficient supply. Don't forget film and batteries for your cameras and buy adapters for any electrical equipment you are taking. If the exchange rate is complicated, take a mini calculator.

Photocopy the following honeymoon planner and tick off each item when completed or confirmed.

## HONEYMOON PLANNER

- As soon as you have confirmed the date of your wedding, start to plan your honeymoon, taking into account the busy times of year.
- When you have booked your flights, confirm your seats and order any special dietary requirements.
- Hotels should be informed you are on honeymoon and the time you are expected to arrive. Ask for any requirements, such as a quiet room, non-smoking, a sea view. If your flight arrives in the early morning, you may have to wait until after midday for your room. Ask if there are any alternative arrangements for checking in early.
- Any car rentals should be reserved and confirmed at the time of booking your flights and hotels.
- Apply for new passports and the bride's passport in her married name.

## THREE MONTHS BEFORE

- Start to plan what you are going to pack and buy any clothing required.
- Arrange visas if required.
- Arrange for inoculations if required.
- Check you have travel and health insurance.
- Check the cameras you are planning to take with you are working properly and buy spare batteries.

## ONE MONTH BEFORE

- Confirm all your travel arrangements.
- Your tickets and vouchers will probably be posted to you. Check all details are correct.
- Buy traveller's cheques and foreign currency.
- Buy toiletries, sunscreen, film for cameras, put together a small first-aid kit.
- Buy the books you will be taking.
- Finish planning and buying outfits for your honeymoon.

## WEEK BEFORE

- Cancel any deliveries.
- Check travel arrangements to and from the airport.
- Confirm with your bridal registry that they will not be sending any gifts while you are away.
- Make sure that someone close has your complete itinerary with hotel addresses and telephone numbers.
- Make a final check that you have confirmed all the arrangements and have everything required.

## DAY BEFORE

- Pack your suitcase.

# the big day

Every element, large or small, contributes to the success of your celebrations. At first, the list can seem

endless and it may be difficult to see the wood for the trees. Concentrate on getting the major elements in

place first and, when those are arranged, you can focus on the details that will make the day a perfect one.

# the run-up to the day

As the day of your wedding comes closer, there are arrangements and duties to plan. These include arranging the bachelor night or hen night, writing speeches, confirming final numbers for the reception, planning the wedding rehearsal and the dinner the night before your wedding. Make a planner to ensure everything runs smoothly, giving clear instructions for the duties of your supporters (refer back to page 34 for more details on who does what on the day).

## THE WEEK BEFORE

Most couples stop working during the week before their wedding as there are so many last-minute details that require their involvement. It's important that you share these responsibilities. What you must not do is start to panic if you think you have forgotten anything. Sit together in a quiet room and go through your checklist to reassure yourself that all the arrangements have been confirmed to the caterers, floral decorators, transport company, photographer and

**You can write the place cards in advance, but someone will need to be on hand to attach the fresh flowers and put them in position.**

videographer and that service sheets have been printed and given to the best man. Domestic details, such as paying household bills, have to be addressed before you depart on honeymoon.

Plan and write your timetable for the day. The groom should also do one for his family and supporters. Write a checklist for the best man and chief bridesmaid. If you are arranging your own flowers for the church, these should be collected and prepared ready to arrange the day before. If your family is arranging and catering for the reception, all the duties and staff briefings should have been finalised. Make sure you have the telephone numbers of the contractors on a separate list for any last-minute changes. You will need to confirm the number of guests attending the reception. If the number of dining tables has increased, inform the floral decorator that you require an extra arrangement. It's the little details that are easily overlooked, not the large ones.

Arrange to have beauty treatments and haircuts about three days before. Do not have a facial the week of your wedding. As luck would have it, you will break out in spots. Collect your wedding clothes. Try on your whole outfit, leaving off one item to ensure good luck, then store your clothes and accessories somewhere safe. On the day before your wedding, gather together your shoes, underwear, veil, jewellery and make-up in one place and check you have everything. Hang your dress so it will not crush.

Make final checks on the seating plan for the reception and service. Rehearse your wedding vows, but don't try to learn them as you may be nervous and forget them on the day. Speeches need to be written and rehearsed. Check you have everything for your honeymoon. Arrange for your going-away outfit and suitcase to be taken to the reception, if it is not being held at home, and finish packing your suitcase the night before. Make sure you have all your documentation for travelling in a safe place – it's a good idea for the best man or chief bridesmaid to look after this.

Arrange separate dinners with your families the night before. Some couples may wish to include guests who are from out of town. There are no hard and fast rules whether to invite them. It's really up to you. Have an early night.

**If you are having a morning wedding, check that you can have access to the church or other venue the night before to arrange the flowers.**

## THE REHEARSAL

One of the most important arrangements is the rehearsal. This normally takes places during the week before your wedding, ideally a few days before the actual day.

The bride and groom and the bridal party should all be present. If your dress has a long train, take fabric and pin this to your clothes so the bridesmaids can practise. Locate the loo as you may need it on the day. The ushers are given the family seating plans to familiarise themselves. During the rehearsal, you should also discuss which ushers will escort members of the bridal party to their seats. This is normally the bride's mother, groom's parents and grandparents of the bride and groom.

Follow the rehearsal with a lunch or dinner, depending on the time of day. It's a nice time for the families to be able to relax and talk about the wedding and any final details that require addressing. Driving to the rehearsal is a good opportunity to check the timing of travel to the place of your service, allowing extra time for any delays due to roadworks or road closures. One other detail you may like to consider is practising your walk to the processional and recessional music at home, just to get the rhythm and timings right.

## YOUR PARENTS

Arranging a wedding can be a rollercoaster of emotions. During this time of looking forward to your new life together, do consider your parents. They have cared and supported you all your life and this is also an emotional time for them. We hear parents saying they have not lost a daughter but gained a son. Think of the meaning behind that statement. You should spare a thought for them. It is very comforting and caring to tell them how much you care for and love them and to thank them for helping you to achieve your goals in life. You might even write a letter thanking them and leave it with a small gift for them to find on the day.

## THE DAY FINALLY ARRIVES

At long last the day dawns. All the plans you have made will, of course, work with military precision. All you both have to do is relax and enjoy the whole day.

If you are marrying late in the afternoon, arrange to have a pampering massage during the day or a relaxing bath with scented oils, but do this before you have your hair and make-up done. Arrange for the delivery of the bridal flowers at least two hours before they are required. Store them in a cool, shady place. If you are having small bridesmaids and pageboys, don't dress them too early as this is almost inviting accidents to happen. The chief bridesmaid helps you to dress. If your mother is there, you can ask her to make sure all the arrangements are running to time.

Before you leave for the church, make sure you have your veil down and your bouquet in hand; place your engagement ring on your right hand. Try to be completely ready before your mother leaves for church with the chief bridesmaid so they can check that you and your father are ready. Don't forget to give your mother or other reliable person a mirror and make-up so you can make one final check before you enter the ceremony. Take time to have a chat with your father. You are probably both feeling nervous and this is the time to try and relax. If you are marrying from the family home, this is the last time you will leave it as a single woman, so turn and take a last look at yourself before you go.

# stag parties or
# bachelor nights

In the not-too-distant past, stag parties were often held the night before the wedding. I am glad this has changed. The thought of marrying when feeling tired and probably suffering a hangover is not really the way to start married life. Today they are more likely to be held at least two weeks before the nuptials, with all the groom's friends and members of his family gathering to celebrate his last days of being a bachelor.

The arrangement and organisation of the stag night are the responsibility of the best man. The party is kept a secret from the groom to make the evening a great surprise. It should reflect the groom's personality and his likes and is usually a dinner followed by other forms of entertainment. The cost of the evening is borne by the guests attending rather than the groom. The best man also has the responsibility to ensure the groom arrives safely and departs with dignity and is not placed on a train to a strange town. As funny as this may seem, it is hardly a friendly gesture.

# hen nights or
# bridal showers

Hen parties or bridal showers have become very popular in the last twenty years. The chief bridesmaid has the responsibility of the planning and organisation of the party. The guests may arrive with a small personal gift for the bride. Aim to make the whole evening a very memorable affair but don't be tempted to arrange anything embarrassing. Don't forget to take photographs and present them in an album when she returns home from honeymoon. The party can be arranged at home or in a restaurant with other entertainment. The chief bridesmaid should make sure the bride arrives safely and departs in dignity. The guests, not the bride, should pay for the party.

# the ceremony

We have to be practical when it comes to the marriage service because it is legally binding. If you are marrying in the Church of England, the minister is also the registrar. Other religious denominations require the services of a registrar at the service. If a registrar is not present, it may be necessary for the couple also to have a civil ceremony for the marriage to be legal.

The law in England states that marriages can take place only between the hours of 8.00 am and 6.00 pm. The reason for this rather strange and quaint law is that by marrying in daylight there can be no case of mistaken identity! So if you wish to marry as the moon rises over Land's End, you would have to have a civil ceremony during the hours of daylight first so the marriage is legal. Certain licences can override this rule. For instance, Jewish, Scottish and Quaker weddings can take place at any time, but not on Saturdays for Jews as that is their Sabbath or on Jewish holy days. In the Church of England it would be very rare to be married on Good Friday, Holy Saturday or Easter Day. Marrying during Lent is allowed, but you must be aware that flowers are not usually allowed in the church.

You have to decide on the type and style of wedding that is suitable for you and your circumstances. A traditional wedding in a place of worship should be for those couples who uphold the values of religious views on marriage. A close friend of mine who is a Church of England minister says if he meets a couple who do not have strong religious views, he would give them time to think about what they want and why and then counsel them to come to the right decision.

However, no Church of England clergy can refuse to marry any couple who meet the legal requirements of residence and haven't been previously married. If the bride or groom have been widowed, remarriage in church is allowed. If one or both of the parties has been divorced, they may be allowed to be married in church, depending on the circumstances. You will need to discuss this with your minister. The Church does offer a Service of Prayer and Dedication after a civil marriage. You must bear in mind this is not a marriage ceremony and does require a civil ceremony first. The tradition is for the couple to enter the church together and a blessing takes place in front of the minister with hymns and readings. Although you will not take vows, you can make a dedication to each other in front of the congregation if you wish. No banns are read in the church.

One of the most important things to remember is not to enter into any financial arrangements with reception venues etc until you have a date booked for your wedding. You must be flexible with your dates and times, remembering the busy times of the year.

## CHURCH OF ENGLAND

Tradition dictates the wedding takes place in the bride's church. There are instances where you can marry in a parish other than the one the bride or the groom lives in. If you wish to marry in another parish, you may need to go on the parish electoral roll and become a regular worshipper for a minimum of six months. Alternatively, you could apply for a special licence or a bishop's licence to marry in that church. If you choose a church simply because you think it is very pretty and will look lovely in the photographs, the Church of England will take a dim view.

Outside every church is a noticeboard displaying the name, address and telephone number of the vicar. Telephone the vicar and arrange an appointment to meet. This will usually take place at the vicarage. Some churches may display a notice specifying a particular time for wedding enquiries, perhaps one evening a week when the couple can call into the church, introduce themselves to the vicar and check they can marry in that parish. You can also find out if the date and time you would like are available.

At the second meeting with the vicar you will be required to complete various forms and show your birth or adoption certificates. If one of you has been married before, a death certificate of the late spouse or a divorce decree absolute must be provided. The vicar will be able to give you details of what the church can offer regarding choirs, organist, pianist, bell ringers and flowers. Some churches offer none of these services. You will be told what fees are payable, not only to the church but also for the organist, bell ringers and choir. Make it clear what you would like.

## CIVIL CEREMONIES

If you choose to have a civil ceremony, there are now many more options available to you than there were ten years ago.

A wedding in a register office is usually a very short affair, lasting only about ten minutes. Some offices can accommodate large numbers of guests, others only a small gathering. The bride and groom stand in front of the registrar and two witnesses, make a declaration that they are free to marry and wish to be man and wife. The registrar declares they are man and wife. The service does not include the exchange of wedding rings, but this can usually be performed at some point.

Each party to the marriage will need to attend the register office to give notice of their intention to marry. Each party will be required to declare their nationality and bring with them passports, birth certificates, ID card or a Home Office travel document or acknowledgment showing nationality. The bride and groom do not have to attend together, but it is preferable if you do. You will need to satisfy the residential qualification of seven days in the district and then wait a further fifteen days before you are eligible to marry. If you would like to marry sooner, you must apply to the Registrar General and they will consider each case on its merits.

Unlike the reading of banns in the church, the register office will display a marriage notice in the register office for fifteen days before the wedding date to ensure there are no objections to the marriage. A certificate is then issued and the marriage can take place.

Do not be late for a register office wedding as the bookings for the offices are timed and you may lose your spot. It is very important to bear in mind that this is purely a legal service. It is not a church. Long white dresses, morning suits and top hats and bridesmaids are inappropriate. A smart suit with a buttonhole is the correct attire for the groom and a suit or dress with a hat and a small bouquet for the bride. Guests who attend should compliment the couple on their choice of dress. Depending on the time of day, a small celebration is normally arranged. Some people marry a few days before and follow with a larger celebration or church blessing. Normally the service is followed by a luncheon party or if late in the afternoon a drinks party, hosted by the couple or a close friend.

A register office wedding can be rather cold and clinical. However, with the recent change in the law, there are now a lot more options available. If you do not wish to marry in a register office, there are many interesting venues from hotels and grand country houses to boats and barns that are licensed for weddings. As an alternative to a register office, it is not surprising these new secular civil weddings are gaining in popularity.

Make a choice of venue that is suitable for your style and budget, ensuring it will give a sense of the occasion. The marriage service will be as at a civil ceremony, but you probably will be able to have a separate area set aside for the service. You can set up chairs so you will have an aisle to walk down. Flowers, music and bridesmaids are permitted, but anything religious is totally inappropriate and is not allowed. You can have music as you enter the room, singing and music during the ceremony and when walking back down the aisle.

One other benefit of having a civil wedding at a venue that has a licence is that the reception will be in the same place. The reception can follow the same structure as a church wedding reception, with cake-cutting, speeches and the bride and groom going away. The style of dress for your guests is determined by the time of day you

have chosen for your ceremony. For an early evening wedding followed by a dinner, I would suggest black tie for the men and evening dresses for the women, but for a lunchtime or afternoon reception, lounge suils for men and smart dresses or suits with hats for the women. Morning dress is inappropriate.

Dress in the case of a bride who has not been married before would normally be as for a first-time marriage; the same goes for the guests. For other remarriages, morning dress is not appropriate. For evening services, black tie for men and evening dresses for women is fine. Widows or widowers should wear a suitable dress or suit.

As far as a wedding list is concerned, if the bride has not been previously married, a wedding list can be compiled as for a first-time couple. I do not feel this is appropriate for widowed couples or second or third time around. Small gifts from friends as a gesture of the new marriage are much more suitable.

## AWAY FROM HOME

Your heart's desire may be to marry on a beach on some tropical isle as the sun sets, surrounded by a few close friends or just yourselves and the celebrant. The idea of marrying in this way is becoming very popular.

If you are planning to marry abroad, make as many enquiries as possible as there are now so many companies offering wedding packages. I would advise you to use a reputable agency that specialises in overseas weddings and is able to help with all the international legalities. You will need to fulfil the legal requirements of this country and the one you are marrying in. If you want to do it yourself, then the embassy or consulates of the country you are choosing will be able to give you the relevant information.

(Below and opposite) From Las Vegas to the deep blue sea (or local swimming pool), possible locations for your wedding are limited only by your imagination. If a quirky and original wedding is what you've always wanted, then maybe you should consider these options.

## SERVICE SHEETS, HYMNS AND READINGS

I always keep the service sheet as well as the invitation as a memento of any wedding I attend. The service sheet is a guide to the ceremony and you can either simply list the prayers, service and readings or also include the words to all the hymns. I prefer to have the complete ceremony on the service sheet as it is far easier than juggling with hymn books, a prayer book and an order of service sheet.

When you have decided the order of service with your clergyman, you need to decide on the design. There are many options. By tradition they are printed on white or cream paper and generally match the style of the invitation. On the front are either the Christian names or initials of the bride and groom, the date and the name of the church. Other options are booklets covered with fabric or ribbon or a plain service sheet with ribbon bindings. I have seen the most beautifully elegant order of service booklets covered with fabric and bound with ribbon, which would always remain a treasured memento.

(Above) If you are marrying in a church, the choice of wedding music need not be limited to the traditional marches. There are plenty of other less familiar options.

## MUSIC

My friend the Rev. Frank Mercurio writes in his booklet about music at weddings: 'Music plays a very important part in a wedding service. If you have hymns, you will obviously want them to be appropriate to the occasion and for guests to be able to join in singing them. You will want to decide whether to have the traditional bridal and wedding marches or have something different, but still suitable. You may like to have a particular anthem that you wish them to sing.' This is very sensible advice.

### Music before the service

*This is usually played for about ten minutes before the service starts.*

Air on a G String — Bach

Sheep May Safely Graze — Bach

Air (Water Music) — Handel

Minuet (Berenice) — Handel

Prière à Notre Dame (Suite Gothique) — Boellman

Behold a Rose is Blooming — Brahms

Air and Gavotte — Wesley

Allegretto in E Flat — Wolstenhome

Cantilena Romantica — Dunhill

Toccatina — Yon

Romance Sans Paroles — Bonnet

Tuba Tune in D — Lang

Romance (Eine Kleine Nachtmusik) — Mozart

Meditation on Brother James' Air — Harold Duke

Improvisation on 'O my Soul Rejoice with Gladness' — Karg-Elert

Canon in D — Pachelbel

Andantino in D Flat (Moonlight and Roses) — Edwin Lemare

Ave Maria — Bach/Gounod

Jesu, Joy of Man's Desiring — Bach

Adagio (Clarinet Concerto) — Mozart

Salut d'Amour — Elgar

## At the entry of the bride

*Only a short piece is required, just sufficient for the bride to proceed down the aisle.*

Bridal March (Lohengrin) – Wagner

Trumpet Voluntary – Clarke

Trumpet Tune and Air – Purcell

The Arrival of the Queen of Sheba – Handel

Hornpipe (Water Music) – Handel

March (Scipio) – Handel

Fanfare for the Bride – Bliss

Coro (Water Music) – Handel

Trumpet in Tune – Carpentier

Minuet (Royal Fireworks Music) – Handel

Concerto in A Minor – Vivaldi

Sonata No 3 in A – Mendelssohn

## Hymns

*Allow for three hymns.*

Praise My Soul the King of Heaven

Morning Has Broken

Lead Us Heavenly Father

Lord of Hopefulness

The Lord's My Shepherd

Praise to the Lord the Almighty

Father Hear the Prayer We Offer

O Perfect Love

O Jesus I Have Promised

Now Thank We All Our God

Come Down, O Love Divine

O Holy Spirit, Lord of Grace

The King of Love My Shepherd Is

Fill Thou My Life

For the Beauty of the Earth

Love Divine All Love Excelling

O Praise Ye the Lord

O Thou Who Camest From Above

O Worship the King

Crown With Love, Lord, This Glad Day

Give Me Joy in My Heart

## Anthem during the signing of the registers

*If you have a choir to sing, here are some suggestions. If you do not have a choir, the organist could play from the list for music before the service.*

Jesu, Joy of Man's Desiring – Bach

Brother James' Air – Jacob

Love One Another – Wesley

God Be in My Head – Walford Davies

Lead me, Lord – Wesley

Ave Maria – Bach/Gounod

## Music as you leave the church

*If you have bells. the music will last only until you reach the church door. Then the bells will start to peal.*

Wedding March (Midsummer's Night's Dream) – Mendelssohn

Toccata in F (Symphony No 5) – Widor

Grand March (from Aida) – Verdi

March on Now Thank We All Our God – Karg-Elert

Final (Symphony No 1) – Vierne

Carillon-Sortie – Mulet

Wedding Day at Troldhaugen – Grieg

Choral Song – Wesley

Sonata in G (first movement) – Elgar

Fantasia in G (slow section) – Bach

Grand Coeur in D – Guilmant

Toccata and Fugue in D Minor – Bach

March Pontificale (Symphony No 1) – Widor

## Readings and Psalms

Psalms 67, 121 or 128

Genesis 1:26 – 28

Romans 12:1 – 2

1 Corinthians 13

John 2:1 – 11

Matthew 7:21

1 John 4

# planning the reception

Wedding receptions were traditionally held in the bride's home. In times gone by, the bride lived at home until her marriage. She would leave for her local church and return to her parents' home for the reception. Times have changed and receptions now take place in hotels, restaurants, grand country houses, galleries, riverboats, museums and marquees. We have catered for weddings based on themes as diverse as an autumnal woodland scene to an ancient Greek temple complete with Greek dancers and statues of gods. At one of the first weddings we organised, the bride wanted to recreate Miss Haversham's table, right down to the cobwebs! All these themes suited the personalities of the couple. When it comes to planning your reception, budget is the first priority followed by the type of celebration you both would like to have.

## WHAT DO WE WANT?

Everything stems from the time of day your wedding will take place. By tradition, the wedding ceremony took place at about 2.00 pm, followed by an afternoon reception with champagne, wines, soft drinks and canapés, lasting for about three and a half hours. The bride and groom's departure would then be closely followed by that of the guests. In the evening, the bride's family would host a small dinner for close relatives.

The other celebration after a morning wedding is the wedding breakfast, a formal lunch with top tables and all the formality the occasion requires. The bride and groom depart in the afternoon followed by the guests. Again the bride's parents would host a small family dinner. These days many couples prefer to have a late afternoon wedding, followed by a two-hour reception that carries on to dinner followed by dancing. They depart after midnight followed by the guests. Another option is to have a lunchtime wedding followed by an afternoon reception. The happy couple leave and guests depart, only to return three hours later for a dinner and dance. This works two

ways. You can have a large reception including everyone in the afternoon and the evening can be a smaller affair. Or vice versa — hold a small afternoon reception and a larger evening party including guests who were not invited to the service. Remember, also, that the reception does not have to be a seated lunch or dinner. Buffets work extremely well, allowing guests to circulate, but remember to have seating otherwise it's a long time to be on your feet.

You have to decide what you both would like. This really depends on where you are getting married. If you cannot hold the reception at home, look at local hotels, restaurants, venues, houses, etc. What you do not want is to have your guests driving for more than half an hour from the ceremony to the reception, otherwise people will rush away from the ceremony, worrying about being held up in traffic, parking and being late.

There are a few other considerations to remember. One is parking for guests. If it is difficult, you must make your guests aware of this — a note with the invitation will suffice. If you are planning to hold your reception at home, it will generate a lot of garbage and it may be worth hiring a skip. Security must also be addressed. Homes left open, cars parked in fields, and marquees set up the day before with equipment could be a target for thieves. You may like to consider security guards. We do this for every large party held in a home and/or marquee. They are not conspicuous and will give you peace of mind.

## PLANNING

Now here comes the planning. Whatever you choose, make a provisional booking; most photographers, transport companies, caterers, florists, entertainers, venues or hotels will hold the date for twenty-eight days. Remember the busy times of year and book early. However, do not feel forced into confirming anything until you are sure it is what you both like and want.

## HOUSE AND GARDEN

Let's start at home. If at all possible, I feel the reception is best held at the bride's parents' home as it is so much more personal. Take some time to work out the space that is available. This may not be readily obvious and will involve a critical eye. Take a good look at familiar usable spaces; see how they could be arranged differently and how guests could be accommodated comfortably. Look at where you could install a bar, store coats and place a buffet or set up dining tables. Do you have enough loos to cope with the number of guests? Is the kitchen large enough for the caterer? Or can you turn the garage or another suitable area into a kitchen for the day? If the time of year is suitable, gardens can be made to look heavenly with some forward planning. Plant flowers that will be at their best on the day. Bars can be placed under trees and large calico umbrellas can cover buffets and tables seating guests. Blankets placed on the ground are ideal for guests to relax on.

## MARQUEES

Some houses and gardens are just right for marquees. If you are marrying in winter, remember that receptions can be very cosy in a well-heated and carpeted marquee. First consider whether you have the space to accommodate the number of guests you wish to invite. Will the marquee company be able to gain access? How long will it take to erect and dismantle? Will you require extra loos? Do you have enough power in the house for lighting, heating and caterers? (You may need to hire a generator.)

Armed with all these questions, the next step is to find marquee companies. As with everything, personal recommendation is the best. You will have been to many weddings and seen what you like and dislike. Marquees come in all shapes and sizes. You should look at them as an extension to your home. All marquee companies will make a site visit – and you must discuss with them the number of guests, the time and style of the reception. Discuss the number of tables required, the number of buffets and bars and the size of dance floor. If you are planning to hold a reception before lunch or dinner, how much space will be required? Try not to be fobbed off with using the dance floor – it's never large enough. Afternoon receptions must allow space for bars, small tables and chairs and a focal point for the speeches and cake-cutting. Service marquees must be large enough for the caterer to operate safely. If you are planning a very large wedding with lots of staff, entertainers and support staff, a separate area must be taken into consideration for storage, changing and eating.

Ask to see samples of linings, photographs of recent constructions and arrange a visit to a marquee under construction. Some marquee companies also supply furniture, lighting, heating and organise the loos. The area you are planning to use may not be flat, so will require scaffolding to create an even floor. If you know it's going to be a very hot day or evening, choose a marquee where the sides can be removed to give a feeling of space. Another nice feature is to have no sides and a clear ceiling at night, but don't think of doing this during the day when the sun is at its height as it will be too hot. If this is the style of marquee you would like, ask the company to wrap the support frames in lining fabric. The marquee can come straight off the house if windows and doors open onto a terrace or garden. If your marquee is a distance from the reception area, you may require an awning, in case of rain or snow.

When it comes to lighting the marquee, this really depends on the time of day and what theme or mood you wish to create. This can include a night sky, tables pin-spotted with tiny lights, bars and buffets bathed in pools of light, decorative features spot-lit to bring them to life and interesting lighting for the dance floor and the band. Don't forget the garden – enhance trees, shrubs and flowers with decorative lighting. Lanterns hung from trees and candles lighting pathways add to a romantic atmosphere.

Everything you discuss with your chosen marquee company must be confirmed in writing. Make sure every detail is included: size of dance floor, colour and type of lining, size of service tent, right down to the time they will have completed their work so other contractors can have clear access. This should be at least twenty-four hours before the wedding, if not sooner. Large marquees really need to be finished two days before. How long will it take them to dismantle? Do they have insurance against damage? All other contractors must remove their equipment before the marquee is dismantled. When you have checked every detail carefully, sign the contract and pay a deposit. If you have been dealing with one person from the company, insist they make regular visits during the construction to make sure all is as it should be. Marquee companies differ in price and quite frankly you get what you pay for. It's not always cheaper for a local company to do the work, so be aware of this when making your enquiries.

## HOTEL RECEPTIONS

If you do not want to have your reception at home, there are so many alternatives. The first choice is often a hotel. Hotels offer a wide range of services, such as recommending a florist and entertainment. Your first point of contact will be the banqueting manager. If your chosen date is available, make an appointment to discuss your plans in detail. Large hotels will have more than one space, so make sure you see all they have to offer.

Talk through every element of the day: the style you like, are you allowed to bring in party designers to change the look, can you bring your own florist, wedding cake, entertainment, photographer and lighting designer? Can you supply your own tablecloths and different style of china and cutlery, or will they only allow recommended suppliers? If you can bring in your own suppliers, at what time will

**(Below) The glory of Glamis Castle would be a memorable place for a wedding. Be sure to check carefully the options and services offered by civil venues as they differ greatly from place to place.**

they have access to the rooms? If you are planning a large party and the rooms have to be decorated in an elaborate style, 3.00 pm on the afternoon of the party will probably not be enough to time, so check what fees are payable for access at the time required.

Ask for sample menus. If there are favourite dishes or foods you like but are not included on the menus, ask if you can have alternatives. Look at the wine list; if you are booking a long time in advance, check they will still have the same wines and vintages. Ask to see samples of linen, china, cutlery and chairs. Most hotels will have photographs of the rooms when they are dressed and ready for parties. Take a good look as there may be designs and ideas you like. Discuss the timings of the day. If the party overruns in the evening, what, if any, are the charges? Is there a room for the bride and groom to change?

You will need more than one visit and your florist and other contractors will require a planning meeting at the hotel. After you have chosen your menu, a tasting will be arranged. If you are planning an afternoon reception, see how they propose to present the canapés. For a wedding breakfast or dinner, request to see the table set and ask the florist to provide a sample of the proposed table flowers. If cocktails are to be served, ask to taste these when tasting the food. Check how they charge for the drinks consumed. Some establishments may charge for opened bottles of spirits that are not consumed. If for some reason you wish to supply your own wines and champagne, ask about the corkage charge.

If there is any element you are not happy with, then say so. Things can be changed and corrected at this stage, but not on the day. When you have all the details in place, the hotel will write to confirm everything. When you are satisfied all is correct, reply to confirm the booking, enclosing the deposit.

## OTHER GREAT VENUES

For a grander or more unusual venue, start by looking at country houses, barns, galleries and museums. Most of these venues will have a very experienced function manager who is there to be as much or as little help as you would like. You may come armed with all your ideas and contractors, or require a lot of help. Some venues may only let you use their approved contractors. My advice is to make an appointment to discuss all your requirements. If you are not happy, then say so. Help is always available. Visit more than one style of venue. Also go and take a look on a grey day to see if you still like it.

When you start to consider where to have photographs taken, choose an area away from the main reception. Check the access is good for older guests, where the coats are stored, whether there are stairs or lifts. Establish the quantity (and quality) of the loos. Find out at what time the hire period starts and finishes. Does the time include set-up for florists? Kitchens are of the utmost importance. Will they be large enough for what you are planning, and if there is no kitchen where do the caterers set up? Is there a separate area for the bride and groom to change? Can you have music? If so does it have to finish at a given time so the residents of the area are not disturbed? If you are having a band, can they arrange for a sound check before the guests arrive? Check the parking. Some venues may not allow candles or smoking. All these questions must be answered before you are satisfied.

## YOUR CARRIAGE AWAITS

On the day of your wedding, most brides will make three journeys. You must choose the right form of transport for your style of wedding. Finding your ideal transport will probably need some research. For years the large black limousine was the car of choice. These days more original transport is available.

So plan your budget, then choose a style to suit you and your personality. When you are choosing the transport to take you to the service, make sure it will be large enough for your dress as you do not want to arrive looking creased. You must be sure the company you have chosen is reliable and takes care of their cars. Ask to see the cars – some companies will bring them to you. If you would like ribbons on the car, these should be the same colour as the bride's dress. Ask to see the driver's livery. Normally the contract is for three hours. The number of cars required depends on the size of the bridal

party. You will need a car for the bride and her father, one for the bridesmaids and bride's mother, another if you have close family. Also allow for transport if you want your hairdresser or dressmaker to arrive at the church before you do. These cars will take the bridal party on to the reception. Send the company maps before the wedding so they know the route. If you live in an area where parking is difficult, it may be wise to reserve spaces.

You may wish to arrange a different style of transport for arriving at the service and leaving the reception. These come in many styles. A couple I met one summer were marrying ten miles from the bride's home. By road it was a long and difficult journey, but there was a quicker route to the bride's home from the church. The couple took a horse-drawn carriage to the river where a family friend kept a boat. This small, pretty boat was decorated with hoops of white and cream flowers and ribbons, fluttering in the breeze and the happy couple were ferried across the river to the delight of a crowd of holidaymakers who applauded them.

Transport we have arranged includes old London taxis, vintage cars, horse and carriage. When leaving the reception, couples have been very inventive, from quad bikes to hot air balloons. But do remember if you are being driven from the reception, have a bottle of champagne on ice in the car with a snack. The chances are you will not have had the time to eat properly. Over a glass of chilled champagne, you can reflect on the day.

## MAGNIFICENT FOOD

Many caterers have good contacts with marquee companies, florists, entertainment, transport, printers, lighting companies, photographers and venues. They are an excellent starting point for helping you to find many other elements of your wedding. You must include your caterer at every site visit to a venue or meetings with other contractors such as the marquee company, lighting, entertainment and florists. They will be running the event on the day. I cannot stress enough how important it is to keep the caterer informed on all the details and timings.

Weddings go hand in hand with entertaining and food. The time of day you are getting married will dictate the style of food you will serve to your guests. Like all the plans you are making, you have to decide what is the most important element. The parts of the wedding most guests will remember are the bride, the flowers and the food and drinks served. There are many combinations to choose from. I have put together ideas from the most popular styles of entertaining your guests. Chapter 3 provides sample menus and recipes.

If you are marrying in the morning, plan a lunch. This could be one of two different styles: a seated wedding breakfast or a buffet lunch. You must remember that a lot of your guests will probably have been up early and will be hungry by lunchtime. Afternoon weddings are followed by a canapé reception as most of your guests will have had a light lunch. Canapés should be an interesting mix of meat, fish and vegetarian options; we also like to include interesting bite-sized tea sandwiches and miniature afternoon teacakes. As well as alcoholic drinks, tea is available for guests.

For a reception of three and a half hours allow at least sixteen canapés per person. Later afternoon weddings would have a reception of about two hours followed by dinner, so allow six to eight canapés per person followed by a three-course dinner. You can approach the dinner with several styles. The first option is a served three- or four-course dinner followed by coffee. If you do not like the idea of formality, serve the first and main course and continue with a dessert and cheese buffet with coffee served from bars. This will allow movement of guests and the buffet can be replenished during the evening. If you have dancing, a dessert and cheese buffet works extremely well. Another option to consider is a buffet dinner. This is an informal way of entertaining and very economical when there are a large number of guests. Whatever your preferences are, the food served should be interesting, with a combination of flavours and textures. Always offer vegetarian alternatives.

When looking for a caterer, personal recommendation is always best. Ask family, friends and work colleagues. You will have been to other weddings and will have ideas of what you want and do not want. My advice is if you do not have a favourite caterer, meet at least three.

Make an appointment at home or the venue you have chosen to discuss the whole day, the style you are planning, your likes and dislikes. Ask to see samples of linens, china, cutlery and glassware. Discuss sample menus and wine lists. If they are providing the waiting staff, ask what uniform they usually wear and if there any alternatives. Do the staff regularly work together or do they contact an agency for casual waiting staff?

Ask for a tasting at their offices. The table should be dressed as you would expect for the wedding reception, complete with a sample arrangement from the florist. If you have asked for the waiting staff to be dressed in a different outfit from their normal style, ask to see these as well. Canapés should be presented in the style discussed. Wines or special cocktails and fruit coolers should also be tasted. Go over the timings for the day in detail (not only your timing but also what time they will set up). Check whether the staff charges for the whole day, or if you run into overtime how much an hour do they charge. Is staff transport included? If you do not have a master of ceremonies, can their head waiter make the announcements? Every detail must be covered. When you are satisfied, ask for a full estimate, detailing every point; then write and confirm with a deposit.

# entertainment

The style of music for your reception will probably be decided when you have agreed on the main elements. Hotels and venues will normally be able to make suggestions and recommendations and there are many agencies specialising in music and entertainment for weddings and parties. If planning a lot of entertainment, an agency should send a representative to oversee the arrangements and timings for the reception.

As a couple you will probably have your favourite style of music, but this must be in harmony with the surroundings. In a grand country house a band playing barn dance music will not be quite right. Music is very important during the reception as your guests will have left the service full of music to arrive to silence. Some hotels and venues may have a time limit on when the music must end. Check the acoustics in the area where you are planning to dance, so the sound is just perfect on the day. When planning your reception, arrange the timings so you will have time for dancing.

String quartets and jazz bands are the obvious choices, if a little predictable. Wind quintets, steel bands, even jazz violins make a change and seem a little less corporate. A harpist will be lost in the conversation; a piano can be too overpowering. If possible, the music should not be in the main reception room, but just as the guests enter. Other reception entertainment we have encountered are one-man bands and barber-shop quartets.

## CHOOSING A BAND

Finding a dance band has to be researched very carefully. Guests will remember a good band, as they will a bad one. The number of guests will determine the size of the band. Dance bands come in all shapes and sizes and styles. Your thoughts may be for a salsa band, but can you realistically dance all evening to that style of music? I would advise a good mix of modern and old favourites. The band must be able to encourage all ages to dance.

Take into consideration that musicians will require breaks. What are you going to do when the music stops? Some bands will rotate their players, so there is continuous music. No music for twenty or so minutes will lose atmosphere and it could be difficult to get your guests to start dancing again. One seamless way is to have a discotheque between the sets. You will need to discuss with the bandleader the music for dancing. Do some research into the music you would like to dance to. Think of the old favourites, such as Gershwin and Cole Porter, as well as modern composers. Add a touch of salsa, samba, as well as waltzes, fox-trots, rock and roll. As the couple you will open the dancing. Some couples we have catered for have taken dancing lessons to surprise their guests. One couple learned how to dance the most amazing tango and completely wowed their on-lookers.

When making your enquiries into choosing the music, consider the following important points. Ask the band for cassettes and if possible a video so you have some idea of their sound and look. Find out their style of dress. If possible, watch the band playing before you make your booking. Ask how long they play for and how they manage their breaks. You will be expected to supply refreshments and this will depend on the time of day and how long the band is booked for. You will need to let the caterer know about this and plan for the extra costs. Does the quote include transportation, hotels if required, VAT, amplification? Not all bands have their own equipment. Do you have to provide chairs? You will need to know what they require for changing and storage, when they want to set up and do a sound check (not, of course, in the middle of the reception). Plan the play list with a good balance of music and specify this in the contract. Sign the contract and return with a deposit. Popular bands can be booked as long as a year in advance during the busy season. Take this into account when making your plans.

## BOOKING A DISCO

Discotheques are probably the first choice of many couples today. As with finding the right band, you will need to do the same for your disco. Play lists have to be planned as it's very important to have the correct mix of styles so everyone wants to dance. Being a disc jockey is not as easy as it may seem. They need to be able to judge the mood

of the party. You do not want one who is continually talking over the music and misjudges what people want. Some discotheque operators can offer lights, smoke machines and lasers; others just bring their music and equipment. What you do not want is music so loud that guests cannot have a conversation. Like all the elements you are planning, ask if you can see them in operation so you can be sure their style is what you like. You should also make enquiries into their style of dress for the evening.

## OTHER ENTERTAINMENT

Also consider other forms of entertainment as well as music. Magicians can wander from table to table, doing close-up magic tricks. Caricaturists can do cartoons for guests. Palm readers, fire-eaters, dancers, jesters, mime artists and circus acts all add to the atmosphere. You may also want to book a children's entertainer.

Fireworks can be a spectacular end to the day. Professional companies can arrange displays set to music and these can be tailored to most budgets. Only have fireworks if your guests can leave the reception area to watch. It could also be cold and many ladies will be wearing thin evening dresses – space blankets work a treat to keep guests warm. If you are planning a firework display and your reception will be near any livestock, such as cattle or horses, it's very important to inform the persons concerned as the noise can be disturbing.

# photographic memories

Finding the right photographer for you is as much about personality as it is about being an excellent wedding photographer. The approach must be professional and an understanding of the bride and her wishes is of utmost importance. You want to be able to recall all the moments of the day. With meticulous planning, this should be achievable.

Start with a list of what you would like recorded. Think not only of the obvious, but also consider informal shots of the preparations for the reception, florists and caterers working, the wedding cake being set up as well as the band's preparations. Firstly, find the person you feel is right for what you want. There are many wedding photographers out there, so start by asking friends and family. Make an appointment to see at least three photographers who are known for their wedding work. Discuss where you are marrying and where the reception is being held. Ask to see samples of their work.

Discuss the charges as they can vary enormously. Some photographers make an all-inclusive charge for the day, including contact sheets, but prints are extra. Others will charge for about three hours and include an album and a certain number of photographs. Ask the charges for extra prints. If you know how many

sets of reprints you would like, it is often less expensive to have them developed together. The copyright of the photographs remains the property of the photographer. They keep the negatives, unless you have come to any other arrangement. Discuss what would happen if you lost your photographs due to any unforeseen circumstances over the years and come to some agreement. It's important you have a full

understanding of the amount of time and the costs involved from the very beginning.

You will need to arrange for your photographer to visit your home, place of ceremony and reception so they see where they can make use of the space and areas available to them. Discuss the style you would like. They will have ideas of what is required.

You will want to have photos taken of the bridal party getting ready; the groom, best man, ushers and guests arriving at church; the bride and her father arriving; the wedding party leaving the church. Have consideration for your guests and don't make them wait around for too long while family photos are being taken. By all means have some photos taken outside the church, but then it is much better to arrive at your reception and disappear for about twenty minutes to have the family photographs taken. Now this is where you become bossy. Instruct the members of your party you wish to be photographed to be nearby, so you are not trying to find them. Informal shots of guests during the reception are a real treasure. You will want the general atmosphere captured on film, with photos of the cake-cutting, the speeches and leaving the reception.

Most photographers will have an assistant who will take the photographs at the church and preparations at the reception. You must be very clear about what you want recorded on the day. A good photographer is so unobtrusive you may wonder if any photos have been taken. If you are

**(Left) The most successful wedding photographs are not always carefully posed. Capturing the joy of the day is often best achieved in a more relaxed picture.**

giving a seated lunch or dinner, consider a disposable camera for each table so guests can take their own candid photos. Don't forget to instruct the waiting staff to collect them at the end of the reception. When you return from honeymoon, you will have photos of all your guests enjoying your wedding.

Many places of service do not allow photography. If you want to have photographs taken during the ceremony, you must ask the minister or registrar if this is possible. Flash photography is not allowed. Some couples may want to have a record of signing the register and certain times of the ceremony.

When you are totally satisfied you have all the details covered, request a detailed estimate. Some photographers ask you to sign a contract. Check that all the details and times are correct. Write and confirm with a deposit, including the agreed timetable of the day. Some photographers, especially the good ones, can be booked as much as a year ahead.

When you receive your wedding photos, one current trend growing in popularity is to set up a special website and post a selection of the shots there. This means that friends and family who live some way away can see the pictures and order prints for themselves. As the copyright remains with the photographer, you may need to check this with him first.

## VIDEOS

You either love or hate them. As with a good photographer, a good videographer is just as unobtrusive. Do you really want the reception ruined by bright lights and cameras in guests' faces? You will need to do a lot of research to find a good one. Ask to see samples of their work. Give clear details of what you would like recorded. You will want to know how many videos are included in the quote. As with the photographer, the master video remains the property of the video company. You will need to discuss this and establish the cost for extra copies. My feeling about videos is they are wonderful to send to family and friends who were unable to attend your wedding due to distance, illness or age, but I doubt you will play a video as much as you will look at your photographs.

# wedding flowers

When you are planning the flowers for the service, reception, your bouquet and those for the bridal party, try to choose flowers that are in season. They are at their best and least expensive. Even in the depths of winter there are some wonderful flowers available. A large bouquet of peonies at that time of year looks completely wrong, but a bouquet of snowdrops and grape hyacinths is magical. Balance is the right description. You want try and carry the theme through all the elements of the day. Now how do you find the right person to do all this for you?

Like all things, ask friends, family and work colleagues. Don't choose someone who may have a very modern style if you are planning a traditional country wedding. There are an enormous number of florists and their ways of working and costs differ. It may take time to find the right person for you, but when you do you will know they are right. Make an appointment, allowing at least an hour. Take along as much information about your dress, hairstyle, timings for the day, where the ceremony and reception are being held. Ask to see photos of their recent work. If they are decorating a church and reception for a wedding in the near future ask if you could visit to see the work. You will need to arrange a site visit to the place of your service and the place of the reception. There may be more than one wedding per day at the place of service which may require a meeting with the other couple or couples to discuss how you could all work together when organising the flowers.

If you are planning to have a marquee, the florist will require a plan of the layout. If you are having a tasting with a table set up, ask for a sample table arrangement. Discuss in detail the style and type of flowers you like. Check there are no hidden charges, such as if the church and reception require the flowers to be removed.

At the reception flowers should be bold and noticeable. Marquee poles can look very unattractive, so wrap these with garlands of flowers and foliage. You could also scatter dried lavender flowers on the floor — as guests walk on them and the marquee warms, the scent will fill the air and banish any mustiness. If you are having a seated lunch or dinner, tables must have arrangements. The wedding cake table, buffets and bars should also be decorated with flowers, perhaps either flower runners or garlands. Tall, slim vases placed on buffets and filled with summer rose petals or autumnal hydrangea heads make a bold statement.

The entrance to the reception is a natural place for flowers. You may feel this is a waste because your guests will only pass by when arriving and leaving, but the flowers make a nice welcome and goodbye, especially if they are scented. If your reception area has large blank walls, there are many ways to make the area a lot more cheerful. Large arrangements in urns or wrought-iron floor-standing candelabras (with non-drip candles) will make the space more welcoming. In marquees fill these areas with plants or make a small flower border or woodland scene. Consider adding fruit or even some vegetables to the arrangements. Frosted fruits look wonderful in the winter. Don't forget herbs as they complement flowers and help to scent the room.

You must take into account the size of your tables. If you have a two-metre (six-foot) round table, a small table centre will look lost. If you are having a lot of tables, consider having some arrangements that are tall as this looks very attractive. Guests' eyes are not drawn to a large space and the tall arrangements give a feeling of intimacy. Don't place them so it is difficult for conversations to be held across the table. The arrangement should be on a tall stand with the flowers and candles above the seated guests' heads, with more candles and flowers around the base of the stand. If you are planning an afternoon reception with small tables, don't forget the flowers for these.

You must have the flowers specified in the quote; you will not want them to be replaced by a flower that is three times the cost. The quote you receive will have all the details of flowers, containers, style of bouquets, buttonholes. Confirm in writing and pay a deposit if necessary. Some florists may offer a visit to a flower market so you can see what is available. This will give you an idea of how different flowers go together to create your perfect day.

# flowers for the service

Flowers for your ceremony must complement the place of worship. For religious ceremonies, there are many focal points. There should be an arrangement in the entrance to welcome guests. Pew ends or chairs look wonderful decorated with posies of flowers. Depending on the scale of the chosen site, large urns can be filled with seasonal flowers. If possible, it is best to decorate the church the day before the service. The day of the wedding a member of the floral decorator's team should check the flowers and top up any containers. The flowers are left in the church after the wedding. Do bear in mind, however, that many churches do not allow any flower arrangements during Lent (see page 56).

If you are planning a civil wedding in a register office, it is almost impossible to decorate the office because the ceremony is short and many couples are married in the same place in one day. There is usually already an arrangement on the table. If you are planning a civil wedding in a licensed venue, you can decorate the area with flowers as you wish, but remember nothing religious is allowed. If your budget is tight for flowers, opt for one large statement rather than small offerings which can seem lost.

# pink flowers

At this summer lunch we have created a table of pink, silver and white with clear glass vases holding bunches of bold peonies. In early summer these wonderful flowers are available in many colours and tones. The table is designed to complement and enhance these abundant flowers.

The blowsy blooms of summer peonies take centre stage in this flower scheme and are complemented by tones of pink and silver used in the place setting and the favour box.

**Boldness pays dividends, as proved by this unusual colour scheme. Its understated elegance is carried through from the bride's bouquet right through to the place card attached to a dramatic single lily.**

# purple calla lilies

At a late winter evening reception bunches of violets and pots of green helxine complement the deep purple tones of the bride's calla lily bouquet. The table design was created to add warmth and a touch of mystery. Amethyst water glasses, jewel-coloured overcloths and candleholders in shades of purple remind guests of the bride's choice of bouquet.

# country church flowers

This lovely Saxon church in the middle of the Suffolk countryside is the setting for a country wedding. The style is very simple and the flowers could have been picked from the gardens, cornfields and hedgerows. The design of the flowers sits well with the simplicity of the church. Glass jars filled with cottage garden flowers are tied to alternate pew ends with fine fishing wire, tall wooden candlesticks stand proud at the remaining pew ends, adding a touch of elegance. The bridal chairs are linked together with a garland of flowers and ivy. The main lighting in the church is metal chandeliers with candles with ivy and trailing foliage to soften them. The frame supporting the flowers over the main entrance door was made by the local blacksmith. The flowers reflect the designs on the chairs. On the path outside, a carpet of dried lavender flowerheads and fresh petals has been scattered while the service is taking place. When the bridal party and guests leave the church the lavender scent is released into the air. The simplicity and elegance of this wedding is carried through to the lunch which is served on long tables, dressed with blue and white checked cloths, wooden platters and simple white china, adding to the charm of the occasion.

**Above: Streamers like maypole ribbons hark back to more innocent times.**

**The style of the flowers complements the age of the church, conjuring up images of bygone weddings. When choosing your flowers you can either choose a style that chimes perfectly with the location or one that contrasts boldly. Here the former most definitely applies.**

The country theme is carried through from the church flowers to the flowers for the reception. Cheery vases of country flowers reflect the bride's bouquet (seen on the previous spread) and are complemented by the checked tablecloth and wooden platters.

# Menu

~

Terrine de Foie Gras
Asperges Anglais

~

Carré d'Agneau
Jus de Menthe
Petits Légumes Nouveaux

~

Symphonie de Desserts
Café, Petits Fours

Guiraud 1986, Sauternes
Château La Louviere,
Graves Pessac Ledgnan 1993
Château Ducru Beaucaillou 1988
Pol Roger Brut 1988

Wrotha
29 Ja

# tables

Whatever style of reception you choose, the tables must be attractive and welcoming. Small tables for an afternoon reception must have decoration. The same applies to the tables used if you are giving a buffet. Candles are never used for a lunch or afternoon reception, unless the wedding is late in the afternoon and it becomes dark early. In the evening lots of candles on the tables give a warm, sensuous and romantic atmosphere.

Candleholders come in many shapes and sizes. They can be made by cutting patterns in hollowed-out fruit and vegetables, such as apples, oranges or pumpkins. Square glass vases wrapped with coloured tracing paper give a warm diffused light, with the candle secured in place by standing in a couple of inches of sea salt or fine white sand. Candles floating in clear glass containers reflect the shimmering light. Lanterns suspended over tables also work well. Hanging clear glass lanterns on transparent fishing line looks magical, even better if you hang flowerheads as well. Consider paper lanterns with the light inside provided by battery candles – a very safe and effective alternative to candles.

The design of your table must be in keeping with the surroundings. If you have a blank space, you can create whatever look you like. China, cutlery, glassware and linen are available in so many styles today. Design a table setting that is creative and memorable. Napkins can be tied with ribbons, ivy, string, garlands of flowers or herbs. Banana leaves are inexpensive and work well for tying napkins folded to hold cutlery or menus.

A colour theme can be created. Colours such as oranges, browns, creams and yellows work extremely well for an autumn wedding. In winter white, dark green and ruby colours are inviting. A summer colour scheme should be cool and crisp. Spring pastel shades harmonise with the colours of spring flowers. Consider graduated colours from

red through to pink or a single colour for a lunch. If you are restricted to plain white tablecloths, make a top cloth from an organza or similar fabric and place flower petals under the semi-transparent layer to soften the look. Place mats made from three colours of grosgrain ribbon woven together are simple but extremely effective, especially if used with a clear glass presentation plate. Placing leaves or flowers under a clear plate is also very attractive. Butter will look appetising decorated with a few flowerheads or herbs. Flowers can be very grand or a small statement.

Chairs can be decorated with small bunches of flowers tied to the backs, but make sure that pollen or sharp foliage will not damage clothing. If you want to hide the rather unsightly chairs available from catering hire companies, make slip covers for the backs.

**Transparent plates are laid on place mats made of ribbon threaded in a chequerboard pattern and the menu is framed by ribbon in a toning shade of yellow.**

## HOW MUCH SPACE

Planning the space for your wedding reception requires some time to work out how to arrange the area to maximum advantage. At home, if space is tight, remove some furniture and store in an area which will not be in use, such as a cellar, garage or garden shed. There are numerous removal companies that will take away furniture for the day, and return it the next, but you will not want to leave the house completely empty.

Before you decide where you wish to hold your reception, it's a good idea to work out the space required for the number of guests you are inviting. For an afternoon reception where guests are standing, you will only need some small tables with chairs, bars and a cake table. You should allow 3 square metres (10 square feet) per person. For a stand-up buffet allow 3.6 square metres (12 square feet) per person.

For a seated lunch or dinner allow 30 square metres (100 square feet) for each 1.8 metre- (6 foot-) round table that seats ten guests. This will allow space for the staff to serve, bars and buffet tables, but not a reception area, stages or dance floor.

The band or disco will be able to tell how much space they require. For a dance floor allow 1 square metre (3 square feet) per person. A dance floor 5.5 metres (18 feet) square will be able to accommodate up to 150 guests. You must remember not everyone will be dancing at the same time.

To work out how many guests you can have in an area that is empty of all furniture, take the measurements, multiply them together and divide by the number of guests to find the capacity. For example, a room 18.2 metres (60 feet) long by 10.6 metres (35 feet) wide will give you 193 square metres (2100 square feet). Using the figures given above, you will be able to work out how many guests it can accommodate. You must allow for fireplaces, furniture that cannot be removed and doors that open into the room (if space is at a premium consider removing them). Ensure windows are accessible so they can be opened.

If you are giving a seated lunch or dinner the following chart lists table sizes and the number of guests they can seat.

## ROUND TABLES

| Diameter | Number of guests |
|---|---|
| 1 m (3 ft) | 4–6 |
| 1.2 m (4 ft) | 6–8 |
| 1.5 m (5 ft) | 8–10 |
| 1.8 m (6 ft) | 10–12 |

## RECTANGULAR TABLES
(Based on 1.2m (4 ft) wide table with a guest either end)

| Length | Number of guests |
|---|---|
| 1.2 m (4 ft) | 8 |
| 1.8 m (6 ft) | 10 |
| 2.4 m (8 ft) | 12 |
| 3 m (10 ft) | 14 |
| 3.6 m (12 ft) | 16 |

**(Opposite above) Paper napkins and flower decorations and plastic glasses can look as effective and dramatic as a far more expensive table setting.**
**(Above right) An original twist on a place card – insert photographs of your guests in wire holders at each place setting.**

Remember that rectangular tables take up more space than round ones, so if you are trying to fit the maximum number of guests into an odd shape, use a combination of different-sized round tables to utilise corners.

For an afternoon reception allow seating for at least one-third of your guests. You must take into consideration the elderly and infirm. For a fork buffet reception, allow seating for half the guests. At a buffet lunch or dinner, allow seating for all your guests (you may need a seating plan if you have a lot of guests).

## THE SEATING PLAN

If you are planning a seated lunch or dinner, you must organise a seating plan. Out of all the arrangements you have made, without doubt this can be the most difficult task. But on the day you will be so pleased you have made the effort. I find by far the best way of organising this is to hand out seating cards when guests arrive. On the envelope is the guest's name, inside a card saying 'you are seated at table A'. You can make changes right up to the last minute, thus

facing the guests: chief bridesmaid, groom's father, bride's mother, groom, bride, bride's father, groom's mother, best man. These days the 'high table' is unfashionable and is being replaced by round tables. This is a very good way of making extended families feel a lot more comfortable. For comfort, if you are planning a round table, use one that measures 1.5 metre (5 feet). The seating plan remains the same.

It is best to seat little bridesmaids and pageboys with their parents. Step-parents, unless they have brought up the bride or groom from a child, are not seated at the top table. Second husbands and wives are not included in the bridal party. Close family tables are placed near to the top table. Friends' tables are further away.

avoiding crossing out on a board which looks awful. Number, letter or name your tables. Make sure the tables are easily identifiable when guests enter the dining area.

Place cards are normally a white or cream tent card with the guest's full name. You can have some fun and make place cards from photographs of your guests. Or use fruit with a label, favours (see page 92) with the guest's name on or biscuits with the guest's name piped in chocolate. The menus can also have your guest's name on the top. Leaves and large stones also make interesting place cards.

There is a traditional order for seating the bridal party. If rectangular, the top table seating is in this order, from left to right

Seating cards, place cards, menus – all are ways of organising your guests with a minimum of fuss. The day will run much more smoothly if everyone knows exactly where they are supposed to be and when.

(Left) Lush roses are
reflected in the patterned
table cloth.
(Above and right) This table
has an Oriental feel thanks
to its exotic fruits and
laquered boxes.

## FAVOURS

Wedding favours are becoming increasingly popular. They have their roots in Europe, where five sugared almonds representing health, long life, happiness, wealth and fertility are presented either in small lace bundles or small boxes. These symbolise hospitality. In France they are called bonbonnières and Italy confetti. They are not meant to be gifts. They are a token of thanks to your guests for taking part in the celebrations, but this does not mean they cannot be something interesting and a reminder of the happy day.

A small box makes an ideal container. It could be filled with a souvenir from the city of your marriage, some home-made sweets or heart-shaped biscuits, flowers, dried herbs or herb seeds, even small soaps. If you want your guests to see the gift, consider a clear box tied with ribbon or coloured cellophane tied into a bundle. Alternatively, choose boxes tied with string then finished with sealing wax stamped with the couple's initials. Allow yourself time, filling and tying over a few days or evenings. Store them in a cool dark place. I think it is a special treat for your guests to receive a favour that has been designed and prepared by the bride and her family.

Plan how you will present them. Arrange them on a table near the door with a sign for guests to help themselves as they leave. At the dining table, they could double as the place card with the guest's name tied to the ribbon or placed in piles in the centre of a dining table.

# the bride's outfit

Every bride should wear the dress of her dreams and with careful planning you will be able to. It's a wonderful feeling to try on a wedding dress for the very first time. Although your wedding is months away, when you look at yourself in the mirror, you will feel like a bride for the first time.

Shopping for the dress of your dreams can be a daunting affair. Firstly, make a list of designers and specialist wedding dress retailers located in your area. Think about the fabric you would like. The huge choice includes silks, duchesse satins, silk chiffons, organzas, velvet trimmed with fur for winter, hand-embroidered fabrics and taffetas. Natural fabrics look and feel wonderful, while synthetic fabrics can look shiny and the colours are not as natural. Delicate embroidery and beading on the bodice of a dress can look beautiful.

Do some research into the style you would like. Buy magazines, chat to your family and friends. If it's a historical style you are after, visit museums and art galleries to get ideas on styles and colours used. There are retailers specialising in original Victorian and Edwardian dresses that would be suitable as wedding dresses. A friend of mine, Clare Signy, chose an Edwardian lace tea dress for her wedding gown with an antique lace veil. It was absolutely perfect for her in so many ways. It suited her slim figure and her personality, and I could not imagine her wearing any other style of wedding dress. She simply looked amazing.

If you can afford the luxury of having your dress made exclusively for you, there are obviously many advantages. An expert dressmaker will make sure her dress fits you perfectly. If you are asking a dressmaker you have known for years to create a style you would like from a pattern, she may be able to adapt or add some ideas and styles of her own. Remember that most dressmakers have had years of experience in making wedding dresses. Don't be talked into using someone who only makes dresses for themselves and, for some reason best known to themselves, would like to make it for you. You do want to wear your dress with confidence on the day, knowing that it feels right and fits like a glove.

The time you should allow for making the dress really depends on the time of year. Some dressmakers require at least six months' notice, others may need longer. You will probably be required to attend at least four fittings. One of the most important points to remember is that most brides lose weight, especially the last few weeks before the wedding, so make sure the dress can be altered right up to the last week.

If buying a made-to-measure dress, there are many shops selling designer wedding dresses. You choose a design from their collection and they have it made up specially for you.

If you are buying an off-the-peg dress, you will have a range to choose from. Some shops take orders and will measure you; when the dress arrives from the manufacturers, alterations are made. Some shops offer a service where they can make any dress from their range to fit you. If you are on a tight budget, sales are a good time to buy old samples or end-of-season dresses. It is likely they will be shop-soiled, but a good dry cleaner should be able to restore it to pristine condition. They may also offer an alteration service.

However you choose your dress, for each fitting you must take with you shoes and underwear, even if they are not the same as you will wear on the day, but they must be similar.

When you feel you have researched your options as thoroughly as you can, contact your chosen designer, retailer or dressmaker. Most will ask you to make an appointment. This is not for any reasons of grandeur. It's purely practical because they will be able to spend time with you to discuss styles and fabrics in detail. Remember they are there to make your dream dress come alive and they have the experience that this requires.

## THE DRESS

Although wedding dresses are not considered to be a fashion statement, styles, fabrics and colours do change from season to season. White can be a very hard colour for most people to wear, whereas ivory, light cream or off-white are far more flattering. When it comes to choosing the style that is right for you, remember that the dress must be very comfortable to wear. You do not want to feel it's too tight to walk, sit down or even to stand up in. The style must suit you and your personality.

**A designer wedding gown (opposite) and a rack of sumptuous dresses (above) illustrate the wide range of styles available.**

Think of your size and shape when choosing a style. If you are short, a full dress with large puffy sleeves will swamp you. If you are tall and slim, you can probably wear any style you like. If you are on the large size, choose a style that is understated with not too many frills. One of the most flattering styles for most figures is a fitted

bodice, dropped waist and scoop neck. Add touches such as beading or embroidery to the bodice, and pearl, bone or fabric-covered buttons. Don't forget some services last up to or beyond an hour and the guests will spend that time looking at the back of your dress, so details are important.

There are also other factors to take into consideration. If you choose a design with very thin shoulder straps, perhaps you should consider having a jacket or a wrap to cover your shoulders during the service. You may have one of those complexions that reacts in small red patches when you become nervous. If this happens to you, I would advise covering your neck and back, perhaps with a thin, translucent fabric such as lace.

Most dresses look wonderful with a train. Long trains will require the help of several little maids, whereas you will be able to cope with a short train with your chief bridesmaid to make sure it is adjusted before you walk up the aisle. If your train is long, it would be sensible to make it detachable for the reception; otherwise attach a loop that

can be slipped over the wrist, to prevent anyone stepping on it.

If you are having a civil wedding in a register office, a bridal dress is the wrong choice. Instead, opt for a very smart suit or dress with a hat. When it comes to older brides, choose a style that is fitting for the occasion. You want to look and feel wonderful. So no white veils or long trains.

Your wedding dress will probably be the most expensive item of clothing you ever purchase. It's important you feel happy with your choice. A beautiful dress will give you bags of confidence on the day. Knowing you look truly wonderful, you will radiate happiness. If you are not happy with your choice, this will also affect you on the big day. You will feel uncomfortable and probably hate looking at the wedding photographs afterwards. The other point to keep in mind is that we are not all super-models. Whatever size and shape you are, you will know what suits you. Don't try to disguise a style that you know is wrong with additions that will serve only to make the design even more unsuitable.

## TRADITIONS AND SUPERSTITIONS

It's bad luck for the bride to make her own wedding dress.

It's bad luck to try on your complete outfit – even during the fittings – until you leave for the service.

The dress should not be finished until your wedding day; the last stitch should be sewn just before you leave for the service.

Something old, something new, something borrowed, something blue: perhaps you could wear an old veil, your dress is new, borrow some jewellery, and sew a small blue ribbon into the lining of your dress.

Did you know that the Armenian tradition is for the groom to deliver the bride's dress in a beautifully decorated box on their wedding day?

## ACCESSORIES

Now you have chosen your dress, it's time to plan the accessories. All really will depend on the style, time of year and the type of wedding you are planning.

Our traditional image of a bride is a beautiful dress, her face slightly hidden and mysterious behind a veil. You will need to match your veil to your dress. This can be done with help of your dressmaker or the shop which is supplying your dress. You will want your veil to drape gently, so choose a fabric that will not stick out. There are many ways to secure your veil: a tiara, a feathered headdress, veil sewn to a hair band, or a flower headdress. It must be comfortable and securely positioned. The veil could be embellished with beads, fake jewels or embroidery.

No wedding dress is complete without jewellery, but you shouldn't choose any that will detract from the overall look. Pearls are the obvious choice. If your dress is very plain, consider wearing a single-strand necklace of light semi-precious stones. Earrings should match the chosen style of your necklace, but make sure they are not too long and dangling or they could become caught in your veil. The only jewellery to wear on your hands is your engagement ring (transfer the ring to your right hand before you leave home); avoid anything on your wrists or arms.

You will be standing for most of the day, so common sense tells you that your shoes must be comfortable, easy to walk up and down the aisle in, dance in and complement your dress. As soon as you have decided on the final design of the dress, start to investigate shoe styles. As with finding the right dress, there are many specialist shoemakers and shops for bridal wear. Spend time deciding on the shoes. Remember your feet will swell so they must be a perfect fit. Fabric should be your choice of shoe, preferably the same as your dress. Leather looks wrong. Choose a heel height you are used to wearing. Once you have found your pair, break them in at home, by wearing them for about half an hour a day for about two weeks. By the time your wedding day arrives, they should be comfortable. Use a specialist spray to protect the fabric on the shoes.

Choosing your underwear is equally important. The type and style will depend on the design of your dress. Start by finding a specialist lingerie shop. You will certainly benefit from the experience of the staff. If possible, take with you a copy of the design of your dress. If you have a strapless dress, you need to find a good strapless bra that is cut low enough at the back not to show. There are many pretty bras on the market, but you may need to choose a flesh-coloured bra in a plain design that will not show through clothing. Nothing worse than seeing a bra through the dress. You could consider the possibility of wearing a corset. This may sound old-fashioned but it will hide any lumps or bumps and will give you a smooth outline throughout the day.

Unless you particularly want to wear stockings, buy a good pair of sheer tights with a cotton gusset which can double as pants and thus avoid the horrors of a visible panty line. Always buy a spare pair of tights just in case you ladder them when getting dressed. Add a garter to wear just above the knee. Save the sexy underwear for your honeymoon – you want to be comfortable and cool on your wedding day.

**Satin (above) or feathered (below), slippers such as these help seal the beauty and elegance of a bride's appearance.**

# bridal flowers

Your bouquet is your most important accessory. The bouquet must complement the colour and style of your dress. If your dress is multi-layered and full, a small bouquet would be lost. If the style of your dress is fitted and slim, an elegant long bouquet would complement the design, as would a simple hand-tied bouquet.

You must also think about your size. If you are petite, you do not want to look overwhelmed by a large bouquet. If you are tall, long-stemmed flowers look balanced. Also take into consideration the comfort factor. The bouquet must not feel too heavy. If you choose a style that drapes over your arm, the stems must be protected to prevent damage to the fabric of the dress. Pollen can stain clothing, so if you decide to have flowers that are likely to cause this problem, make sure all the stamens are removed before you pick it up.

Choosing flowers is very personal as certain flowers may be symbolic in your relationship, such as the first flowers your fiancé gave you or flowers you both love. Seasonal flowers represent the most sensible choice, as they are at their best and most economical. Although you will probably have ideas of colours, shape and style, you must be practical as well. Very soft, easily bruised flowers will not last through the service. The time of day and season are also important. A daytime spring wedding suits pale, fresh colours, while a dark winter's day demands rich, jewel-coloured roses with their intense warmth. In summer, consider garden flowers such as peonies and sweetpeas. Early summer brings lily of the valley, which makes the most stunning yet simple bouquet. Sunflowers wrapped with golden corn reflect the colours of late summer. Autumn brings berries, crab apples and rose hips. Don't forget to have a little rosemary for remembrance and myrtle for love.

You will probably want to preserve some or all of your flowers. Before you throw your bouquet to your female guests, remove the flowers you wish to keep. They can be pressed or preserved. There are companies who specialise in preserving flowers from bridal bouquets. If you are considering this, ask someone whom you know to be reliable to carry out your wishes as you will be on honeymoon.

Flowers for your hair must be chosen with care. If the hairstyle you are planning is elaborate, it will not require flowers. A floral headdress could present problems with a veil, and thorns, spikes and pollen could damage the fabric.

Flowers for your attendants should complement your bouquet. Small bridesmaids with floral headdresses, carrying decorated baskets filled with roses petals, present a charming picture. Don't forget to tuck some sweets into the basket, choosing only non-sticky, non-

**A striking, densely packed bouquet of vibrant red roses (far left), a springtime bunch of grape hyacinths, lily-of-the-valley and hellebores (below left), an autumn arrangement of berries and foliage (above left) and a contemporary bouquet of steel grass and white phaleonopsis orchids (above). Each is suited to a different season and style of dress.**

staining ones! Pomanders of violets or small roses are also dainty. Older bridesmaids and the maid of honour carry small bouquets, normally a scaled-down version of the bride's.

The groom, best man, ushers and fathers of the bride and groom usually have a simple single buttonhole for their jackets. If the mothers of the bride and groom care to wear a corsage, the design must be only a little larger than a buttonhole and match the colour of the chosen outfit and the bridal flowers.

# hair and make-up

Your wedding will be the most important day of your life. More photographs are taken of you than at any other time. You want to feel and look absolutely wonderful. Your dress and accessories have been chosen with great care. Now for want the finishing touches.

You are spending a lot of time and money on the whole day so it really is worth spending that little bit extra to have your hair and make-up done by a professional. You know how the hand of fate works. If you do your own hair and make-up on the day, you can almost guarantee it will go wrong, especially if you feel nervous. If you are really confident that you can manage it, then congratulations.

You have to choose whether to have a hairdresser and make-up artist come to your home or whether to visit them in their salons. I feel there are very good reasons for having them both with you on your wedding day. You will feel more relaxed at home or in a hotel. You do not have to drive anywhere, have the problems of parking, perhaps visiting two different salons or battling with the weather. You may have to struggle with your headdress and veil. You may even have to make an appointment hours before your wedding. The following advice is given by well-known hairdresser and make-up artist Derek Thompson, known as the 'Wedding King'. He has looked after many brides on their wedding day.

With your hairdresser with you in a relaxed atmosphere, you will feel pampered and well looked after, but whatever your choice you will need to make an appointment with your hairdresser to discuss the style you would like. If possible, take with you a sketch or photograph of your dress with a sample of the fabric and your headdress or hat. Much will depend on what time of day you are getting married and where. Is it a grand wedding reception or a simple country wedding? Spend time discussing the look you want. Do you want to look chic, natural or glamorous? However, you do not want to look radically different from normal – just a subtly enhanced version. If possible, wear your hair up and choose make-up to suit your style and personality. You must feel very confident and, above all, radiant and beautiful.

When having a trial hair and make-up session, do not allow yourself to be talked into anything you know is not right. We all know that when we look in the mirror it is either instantly right or wrong, so keep that in mind. So if it's not you, if the hair is wrong or the make-up too heavy, it will always be wrong. When you look at yourself it should feel comfortable. You may require more lipstick or a little more eye shadow but it will feel right. You must communicate now if you don't like what you see.

When you have chosen your hairdresser and make-up artist, remember to confirm the booking in writing. Make sure you tell them in advance if they will also be expected to attend to bridesmaids or any other female relatives.

If you would like to wear fresh flowers in your hair, speak to the florist. The flowers have to complement your bouquet, but make sure they are robust enough to stand up to the rigours of the day and will not flop within twenty minutes.

Your hairdresser should arrive at least two hours before you need to put on your dress. Allow at least one hour for your hair and thirty minutes for your make-up and fifteen minutes for a gossip! Wash your hair when you are bathing. If you want to wear your hair up, wash it the day before. This is a very calming time. Do not allow anyone in the room with you; they will be seeing you for the rest of the day.

When dressing, cover your face to protect the fabric, then lift the dress over your head. You may need help with this manoeuvre. Your make-up may require a little adjustment, so drape a cloth over your dress to protect it. Some dresses come with what can only be described as a large mesh bag to slip over your dress and protect it from make-up when you are dressing.

If you are doing your own hair and make-up, sit down at least three times and practise with styles of hair and make-up. Apply your make-up before you do your hair. You do not want to spoil your hair by scraping it back. Your headdress might take some time to get right so make sure you practise this. Some beauty salons will give you make-up lessons in advance of the big day. Do not be talked into wearing extra make-up for the photographs. Use a matt foundation as this is much more flattering in photographs. When properly applied, make-up will last all day so give yourself time. Stay calm and do this in a very relaxed atmosphere, even if it means pinning a 'do not disturb' note to the door.

Remember to take make-up such as lipstick or powder with you to touch up later on – ask your mother or a close friend to carry it in their handbag for you.

**A sparkly tiara (left) will look glamorous, or you can opt for elegant arrangement of fresh flowers in a simple hairstyle for an understated look.**

# clothes for the groom

Although all the eyes will be on the bride as she arrives for the service, it's just as important that the groom is as immaculately turned out as the bride. Somehow it seems to be easier for the man.

The traditional morning suit of black coat, grey waistcoat and pinstripe grey trousers looks very elegant and dashing. If you wish to change details, then a wing collar with a stock can replace the white shirt with a stiff collar and tie. Try to have some idea of the colour of the bride's dress so you can match the stock. If you choose to wear a tie, chose one that is not too loud but is jolly. Waistcoats are grey or buff colour, single or double breasted. A brocade waistcoat adds style. If you are planning to wear a stock it should match the waistcoat. – Stock pins, cuff links should be elegant and not too loud. Plain, highly polished black leather lace-up shoes with grey socks complete the suave groom. Don't forget to remove all traces of shoe polish – if you inadvertently step on your bride's dress, you do not want to leave polish marks. No handkerchief is worn in the morning jacket pocket as it would conflict with the buttonhole. With morning suits comes the top hat. They are very cumbersome to carry, the groom never wears it and it is just an accessory – my advice is not to bother.

If you are marrying in the evening, followed by a dinner and dancing, traditional black tie is the correct dress. Worn either with a wing collar or Eton collar, the choice of tie can add a little colour and, depending on the style of the wedding, some humour.

If you are marrying in a register office, wear a formal dark suit with suitable accessories or maybe some other form of dress that suits your personality – and you know you can carry off with style and humour. Morning or evening dress is not really appropriate.

# the supporting cast

The best man and ushers must be as smart as possible, since they are greeting and looking after the groom and the guests. The ushers are always the first contact and looking immaculate sets the tone for the day.

The best man and ushers wear morning dress without hats as they are cumbersome to carry and never worn. They may like to theme the waistcoat with a stock. If morning dress is not the order of the day, opt for a dark lounge suit with white shirts and matching ties. This also applies to evening dress – choose matching bow ties. Shoes worn with morning dress are plain black, polished lace-ups, with black or dark grey socks.

As most men will need to hire their outfits, arrange to do this as soon as you have set the date, especially if you are getting married at a busy time of year. You will be measured and fitted and asked to pay a deposit. Don't forget to return all the items of clothing in order to have the full deposit repaid. If the groom has also hired his outfit, the best man is responsible for collecting and returning it and reclaiming his deposit.

When you have chosen your wedding dress, think about your bridesmaids and pageboys. By tradition their parents pay for the outfits, but you must give thought to the costs as it is very unfair for you to expect the parents to pay a fortune. If you want to have a certain style and fabric, offer to pay for some of the costs. It's much better to have the outfits made by a friend or someone you know would like to help. Bridesmaids' dresses should be made to ensure they fit correctly. Have the dresses made as late as sensibly possible; children grow very quickly. Don't have long dresses as the children can trip over or step on and tear the fabric. Girls look charming in three-quarter-length dresses and after the wedding they can be made into party dresses. Don't choose strong colours or patterns as they can overwhelm the child. Little bridesmaids look sweet in ballet shoes and they are comfortable. The colours of the shoes can easily be made to match the fabric of their dresses.

Older bridesmaids' dresses must be elegant and understated. It's rather unfair to put them in an unflattering design full of bows, frills and layers of fabric.

When choosing on your pageboys' outfits, there are many styles to choose from, but they must be in harmony with the bridesmaids. The sash of the bridesmaids' dresses can match the sash of the pageboys' outfits or the colour of their knickerbockers. Other outfits are military, kilts, sailors, or whatever style you want to develop. Shoes depend on the outfit, but are usually black patent or a plain shoe with buttons. Break the shoes in a few weeks before the wedding.

The most important person after the bride is her mother. The outfit should be chosen with care so as not to upstage the bride in any way. After all, it's the bride's day. Choose an outfit that is comfortable, a style that is classic and elegant. One colour always works well. Team the dress or suit with a hat. Shoes are so important for comfort as you will be on your feet most of the day. Choose a handbag that is not too large, but can carry the bride's lipstick and a small make-up bag and mirror. The groom's mother nearly always worries about what the bride's mother has chosen. After the outfit is decided, tell the groom's mother so she can avoid choosing a clashing colour.

# food & drink

The food and drink at your wedding reception represent one of the most important elements of the day, so take the time to decide what you really want. Champagne and wedding cake may be the most traditional elements of a wedding feast, but there are plenty of other options.

# celebratory drinks

A wedding and champagne go hand in hand – one's first thought of celebrating is to toast the bride and groom with a chilled glass of champagne but of course there are plenty of other choices.

## WHAT TO SERVE AND WHEN

Planning the drinks you wish to serve is as important as deciding on the menu. The time of day and your budget are important considerations. For a late morning and lunchtime wedding reception consider serving champagne, as well as something light such as Bellinis (puréed fresh peaches mixed half-and-half with Prosecco) or sparkling white wine with fresh raspberry juice. These two drinks are particularly delicious during the spring and summer when the fruit is inexpensive and readily available.

Fresh fruit coolers, punches and cocktails, displayed in large jugs, are wonderful to look at and taste divine. Displaying them in this way makes it easy for guests to serve themselves from the bar. With so many mouthwatering fruit drinks available today, to serve plain orange juice is very unimaginative. Pitchers of ice-cold Bloody Mary made with tequila or flavoured vodkas are perfect for a late morning reception, followed by an early lunch or brunch. I personally do not like serving Bucks Fizz as I feel it is a waste of good champagne and fresh orange juice.

For an afternoon reception, champagne and sparkling wine mixed with fresh fruit purée is refreshing, as are jugs of white wine punch garnished with fresh fruits and flowers. Remember if you are planning an afternoon reception that there may be guests who would welcome a cup of tea so set up a tea bar just before they leave. In winter,

glasses of mulled wine with lots of spices and citrus peel, or hot buttered spicy rum, warm the coldest of hands. Chilled beers and soft drinks, including water, should also be available for your guests. At a large evening reception, a cocktail bar is lots of fun. Many cocktails can be made up in advance and stored on ice or in a fridge. When there is dancing plenty of soft drinks and water must be on hand. If your budget does not stretch to serving champagne during the reception, white wine or sparkling wine such as good Prosecco are also very good.

If children will be present, have plenty of fresh fruit drinks and water on hand. Children are notorious for not eating very much at a wedding as they are so excited. To tempt them we have started to serve interesting-flavoured and layered thick milk shakes made with lots of ice-cream.

## HOTELS, VENUES AND CATERERS

Discuss in detail with your chosen hotel, venue and/or caterer what you would like. If you are selecting your wine six to eight months in advance, enquire if the same vintages will be available. All drinks will probably be on a sale or return basis. Discuss quantities, and be generous in the calculations – it's better to have more than to run out. Another point to consider is to ask for a bottle count at the end of the evening. They will be quite used to people asking, so do not be embarrassed. If you wish to supply your own champagne, wines and soft drinks, some venues and caterers will have a corkage charge. Determine how much this charge is and allow for it within your budget. Some caterers do not have corkage charges but may charge for removing the empty bottles and taking the leftover drink back to their base for you to collect or they may deliver for you.

## DESIGNING A BAR

If you are arranging your own bar for drinks there are a few important points to remember. Your bar or bars should be inviting, convenient for guests to serve themselves and easy to keep uncluttered and clean. Place the bar in a convenient position, so that it is easily accessible for guests to serve themselves. Place a waterproof

**(Left) An inviting bar for guests to serve themselves at an informal outdoor reception.**

protection on the floor, taping down the edges to prevent accidents. The bar table should be at least 2 metres (6 feet) long and 1 metre (3 feet) high. Cover with a cloth to the ground, so storage of ice bins and glasses is hidden. If you are serving cocktails, make sure you have a supply of electricity to the bar for the blenders. Tape down the flex. On the bar place snacks so your guests can nibble while waiting for a drink. Fill tall vases with fruits in season. Place garnishes and ice in glass containers. Make garlands of flowers to decorate the front of the bar. Large cookie jars or jugs, labelled and filled with fresh fruit coolers or cocktails with a ladle by the side can stand ready for guests to serve themselves. Write a menu and place on the bar. Arrange the glasses in matching rows. I like to use attractive and fun glasses. Tie ribbon or ivy around the stems of champagne glasses. In summer use French lavender for stirrers in fresh fruit coolers. This is unusual and looks very pretty placed in the glass ready to be served. Fruit or flower ice cubes look particularly lovely in glasses of mineral water and white wine punches.

## COOLING DRINKS

Use large, waterproof containers to cool champagne, wines, beers and mineral water. A new dustbin, a smart galvanised container, plastic toy box, a large cooler or half-wooden barrel are all suitable. When using ice bins, place them in large rubbish bins to protect the floor from condensation. Cover the bottom of the container with ice, place the bottles in the bin and cover with more ice. For large receptions, use separate ice bins for champagne, wines, beers and soft drinks. To make serving easier, before chilling down, remove the foil from around the champagne corks. Remove and replace the corks in the white wine bottles. Allow at least two hours for the drinks to cool. When serving beers for guests to help themselves, tie the bottle opener to the ice bin so it does not go missing.

## QUANTITY OF ICE REQUIRED

For a lunchtime reception (4 hours) with 100 guests, allow 10 x 3.6kg (30lb) bags of ice.

For an afternoon reception (5 hours) with 150–200 guests, allow 18 x 13.6kg (30lb) bags of ice.

For an evening reception (6–7 hours) with 100–150 guests followed by dinner and dancing, allow 25 x 13.6kg (30lb) bags of ice.

This allows ice for chilling the drinks and ice cubes for placing in drinks. If the weather is very hot, allow for another delivery of ice about halfway through the reception. Remember to store the ice out of direct sunlight.

## HIRING GLASSWARE

It's unlikely that, unless you are planning a very small lunch, dinner or reception, you will have the quantity of glassware required. There are many wonderful styles available for rental these days and for your wedding it is worth spending just that little bit more. For a small extra charge, you can return the glasses unwashed. When buying your drinks, some suppliers offer free glass hire. Make sure they are sparkling clean before use and just as sparkling when you return them.

## QUANTITY OF DRINK PER PERSON

### LUNCH

$1/4$ bottle champagne

$1/4$ bottle white wine

$1/4$ bottle red wine

1 litre bottle mineral water

$1/2$ litre fresh fruit juice

### AFTERNOON RECEPTION

$1/3$ bottle champagne

$1/4$ bottle white wine

$1/4$ bottle red wine

1 70cl bottle mineral water

### EVENING RECEPTION FOLLOWED BY DINNER AND DANCING

$1/2$ bottle champagne

$1/2$ bottle white wine

$1/2$ bottle red wine

2 bottles beer

$1/2$ litre fresh fruit juice

1 litre mineral water

### EQUIPMENT FOR SETTING UP THE BAR

Bottle openers

Cloth for mopping up spills

Cocktail shaker

Containers for garnishes and ice cubes

Corkscrews

Crushed ice

Cutting board and knife

Drink napkins to wrap around glasses

Ice bins

Ice cubes

Jugs

Large containers for chilling drinks

Serving trays

Spoons, ice tongs or scoop

Stirrers

Strainer

Straws

Tin opener

# cocktails and soft drinks

## COCKTAILS

### CANALETTO

Many years ago I had the great pleasure of drinking one of these delicious cocktails at a fiftieth birthday party at the Gritti Palace in Venice. Made with puréed fresh raspberries mixed with very cold Prosecco and garnished with fresh raspberries and mint, this is a wonderful alternative to the classic Bellini. We have served these drinks on many occasions and they are extremely popular. They are also easy to prepare in jugs, ready for serving.

SERVES 100 IN 100ML (4FL OZ) GLASSES

*4 kilos (8lb) fresh raspberries (this yields 4 litres (7 pints) of fresh raspberry juice)*
*10 bottles of chilled Prosecco*
*130 raspberries, variegated mint leaves and viola flowers, to garnish*

Place the fresh raspberries in a blender and blend until smooth. Sieve the purée through a strainer set over a large jug or bowl, pour into an airtight container, seal and place in the fridge until ready to use. To serve, place the juice and Prosecco into a large container, mix well and pour into jugs. Serve in glasses garnished with raspberries, mint and viola flowers.

### CHOCOLATE MARTINI

A very popular cocktail. For a fun look, add a few Smarties.

SERVES 10

*500ml (17fl oz) chocolate vodka or a good Polish vodka*
*250ml (7¹/₂fl oz) chocolate liqueur*
*Ice*
*Smarties, to garnish (optional)*
*Cocktail shaker*

Mix the vodka and liqueur together. Cover and place on ice or in the fridge. To serve, pour about 75ml (3fl oz) into a cocktail shaker filled with ice. Shake until very cold, pour into a cocktail glass and garnish with the Smarties.

### RASPBERRY MARTINI

Refreshing on a summer day and very different.

SERVES 10

*500ml (17fl oz) raspberry vodka or a good Polish vodka*
*150ml (¹/₄ pint) fresh raspberry juice*
*100ml (3¹/₂fl oz) raspberry liqueur*
*100ml (3¹/₂fl oz) crème de mûre*
*Ice*
*Frozen raspberries, to garnish*
*Cocktail shaker*

Mix all the ingredients except the ice and the garnish, and stir well. Place on ice or in the fridge until required. To serve, fill the cocktail shaker with ice, pour in one-tenth of the mixture, shake until ice-cold, pour into a cocktail glass and garnish with a frozen raspberry.

**(Left) Canaletto. (Top right) Mango Berry Coolers (see page 122). (Bottom right) Chocolate Martinis.**

## WHITE WINE PUNCH

White wine with a kick which looks very inviting.

MAKES 9 x MEDIUM-SIZED WINE
GLASSES
2 bottles good white wine (not sweet), well
    chilled
100ml (3½ fl oz) brandy
100ml (3½ fl oz) vodka
Ice
Berries and flowerheads, to garnish

Pour the wine, brandy and vodka into glass
jugs with an ice lip. Add the ice and stir. Place
the garnish in the glasses, pour in the punch
and serve.

## PLANTERS PUNCH

My friend Stephen Camacho is the best drinks-
mixer and cocktail-maker I have ever known.
This is his family recipe for planters punch.
Rather than the sweet and sticky variety, this
version is made with fresh fruit juices and
matured for 36 hours.

SERVES 10
1 litre (1¾ pints) light rum (Mount Gay or
    Cavalier)
1 litre (1¾ pints) fresh pineapple juice
250ml (7½ fl oz) fresh passion fruit juice
250ml (7½ fl oz) fresh lime juice
Grated nutmeg
Ice
Slices of mango and pineapple, to garnish
Straws

Place all the ingredients except the ice and
garnish in a large airtight container. Stir well
and place in the fridge for 36 hours to mature.
To serve, pour over ice in tall glasses, add a
straw and fruit to garnish.

## MOJITO

This is an extremely refreshing drink to serve
on a hot summer's day.

SERVES 8
200ml (7½ fl oz) white rum
120ml (4fl oz) fresh lime juice
60ml (2fl oz) sugar syrup
240ml (½ pint) sparkling water
Ice
A good handful of mint leaves, washed
Stirrers

Place all the ingredients except the water, ice
and mint in a container and place on ice or in
the fridge. To serve, place about 8 mint leaves
in the bottom of each tall glass, crush the mint
with a long spoon, add the mix to three-quarters
of the way up the glass, fill with ice and top up
with water. Place a stirrer in the glass.

# SOFT DRINKS

## MANGO BERRY COOLER

When mangoes and raspberries are in season,
this makes a delightful drink, served ice-cold.
Lavender is in season at the same time and a
stalk of lavender acts as an unusual stirrer.

SERVES 10
1 liltre (1¾ pints) fresh mango juice
500ml (15fl oz) fresh raspberry juice
500ml (15fl oz) still mineral water
Ice
Lavender stirrers

Mix the juices and water together, stir well.
Place in a container on ice or in the fridge. To
serve, fill the glasses with ice, pour over the
juice and add the lavender.

**(Top left) White Wine Punch. (Bottom left)
Mojitos. (Right) Planters Punch.**

## THE BIG APPLE

This is a classic combination of apple juice and ginger beer.

MAKES 5 x 250ML (8FL OZ) GLASSES
*1 litre (1³/4 pints) organic apple juice (choose a sharp variety)*
*1 x 330ml can of Old Jamaican ginger beer, or a good old-fashioned brand*
*Ice*
*Fresh mint, to garnish*
*Straws*

Pour the apple juice and ginger beer into a jug and mix. Fill the glasses with ice and drink, garnish with the mint and straws, and serve.

## COOL VANILLA CHERRY

Vanilla and cherry work so well together. If you don't want to serve just juice, a shot of vodka or grappa makes a great cocktail.

MAKES 5 x 140ML (¹/4 PINT) GLASSES
*500ml (15fl oz) dark cherry pulp*
*200ml (7¹/2 fl oz) sparkling mineral water*
*1 teaspoon vanilla essence*
*Ice*
*Cherries, to garnish*
*Straws*

Mix the cherry pulp, water and vanilla essence together, stir well, and pour into jugs. Fill the glasses with ice, pour over the juice, garnish with the cherries, add a straw and serve.

## PEAR AND APPLE CRUSH

A refreshingly different fruit cooler for your guests who enjoy soft drinks. This is very easy to mix ahead of time and leave on ice or in a fridge. Try to find a good brand of organic juice; the apple will be nicer if you can use a fairly sharp variety.

SERVES 100 IN 200ML GLASSES
*20 x 980ml (1³/4 pint) bottles organic apple juice (such as Bramley)*
*5 x 980ml (1³/4 pint) bottles organic pear juice*

*1 litre (1³/4 pints) fresh lemon juice (squeezed from approximately 20 lemons)*
*Ice*
*Thinly sliced whole apples, to garnish*
*Stirrers*

Mix together all the ingredients apart from the garnish. Store in an airtight container on ice or in a fridge. To serve, stir well and pour into jugs. Fill the glasses with ice, garnish with whole apple slices, add a stirrer and pour over the juice.

## SUMMERTIME PEACH

Like the berry cooler, it's wonderful to use fruits when they are plentiful to create delicious, refreshing drinks like this one.

MAKES 10 x 200ML (7 1/2 FL OZ) GLASSES

500ml (15fl oz) fresh mango juice
1 litre (1 3/4 pints) fresh peach juice
500ml (15fl oz) still mineral water
Ice
Slices of peach or mango, to garnish

Mix the juices with the water, stir well, store in a container on ice or in the fridge, until ready to serve. To serve, fill the glasses with ice, pour over the juice, garnish with the fruits and serve.

## CAPE CRANBERRY

I created this soft drink for the wedding of Ming Veevers Carter who married on Cape Cod this year. It combines two loves in her life: the Cape and the tropics.

MAKES 5 x 250ML (7 1/2 FL OZ) GLASSES

1 litre (1 3/4 pints) cranberry juice
250ml (7 1/2 fl oz) fresh mango juice
Ice
Fresh cranberries, to garnish

Mix the juices together and stir well, place in a container on ice or in the fridge. To serve, fill the glasses with ice, pour over the juice and garnish with cranberries.

## MILK SHAKES

I first had one of these delicious three-colour milk shakes eighteen years ago in Boston. This year I returned, looking forward to enjoying another one. Alas the ice-cream parlour had been replaced by a coffee shop. Great for children (and adults) at an afternoon wedding.

SERVES 6

Place six glasses in the freezer. If you have the luxury of being able to use three blenders, all the better. If not, fill each glass with a layer of shake, then place in the freezer, wash the blender, and repeat the process until the milk shakes are complete.

VANILLA LAYER

100ml (3fl oz) full-fat milk
1 litre (2 1/4 pints) vanilla ice-cream
Seeds from a vanilla pod or a teaspoon of
    pure vanilla essence

STRAWBERRY LAYER

100ml (3fl oz) full-fat milk
1 litre (2 1/4 pints) strawberry ice-cream
4 fresh strawberries, washed and chopped

CHOCOLATE LAYER

100ml (3fl oz) full-fat milk
1 litre (2 1/4 pints) bitter chocolate ice-cream
2 tablespoons Ovaltine

FOR THE VANILLA LAYER:
Place the milk and half the ice-cream in a blender, add the vanilla seeds or essence. Blend until smooth. Add the remaining ice-cream, blend until smooth, pour into glasses; place in the freezer for about half an hour.

FOR THE STRAWBERRY LAYER:
Place the milk, half the ice-cream and the strawberries in a blender, blend until smooth, add the remaining ice-cream and blend until smooth. Pour into the glasses and place in the freezer for about half an hour.

FOR THE CHOCOLATE LAYER:
Place the milk, half the ice-cream and the Ovaltine in a blender, blend until smooth, add the remaining ice-cream, blend till smooth. Pour into the glasses and serve immediately with long spoons and straws.

# wedding food

Planning the style of food for your reception is dictated by the time of day you are marrying. There are four options: a seated lunch, an afternoon wedding with canapés, an evening dinner or a buffet for lunch or dinner. If you are thinking of catering your own reception, forward planning is essential.

Planning the style of food within your budget is not too difficult. Instead of canapés served before lunch or dinner, place snacks on tables for guests to help themselves. You could hire a chef or chefs to do the cooking, along with waiting staff to set up the bar and tables as well as serve and clear away. If you are considering providing your own ingredients for someone else to prepare, I would advise having a trial run. You will need to be detailed in your instructions and what you like and dislike. What you cannot do is spend your wedding day in the kitchen, or expect your family and friends to do the same. Plan to use seasonal foods as they are at their best in flavour and price.

Kate Dyson, who owns the Dining Room Shop in London, decided she would cater for both her daughters' weddings. At the first wedding she entertained 150 guests with a barbecue supper; for the second a year later, she organised picnic baskets for 350 guests. Armed with a Victorian afternoon tea cookbook, they set about planning the contents of the baskets for adults and children. While they were at the church, twelve people at home filled the baskets, ready to hand to guests as they arrived. This idea inspired our picnic on the lawn (see page 147).

I have put together five styles of wedding receptions, all developed from menus we have served at weddings. The food should be memorable, a feast for the eye and a combination of flavours and textures. At weddings people will remember bad food as well as excellent creations. Balance the menus and think of the age range of your guests. Children and more elderly guests would probably not eat hot and spicy foods. Chocolate is always a winner for dessert and lamb is the most requested main course. The food you both like becomes part of the menu. Don't forget the vegetarians and don't simply offer the vegetables that are served with a main course. Whatever the style of reception you are hosting, the food must be presented in an elegant way.

This chapter contains a grand five-course dinner, a simple three-course menu that could be served for a lunch or dinner, canapés for an afternoon reception, a buffet inspired by the flavours from the Mediterranean and a summer's afternoon picnic for adults and children. Some elements can be prepared in advance and stored in the freezer.

**(Left and below) Simple or sophisticated, appetisers are important ingredients of the wedding reception. (Right) Tower of Asparagus.**

# informal lunch

This light summer lunch for 20 is an interesting mix of modern and traditional styles using seasonal ingredients full of flavour. Fresh asparagus is tied neatly into bundles that are filled with artichokes and wild mushrooms. Succulent scallops are lightly grilled and drizzled with a sweet chilli dressing. For dessert there is a classic fruit fool with pretty heart-shaped cookies sparkling with sugar.

FIRST COURSE
*Tower of Asparagus*

MAIN COURSE
*Scallop and
Langoustine Salad with
Sweet Chilli Dressing*

DESSERT
*Gooseberry and Elderflower
Fool, served with Sugared
Heart Biscuits*

## TOWER OF ASPARAGUS

These towers can be prepared and stored in the fridge 6 hours before they are required.

FOR THE TOWER:

*60 red cherry tomatoes, halved*

*8 shallots, peeled and finely chopped*

*2 cloves garlic, peeled and finely chopped*

*2 tablespoons soft thyme leaves*

*Olive oil, for frying*

*600g (1lb 4oz) wild mushrooms, brushed*

*20 artichoke hearts, cooked and chargrilled*

*160 green asparagus spears, blanched and cut into 8cm (3¹/₂ in) lengths*

*160 white asparagus spears, blanched and cut into 8cm (3¹/₂ in) lengths*

*2 large leeks, washed, cut into 20 1cm (¹/₂ in) strips, blanched and dried*

**FOR THE DRESSING:**

*200g (6¹/₂oz) goat's cheese, outside ash removed, cut into small pieces*
*300ml (¹/₂ pint) warm water*
*2 tablespoons good sherry vinegar, warmed*
*300ml (¹/₂ pint) balsamic vinegar, reduced by half*
*Sea salt and freshly ground black pepper*

**SPECIAL EQUIPMENT:**

*20 metal rings, 6.5cm wide x 4cm deep (2¹/₂in x 1³/₄in)*

Preheat the oven to 100°C/210°F/gas mark ¹/₄. Place the cherry tomatoes cut side up on a metal baking tray. Sprinkle with half the shallots, the garlic and thyme; season. Place in the oven for 6–8 hours. Remove from the oven. Cool and carefully store in an airtight container in the fridge.

Heat a sauté pan with a little olive oil, and sauté a few mushrooms at a time with the remaining shallots. Season and place in a colander to drain. When cooled, place in an airtight container in the fridge.

Cut a 3cm (1¹/₄in) disc from each artichoke. Place the discs in a bowl, cover and set aside. Cut the remaining artichokes into small pieces and place in a large bowl. Add the tomatoes and wild mushrooms, season well, cover and set aside.

Place the rings on a metal tray. Put an artichoke disc on the base of each ring. Season. Place the asparagus in two separate bowls and season well. Arrange the spears around the rings in alternate colours. Fill the centres of the rings with the tomato and mushroom mixture. Place the blanched leeks around the top edge of the rings and tie tightly in place. Cover and place in the fridge.

**TO MAKE THE DRESSING:**

Heat a pan of water. When warm place a metal bowl over the pan, add the goat's cheese and slowly melt. Do not over-heat the cheese or it will split. Remove the bowl. Whisk in the warm water a little at a time, then whisk in the vinegars. Check the seasoning. Do not place in the fridge.

To serve, place the towers in the centre of the plates, remove the rings and drizzle around the dressing.

## SCALLOP AND LANGOUSTINE SALAD WITH SWEET CHILLI DRESSING

**FOR THE DRESSING:**

*6 tablespoons sweet chilli sauce*
*5 tablespoons fish sauce*
*2 tablespoons light soy sauce*
*Juice of 3 large limes*
*3 cloves garlic, peeled and finely chopped*
*3 tablespoons peanut oil*

**FOR THE SALAD:**

*40 medium-sized scallops, roes removed*
*100 langoustine tails, poached and peeled*
*Vegetable oil*
*400g (13oz) spring onions, finely sliced*
*400g (13oz) red onions, peeled and finely sliced*
*400g (13oz) bok choy leaves, washed and dried*
*800g (1lb 10oz) carrots, peeled and cut into strips*
*500g (1lb 1oz) French beans, split and blanched*
*400g (13oz) snow pea shoots, washed and dried*
*2 cups coriander, washed and dried*
*1 cup Thai basil, washed and dried*
*1 cup mint leaves, washed and dried*
*2 radishes, washed and cut into strips*
*Sea salt and freshly ground black pepper*

**FOR THE GARNISH:**

*1kg (2lb 2oz) cashew nuts, roasted*
*40 crayfish, poached and cooled*

**(Above) Scallop and Langoustine Salad with Sweet Chilli Dressing. (Right) Gooseberry and Elderflower Fool with Sugared Heart Biscuits.**

In a bowl mix the sweet chilli sauce, fish sauce, soy sauce, lime juice and garlic. Whisk in the peanut oil and set aside. Heat a chargrill plate; slice the prepared scallops in half lengthways, brush with a little oil and season with salt and pepper. Chargrill the scallops for approximately 15 seconds per side, then leave to cool.

Place the langoustines and scallops in a bowl. Place all the other salad ingredients in a separate bowl. Lightly dress the langoustine and scallops and the salad with the dressing. In a serving bowl, layer up the langoustine, scallops and salad, seasoning between the layers. Scatter with cashew nuts, garnish with crayfish, drizzle over any remaining dressing and serve.

## GOOSEBERRY AND ELDERFLOWER FOOL

2.5kg (5lb 5oz) gooseberries, trimmed
900g (1lb 14oz) caster sugar
120ml (4fl oz) elderflower cordial
1 litre (1³/₄ pints) double cream, lightly
  whipped
Elderflowers, to garnish

Place the gooseberries, sugar and cordial in a heavy-bottomed saucepan, slowly bring to the boil, cover and simmer until the fruit is tender. Remove from the heat. Place into a bowl, cover and leave to cool. When cold, place into a food processor and purée until smooth. Sieve into a bowl. Fold in the cream. Cover and place in the fridge. To serve, fill 200ml (6¹/₂fl oz) glasses with the fool and garnish with the elderflowers.

## SUGARED HEART BISCUITS

### FOR THE DOUGH:
240g (8oz) unsalted butter
400g (13¹/₂ oz) caster sugar
2 large free-range eggs, beaten
560g (1lb 3oz) plain flour
¹/₂ teaspoon salt
1 teaspoon vanilla essence
Zest of 2 lemons

### FOR THE ICING:
2 free-range egg whites
300g (10oz) icing sugar
Juice of ¹/₂ lemon
Various food colours and sanding sugars

Preheat the oven to 170°C/325°F/gas mark 5. Line a baking tray with nonstick baking parchment paper or a silicon baking mat. Cream the butter and caster sugar in an electric mixer until light and fluffy. Add the eggs gradually and beat until smooth. Carefully fold in the remaining ingredients. Place the dough on a floured surface and knead until smooth. Cover with cling film and rest in the fridge for 1 hour or until firm. Remove and place on a floured work surface. Roll out to 5mm (¹/₂in) thickness. Cut out with a heart cutter and place on the tray. Bake in the oven for 15–20 minutes or until golden brown.

Remove from the oven and cool on a wire rack, then store in an airtight container in a cool place.

To make the icing, place the egg white and icing sugar in an electric mixer and beat until stiff. Add the lemon juice and beat until smooth. Colour as required and decorate as desired.

# afternoon reception

The dishes chosen for this afternoon reception for 50 people provide an interesting mix of flavours and styles of food.

*Rillettes of Salmon with Caviar and Crème Fraîche*

*A Selection of Sushi*

*Little Spoons of Lobster with Avocado*

*Heart-shaped Quesadillas with Smoked Chicken*

*Sesame-crusted Tuna with Mango and Chilli Salsa*

*Banana Leaf Cones filled with Noodle Salad*

*Chinese Duck Wrap*

*Parmesan Baskets filled with Butternut Squash Risotto*

*Toasted Bread Boxes filled with Creamed Wild Mushrooms*

*Crab Cakes with Corn Chowder Dip*

*Red Pepper and Ginger Soup Sip*

*Muffalata*

*Sandwiches*

*Heart Pavlovas*

*Passionfruit Heart Tartlets*

*Little Heart Fruit Tarts*

*Ginger Chocolate Box*

## RILLETTES OF SALMON WITH CAVIAR AND CRÈME FRAÎCHE

FOR THE SALMON POACHING LIQUID:

1 leek, washed and sliced

1 onion, peeled and sliced

1 bay leaf

2 sprigs of thyme

10 whole black peppercorns

1 glass of white wine

2 litres (3½ pints) fish stock or water

FOR THE RILLETTES:

500g (1lb 1oz) skinless salmon fillet

120g (4oz) gravlax, finely chopped

2 shallots, peeled and finely diced

2 tablespoons chives, finely chopped

2 tablespoons dill, chopped

Juice and zest of ½ lime

Juice of ½ lemon

3 tablespoons crème fraîche

Salt and freshly ground black pepper

FOR THE GARNISH AND BASE:

250g (8½oz) packet pumpernickel bread

500g (1lb 1oz) oak-smoked salmon, thinly sliced

4 tablespoons crème fraîche

120g (4oz) Sevruga caviar

Place all the ingredients for the poaching liquid in a large saucepan, season and bring to the boil. Place the salmon fillet in the pan, bring back to the boil, then remove the pan from the heat and leave to cool. Once cold, drain and flake the fish into a bowl.

Combine the rest of the ingredients apart from the crème fraîche with the salmon, mix well, season and fold in the crème fraîche. Once all the ingredients are combined, place the mixture into a piping bag with a 2.5cm (1in) nozzle, and pipe a long 'sausage' onto cling film. Roll up the cling film and twist the ends tightly. Repeat this until all the mixture is used. Place in the freezer.

Cut out 50 discs of pumpernickel bread with a 2.5cm (1in) cutter; repeat this with the smoked salmon. Place in separate airtight containers and refrigerate.

To serve, remove the salmon from the freezer and leave for 5 minutes. Lay out the pumpernickel bread on a serving plate and slice the salmon rillettes into 1.5cm (½in) slices, remove the cling film and place on the pumpernickel bread. Top with smoked salmon discs, a swirl of crème fraîche and caviar.

## A SELECTION OF SUSHI

1kg (2lb 2oz) sushi rice

300ml (½ pint) seasoned sushi vinegar

200g (6½oz) very fresh fillet of salmon, skin and brown flesh removed

200g (6½oz) very fresh loin of tuna, skin removed

20 large Mediterranean prawns, shelled with the tail on

7 sheets of nori

60g (1oz) tube wasabi

120g (4oz) salmon roe (keta)

5 tablespoons white sesame seeds

5 tablespoons black sesame seeds

1 x 500g (1lb 1oz) lobster, cooked, shell removed and cut into strips

1 cucumber, deseeded and cut into strips the length of the nori sheets

½ daikon radish, cut into strips the length of the nori sheets

1 avocado, peeled and cut into strips the length of the nori sheets

juice of ½ lemon

600ml (1 pint) Kikkoman soy sauce

SPECIAL EQUIPMENT:

Japanese rice cooker

Fan (uchiwa)

Rice cooling tub

Wooden paddle

Bamboo rolling mats

Heavy chopping knives

**(Left) Rillettes of Salmon. (Above) Sushi.**

TO COOK THE RICE:

Place the rice into a fine sieve, wash well. Leave to drain, then wash again and leave for about 1 hour in a cool place. Place the washed rice into the cooker, pour over 1.3 litres (2½ pints) water and cook to the packet instructions. When cooked, drain the rice and place in the cooling tub or on a large plastic tray. Toss the rice with the wooden paddle and add the seasoned vinegar, fanning the rice all the time (you will need someone else to help with this). The best way is to lift the rice with the paddle as you add the vinegar. When all the vinegar is absorbed, cover the rice with a damp cloth and leave in a cool place.

Take a clean plastic tray lined with cling film. With large teaspoons, make 60 quenelles with the rice (the remainder of the rice is for the sushi rolls). Place on the tray, cover and place in the fridge.

TO PREPARE THE FISH:

Cut the salmon and the tuna into rectangular blocks, and slice thinly to the width and length of the rice quenelles. Place on a tray, cover and place in the fridge. Cut the prawns along the underside, open out to a butterfly, leaving the tails on. Cover and place in the fridge. Cut 20 5mm (1/8 in) strips of nori. Place into an airtight container.

### TO MAKE THE SUSHI:

Remove the rice quenelles and prepared fish from the fridge. Spread a little wasabi on the top of the rice. Top the rice with the fish. Place the prawns on the rice and place a strip of nori around the prawn.

### TO MAKE THE SALMON ROE SUSHI ROLLS:

When handling the rice, it is important to moisten your hands with sushi vinegar to prevent the rice sticking to you. Also have a clean cloth by your work area to clean your hands between each handling of the rice.

Lay a nori sheet on a bamboo rolling mat, rough side up. Spread the nori with the rice, leaving a 2cm (1/2in) edge on the far side. Roll the mat away from you, pressing the rice to keep it firm. Wet the far edge of the nori with water, so on the final roll the nori will stick together. Repeat with another 2 sheets of nori. Cut each roll into 10 even pieces, place a dot of wasabi on the top, and top with the salmon roe.

### TO MAKE THE INSIDE OUT ROLLS:

Cover the bamboo rolling mat with cling film. Place a nori sheet on top. Spread the nori with the seasoned rice. Sprinkle with sesame seeds, covering the rice. Turn the sheet over and spread a little wasabi down the centre of the nori side, then place the lobster, cucumber, radish and avocado down the centre. Squeeze over the lemon juice. Make the roll by holding the base of the mat and pressing the ingredients with your fingers, roll up tightly, then gently mould into a square. Repeat with another 2 nori sheets and cut each roll into 10 even pieces.

### TO SERVE THE SUSHI:

Arrange the sushi on a black lacquer tray. Pour a little soy sauce into dipping bowls and serve.

## LITTLE SPOONS OF LOBSTER WITH AVOCADO

*3 x 500g (1lb 1oz) lobsters, poached and*
*  cooled, all the meat removed*
*10 red cherry tomatoes*
*1 Hass avocado*
*1 lime, halved*
*1 large bunch of coriander leaves, washed and*
*  dried*
*2 chillies, deseeded and cut into 3cm (1 1/2 in)*
*  strips*
*50 crayfish, poached and peeled*
*150ml (1/4 pint) good quality lemon olive oil*
*Sea salt and freshly ground black pepper*

Cut the lobster meat into 5mm (1/8in) round slices. Using a sharp serrated knife, cut each cherry tomato into 5 slices. Cut the avocado in half, peel and cut into 5 segments lengthways and slice each segment into 20. Squeeze the juice of the lime over the avocado, season.

To serve, lay out the teaspoons. Layer the avocado, lobster, cherry tomato, coriander and chilli strips, seasoning each layer. Top with the crayfish and drizzle with a little lemon olive oil and serve.

## HEART-SHAPED QUESADILLAS WITH SMOKED CHICKEN

FOR THE SALSA:
*6 large plum tomatoes, blanched, peeled, deseeded and finely diced*
*1 small red onion, peeled and finely diced*
*1 red chilli, deseeded and finely diced*
*1/2 cup chopped coriander, washed and dried*
*Juice of 2 limes*
*2 tablespoons extra virgin olive oil*

*3 x 30cm (12in) flour tortillas*
*150ml (5fl oz) crème fraîche*
*2 smoked chicken breasts, thinly sliced and cut into strips*
*3 large pickled walnuts, sliced*
*60g (2oz) Manchego cheese, cut into small dice*
*Coriander leaves, to garnish*
*Sea salt and finely ground black pepper*

To make the salsa, place all the ingredients into a bowl, season, cover and place in the fridge.

To make the quesadillas, preheat a deep-fat fryer. Cut the tortillas into hearts using a small heart-shaped cookie cutter. Deep-fry

**(Left) Little Spoons of Lobster with Avocado.**

until golden, drain on absorbent paper. When cold, layer in an airtight box. Store in a cool place.

To serve, place the hearts on a work surface. Pipe a little crème fraîche into the centre of each heart, spread it slightly but do not go over the edges. Place a few strips of chicken on each heart, followed by the walnuts and cheese. Season, top with the salsa, garnish with the coriander and serve.

## SESAME-CRUSTED TUNA WITH MANGO AND CHILLI SALSA

*3 large free-range egg yolks*
*3 tablespoons runny honey*
*6 tablespoons black sesame seeds*
*6 tablespoons white toasted sesame seeds*
*800g (1lb 10oz) loin of tuna cut into squares, 2.5 x 2.5cm (1 x 1in)*
*Unscented vegetable oil*
*Sea salt and freshly ground black pepper*

*For the salsa:*
*1 large ripe mango, peeled and finely diced*
*1 red chilli, deseeded and finely diced*
*1 small red onion, peeled and finely diced*
*1 clove garlic, peeled and finely diced*
*Juice of 1 large lime*
*2 tablespoons fish sauce*
*2 tablespoons coriander, washed, dried and chopped*

Whisk the egg yolks in a bowl with the honey. Place the sesame seeds into a bowl and season well. Coat the tuna in the egg and honey, then in the sesame seeds, coating well. Heat a large sauté pan with a little oil. Seal the tuna on each side for 20 seconds, remove and leave to cool. When cold, place in an airtight container in the fridge.

To make the salsa, place all the ingredients into a bowl, mix well, pour into a container, cover and place in the fridge.

To serve, remove all the ingredients from the fridge. Cut the tuna into 2cm (1/2in) thick slices, top with the salsa and serve.

## BANANA LEAF CONES FILLED WITH NOODLE SALAD

TO MAKE THE CONES:
*6 whole banana leaves*

FOR THE NOODLE SALAD:
*Vegetable oil*
*1kg (2lb 2oz) thin fresh egg noodles*
*4 cloves garlic, peeled and finely chopped*
*1 walnut-sized piece of ginger, finely chopped*
*500g (1lb 1oz) carrots, peeled, sliced on a mandolin and cut into triangles*
*500g (1lb 1oz) spring onions, finely sliced*
*500g (1lb 1oz) shiitake mushrooms, finely sliced*
*10 red peppers, quartered, deseeded and cut into diamonds*
*500g (1lb 1oz) mangetout, cut into triangles*
*1 cup coriander leaves, washed and dried*

FOR THE DRESSING:
*450ml (3/4 pint) light soy sauce*
*3 tablespoons sweet chilli sauce*
*Juice of 3 limes*
*3 tablespoons caster sugar*
*3 tablespoons peanut oil*

FOR THE GARNISH:
*2 tablespoons black sesame seeds*
*2 tablespoons white sesame seeds*

Place a large dinner plate approximately 25cm (10in) across on the banana leaves, cut out 25 circles the size of the plate, cut each circle in half. Wrap to create a cone and staple to secure.

Heat a large pan of water, add a little salt and vegetable oil and bring to the boil. Take a large container of ice-cold water and keep to

## CHINESE DUCK WRAP

FOR THE MARINADE:

300ml (½ pint) light soy sauce

3 tablespoons dry sherry

2 tablespoons yellow bean paste

2 tablespoons caster sugar

4 star anise

2 teaspoons five-spice powder

1 walnut-sized piece of fresh ginger, peeled
    and finely grated

3 cloves garlic, peeled and crushed

600ml (1 pint) dark chicken stock

Vegetable oil

3 duck breasts

FOR THE WRAP:

5 x 30cm (12in) spinach tortillas

500g (1lb 1oz) sour cream

½ cucumber, peeled, deseeded and finely
    sliced

5 spring onions, washed, dried and cut into
    fine strips

2 baby gem lettuces, washed, dried and finely
    shredded

200g (6½oz) plum sauce

Place all the ingredients for the marinade into a large saucepan. Bring to the boil, then turn down to a simmer for approximately 10 minutes to infuse the flavours. Meanwhile, heat a sauté pan with a little oil and seal the duck breasts until golden all sides. Add the duck to the marinade, return to the boil, remove from the heat, and leave to cool. When cold, put the duck and marinade in an airtight container, and place this in the fridge.

To make the wraps, remove the duck breasts from the marinade and pat dry. Slice each duck breast into 8 strips. Place the tortillas on a work surface, spread evenly with the sour cream, followed by the cucumber, spring onions and lettuce. Lay the strips of duck on top and drizzle with plum sauce. Roll up the wraps and seal with cling film. Chill until ready to serve, then cut each wrap into ten at an angle.

one side. Cook the egg noodles in the boiling water for 4–5 minutes, then drain in a colander and drop into the ice-cold water to refresh. Once cold, drain and place into a large bowl, drizzle with a little vegetable oil and toss to prevent the noodles sticking.

Heat a wok, add a little vegetable oil, add the garlic and ginger and sauté the vegetables. Place in a large bowl and mix in the noodles. Leave to cool, then cover and place in the fridge.

To make the dressing, put the soy sauce, sweet chilli sauce, lime juice and sugar in a bowl. Mix well until the sugar is dissolved. Stir

**(Above) Banana Leaf Cones filled with Noodle Salad. (Right) Parmesan Baskets filled with Butternut Squash Risotto.**

in peanut oil; pour into a container with a lid and place in the fridge.

To serve, dress the noodles, add the coriander and mix well. Place the banana cones in ice-cream stands or baskets. Fill with the noodles and sprinkle with a few sesame seeds. Serve with a fork.

## PARMESAN BASKETS FILLED WITH BUTTERNUT SQUASH RISOTTO

### FOR THE PARMESAN BASKETS:

*500g (1lb 1oz) grated Padano Parmesan*
*4 wine corks*

### FOR THE RISOTTO:

*1 litre (1¹/₂ pints) vegetable stock*
*Extra virgin olive oil*
*1 medium butternut squash, peeled and finely diced*
*90g (3oz) unsalted butter*
*3 shallots, peeled and finely chopped*
*2 cloves garlic, peeled and finely chopped*
*250g (8¹/₂ oz) Arborio rice*
*1 glass of dry white wine*
*60g (2oz) Reggiano Parmesan, grated*
*¹/₂ cup flat leaf parsley, washed, dried and chopped*
*Sea salt and finely ground black pepper*

### TO MAKE THE BASKETS:

Preheat the oven to 180°C/350°F/gas mark 4. Do not put the oven on a fan cycle or the Parmesan will blow over the oven. Line a baking tray with nonstick baking paper or a silicon baking mat. Place a 5cm (2in) round cutter on the prepared baking tray, place a heaped teaspoon of the grated Parmesan inside the cutter, remove the cutter and repeat this five times. Place in the oven for about 5 minutes until the cheese is bubbling and golden. Remove and while the discs are still hot, mould over the corks to form a basket. You will have to work quickly while the cheese is hot. Repeat until all the Parmesan is used. When cold, place in an airtight container in a cool place. These can be made a day in advance.

### TO MAKE THE RISOTTO:

Place the vegetable stock in a saucepan and bring to the boil, then reduce to a gentle simmer. Meanwhile, heat a large sauté pan with a little olive oil. When the oil begins to smoke, add the squash and sauté until golden and soft. Season and place to one side. In a saucepan, melt 30g (1oz) of the butter, add the shallots and cook until transparent, then add the garlic and cook but do not brown, add the rice, and coat each grain, add the wine, reduce by three-quarters, then slowly add the stock. When the rice has absorbed all the stock and is cooked through but still al dente, add the Parmesan, the remaining butter, parsley and squash, reserving some to garnish the tops of the baskets.

To serve, place the Parmesan baskets on a serving tray, fill with the risotto and garnish with the reserved squash.

## TOASTED BREAD BOXES FILLED WITH CREAMED WILD MUSHROOMS

### FOR THE BOXES:

*1 x 800g (1lb 10oz) white tin loaf, unsliced but with all crusts removed*
*300ml (¹/₂ pint) extra virgin olive oil*

### FOR THE FILLING:

*3 shallots, peeled and finely chopped*
*2 cloves garlic, peeled and finely chopped*
*2 teaspoons soft thyme*
*250g (8¹/₂ oz) mixed wild mushrooms, brushed*
*150ml (5fl oz) medium Madeira*
*450ml (³/₄ pint) double cream*
*¹/₂ cup flat-leaf parsley, washed, dried and chopped*
*Sea salt and finely ground black pepper*

### TO MAKE THE BOXES:

Preheat the oven to 200°C/400°F/gas mark 6. Line a baking tray with nonstick baking paper or a silicon baking mat. Using a sharp bread knife, cut the loaf into 2.5cm (1in) cubes. Place the cubes in a bowl and pour over the olive oil and toss well until all the cubes are covered.

# buffet of mediterranean flavours

This colourful buffet menu for 20 people has been inspired by the flavours of the Mediterranean. The creations have proved very popular and there are dishes here that appeal to everyone.

**(Below) A selection of antipasti.**

## ANTIPASTI

*Chargrilled Vegetable Stack*

*Grilled Asparagus with Portobello Mushrooms*

*Grilled Baby Aubergines with Red Onion Jam*

*Baby Peppers filled with Caponata*

*Grilled Figs and Baby Mozzarella Salad with Basil*

### MAIN COURSES

*Tuscan Chicken*

*Herb-crusted Tuna with Shaved Fennel Salad and Red Pepper Aïoli*

*Goat's Cheese, Lemon and Herb Risotto with Parmesan Crisps*

### DESSERTS

*Individual Panettone*

*Lemon Pots*

*Crème Brûlée*

*Bitter Chocolate Mousse*

*White Chocolate Tart*

## CHARGRILLED VEGETABLE STACK

2kg (4$^{1}/_{2}$lb) courgettes, cut lengthways into
   5cm (2in) wide strips
2kg (4$^{1}/_{2}$lb) aubergines, cut lengthways into
   7.5cm (3in) wide strips
Olive oil
25 red peppers, halved, roasted and peeled
120g (4oz) Reggiano Parmesan, grated
5 tablespoons pesto sauce
Sea salt and freshly ground black pepper

Preheat the oven to 200°C/400°F/gas mark 6.
Line a 40 x 25 x 6cm (16 x 10 x 2$^{1}/_{2}$in) baking
tray with baking parchment. Heat a chargrill
plate. Brush the courgettes and aubergines
with olive oil and season. Chargrill until bar
marks are visible. Place half the peppers
presentation open side up on the lined tray,
sprinkle with Parmesan and layer with half
the courgettes. Spread with pesto and
sprinkle with more Parmesan. Repeat with
the aubergine, followed by more red pepper,
courgette and aubergine layers, ending
with red pepper on the top. Season between
each layer. Cover with foil and bake in the
preheated oven for approximately 15 minutes.
Remove from the oven, leave to cool and
refrigerate. To serve, place on a board and
cut into small squares, then transfer to a
serving plate.

## GRILLED ASPARAGUS WITH PORTOBELLO MUSHROOMS

12 Portobello mushrooms
Olive oil
180 spears of asparagus, blanched, refreshed and cut into 10cm (4in) lengths
4 cloves garlic, peeled and finely sliced
3 shallots, peeled and finely sliced
Sea salt and freshly ground black pepper

Heat a chargrill plate, brush the mushrooms with olive oil, season and chargrill on both sides for approximately 5 minutes. Place on a baking tray and set aside. Repeat with the asparagus and place on the tray with the mushrooms. Then sprinkle with garlic and shallots and drizzle with olive oil. Cover and refrigerate.

## GRILLED BABY AUBERGINES WITH RED ONION JAM

10 baby aubergines
Olive oil
5 tablespoons red onion jam
Sea salt and freshly ground black pepper

Heat a chargrill plate. Halve the aubergines lengthways, score the flat side with a knife, brush with olive oil, season and cook for approximately 5 minutes until soft. Remove and leave to cool. When cold, cover and refrigerate. Serve topped with red onion jam.

## BABY PEPPERS FILLED WITH CAPONATA

10 baby red peppers
10 baby green peppers
Olive oil
30g (1oz) red onions, peeled and finely diced
30g (1oz) courgettes, finely diced
30g (1oz) aubergine, finely diced
30g (1oz) fennel, finely diced
30g (1oz) red pepper, finely diced
2 cloves garlic, puréed
1/2 cup flat-leaf parsley
5 plum tomatoes, peeled, deseeded and finely diced
3 tablespoons good balsamic vinegar
Sea salt and freshly ground black pepper

Preheat the oven to 200°C/400°F/gas mark 6. Remove the tops of the baby peppers, discard the seeds, place in a bowl and dress lightly with olive oil; season. Place on a baking tray and bake in the oven for approximately 8 minutes until soft and blistered. Remove and leave to cool.

Heat a large sauté pan and individually sauté the vegetables except the tomatoes, adding the garlic and seasoning. Remove from the heat and place in a bowl. When cold, add the parsley, tomatoes and balsamic vinegar, mix well and fill peppers. Cover and put in the fridge.

## GRILLED FIGS AND BABY MOZZARELLA SALAD WITH BASIL

1kg (2¼ lb) baby Mozzarella balls
300ml (½ pint) olive oil
3 shallots, peeled and finely sliced
2 cloves garlic, peeled and finely sliced
10 black figs, cut into quarters
60g (2oz) caster sugar
1 cup green basil leaves
1 cup purple basil leaves
Salt and freshly ground black pepper

Place the baby Mozzarella in a large bowl, pour in the olive oil, add the shallots and garlic and set aside. Heat a large frying pan, dip the figs in sugar and pan-fry until caramelised. Arrange the Mozzarella, figs and basil leaves on a serving dish, season and drizzle with the marinade.

(Above) Goat's Cheese, Lemon and Herb Risotto served in Squash with Parmesan Crisps.

## GOAT'S CHEESE, LEMON AND HERB RISOTTO

150ml (6 fl oz) olive oil
6 cloves garlic, unpeeled
2.3 litres (4 pints) vegetable stock
120g (4oz) unsalted butter
5 shallots, peeled and finely diced
3 cloves garlic, puréed
2 tablespoons soft thyme leaves
1kg (2lb 2oz) Arborio rice
1 glass of dry white wine
120g (4oz) unsalted butter
Juice and zest of 3 lemons
120g (4oz) grated Parmesan
1kg (2lb 2oz) of goat's cheese such as Golden Cross
1 cup flat-leaf parsley
2 squash, hollowed
Sea salt and freshly ground black pepper

In a saucepan heat the olive oil. When it is hot, add the whole garlic cloves and slowly cook for about 30 minutes. It should be soft, not brown. Remove from the heat, leave to one side in the pan. In a large pot bring the stock to the boil. Heat a large pan with the butter; when foaming, add the shallots and the garlic and sauté for about 5 minutes; do not colour. Add the thyme and rice; coat the rice grains with the butter. Add the white wine and slowly add the stock a ladleful at a time, stirring all the time. After 20 minutes the rice should be cooked through but still al dente. Stir in the butter, juice and zest of lemons, Parmesan, goat's cheese and parsley. Check consistency; if too thick add a little boiling water. Season. Pour into the squashes and garnish with the whole garlic cloves and parmesan crisps.

## PARMESAN CRISPS

### MAKES 30 ROUNDS

*Experiment with various shapes and sizes. They also make tasty snacks with cocktails. Store in an airtight container, layered with greaseproof paper. They are fragile so take care. I usually make a few extras to allow for breakages.*

*300g (11oz) Parmesan cheese*

Preheat oven to 190°C/375°F/gas mark 5. Grate the Parmesan with a fine grater. Line a baking tray with a sheet of greaseproof paper or (for better results) a silicon mat. Place a 10cm (4in) ring cutter onto the greaseproof paper or a silicon mat; evenly sprinkle grated Parmesan inside the cutter. Remove mould and bake for 4 minutes. When the crisps are ready they should be slightly bubbling and golden. Remove tray from oven. Using a palette knife place the discs on a wire cooling rack, cool and store.

## TUSCAN CHICKEN

*2 litres (3$^{1}/_{2}$ pints) white chicken stock*
*4 teaspoons saffron*
*20 skinless chicken breasts*
*3 fennel bulbs, cut into medium sized pieces*
*2kg (4$^{1}/_{2}$lb) medium-sized potatoes, peeled with a knife*
*6 tablespoons cornflour, dissolved in a little cold water*
*4 large artichokes, cut into medium-sized pieces*
*5 red peppers, roasted and cut into strips*
*10 plum tomatoes, peeled, quartered and deseeded*
*$^{1}/_{2}$ cup flat-leaf parsley, chopped*

Bring the stock to the boil in a large saucepan, then turn down to a simmer. Add 3 teaspoons of the saffron and the chicken breasts and poach for about 10 minutes until chicken is cooked. Remove the chicken from the saucepan, bring the stock back to the boil, add the fennel and cook for about 5 minutes. Remove and set aside. Place the potatoes in the saucepan with salt and the remaining saffron and cook for about 15 minutes. Drain (reserving the stock) and set aside.

Cut the chicken into cubes, bring the stock back to the boil, whisk in the cornflour and cook for about 5 minutes. Add the chicken, fennel, potatoes, artichokes and red peppers. When hot, add the tomatoes and parsley and ladle into a warm dish to serve.

## HERB-CRUSTED TUNA WITH SHAVED FENNEL SALAD AND RED PEPPER AÏOLI

*Olive oil*
*300ml (11fl oz) runny honey*
*3 tablespoons Dijon mustard*
*4 free-range egg yolks*
*2.5kg (5$^{1}/_{2}$ lb) tuna loin, skin removed*
*2 cups parsley, chopped*
*1 cup marjoram, chopped*
*1 cup dill, chopped*
*$^{1}/_{2}$ cup flat leaf parsley*
*Sea salt and freshly ground black pepper*

FOR THE SALAD:
*6 fennel bulbs*
*4 shallots, peeled and finely sliced*
*1 cup dill*

**(Left) Grilled Figs and Baby Mozzarella Salad with Basil.**

FOR THE DRESSING:
*Juice and zest of 3 lemons*
*2 cloves garlic, peeled and sliced*
*300ml (11fl oz) olive oil*

FOR THE RED PEPPER AÏOLI:
*6 red peppers, roasted and peeled*
*3 cloves garlic, peeled and puréed*
*Juice of 2 lemons*
*900ml (1½ pints) mayonnaise*
*Sea salt and freshly ground black pepper*

Preheat the oven to 200°C/400°F/gas mark 6. Pour some olive oil into a roasting tray to a depth of about 2mm (⅛ in). Place in the oven and heat for approximately 10 minutes. In a bowl mix the honey, mustard and egg yolks; season the tuna with salt and pepper, roll in the honey mix, then roll in the mixed herbs. Place the tuna in the roasting tray. Bake for approximately 10–15 minutes, remove and cool.

To make the aïoli, finely dice one of the red peppers and place in a bowl. Place the remaining peppers, garlic and lemon juice in a food processor and blend until smooth; add the mayonnaise. Blend again, ensuring all the ingredients are mixed well. Pour into a bowl and mix with the diced pepper. Season and pour into a serving bowl.

Cut the fennel in half lengthways and thinly shave on a mandolin. Place in a bowl, add the shallots and dill. When ready to serve, add the juice and zest of the lemons, sliced garlic, olive oil and season with salt and pepper and arrange on a serving dish. Slice the tuna into thin steaks, layer over the fennel salad and serve with red pepper aïoli.

## INDIVIDUAL PANETTONE

FILLS 12 DARIOLE MOULDS SIZE 5 X 5.5CM (2 X 2½IN)
*300g (10oz) strong flour*
*1 teaspoon salt*
*1 tablespoon sugar*

*2 teaspoons yeast*
*75ml (3fl oz) milk*
*2 free-range eggs*
*1 free-range egg yolk*
*90g (3oz) butter, cubed*
*30g (1oz) sultanas*
*30g (1oz) candied peel*
*Butter, for greasing*

Mix the flour, salt and sugar together. Dissolve the yeast in the milk and combine with the eggs and egg yolk. Stir into the flour and mix until smooth. Pour into the bowl of an electric mixer and with the mixer on a slow speed, add the butter cube by cube, then add the sultanas and mixed peel. Transfer the dough to a clean bowl, cover with cling film and leave in a warm place to prove for about 1 hour or until doubled in size.

Turn the dough out onto a floured surface and knead until smooth. Divide into 12 even-sized pieces. Roll into balls and place into greased dariole moulds. Leave in a warm place to prove for 30–40 minutes or until doubled in size. Brush the tops with a little beaten egg and bake at 180°C/350°F/gas mark 4 for 15–20 minutes or until well risen and golden brown. Remove from the oven and demould while still warm. Once cold, wrap in brown paper collars and tie with a raffia bow.

## LEMON POTS

FILLS 6 TEA GLASSES EACH HOLDING 100ML (4FL OZ)
*600ml (1 pint) double cream*
*120g (4oz) caster sugar*
*Juice of 2 lemons*
*Redcurrants, to garnish*

Bring the cream and sugar to the boil in a saucepan. Add the lemon juice and pass through a fine sieve or chinois. Leave to cool slightly then fill the tea glasses and leave in the fridge to set. Garnish the tops with a strand of 3–5 redcurrants

## CRÈME BRÛLÉE

FILLS 6 100ML (4FL OZ) TEA GLASSES.
*600ml (1 pint) double cream*
*1 vanilla pod, split in half*
*2 free-range eggs*
*5 free-range egg yolks*
*60g (2oz) caster sugar*

FOR THE CRAQUELIN:
*60g (2oz) caster sugar*
*15g (½oz) flaked almonds*

Boil the double cream and vanilla pod together in a pan. Whisk the eggs, egg yolks and caster sugar together until smooth, then pour on the boiling cream and whisk until combined. Continue to whisk over a pan of boiling water until the mixture thickens (this should take about 5–10 minutes). Remove from the heat and pass through a fine sieve or chinois, then fill the glasses and leave in the fridge to set.

To make the craquelin, boil the sugar to a light caramel and pour onto a silicon baking mat or sheet of baking parchment. Sprinkle with the almonds and leave until cool. Blitz in a food processor until fine. Sprinkle evenly onto a greased tray and return to the oven at 180°C/350°F/gas mark 4 until fully melted and golden brown. Remove from the oven and leave to cool slightly, then cut into triangles and remove from the tray while still warm. Stick into the tops of the brûlée just before serving.

## BITTER CHOCOLATE MOUSSE

FILLS 6 100ML (4FL OZ) TEA GLASSES
*30g (1oz) glucose*
*120g (4oz) bitter chocolate*
*1 leaf gelatine*
*200ml (⅓ pint) double cream, whipped*
*Chocolate pieces, to garnish*

Dissolve the glucose in a pan with 30ml (1fl oz) water. Melt the chocolate in a bowl over a pan of hot water. Soak the gelatine in a little cold water and dissolve in the glucose mix. Stir the glucose mix into the melted chocolate and fold in the whipped cream. Pour into the tea glasses and leave in the fridge to set. Serve garnished with abstract chocolate pieces.

# WHITE CHOCOLATE TART

MAKES 1 TART 35 X 11CM (14 X 4¹/₂IN)

FOR THE PASTRY:
150g (5oz) plain flour, sifted
60g (2oz) icing sugar
60g (2oz) unsalted butter, cubed
1 free-range egg

FOR THE FILLING:
300ml (¹/₂ pint) double cream
6 free-range egg yolks
60g (2oz) caster sugar
210g (7oz) white chocolate, melted

FOR THE FROSTED REDCURRANTS:
1 punnet redcurrants
1 free-range egg white
30g (1oz) caster sugar

To make the pastry, mix the flour, icing sugar and butter in an electric mixer until it has the consistency of breadcrumbs and all the butter is combined. Add the egg and mix to a smooth dough. Wrap the pastry in cling film and leave to rest in the fridge for 2 hours or until the dough is firm.

Roll out the pastry and line the tin, making sure there are no holes in the lined case. Rest in the fridge for a further 30 minutes. Preheat the oven to 160°C/325°F/gas mark 3. Line the inside of the case with greaseproof paper and fill with baking beans and bake for about 30 minutes. Remove the beans and bake for a further 10 minutes or until the case is golden brown. Remove from the oven.

To make the filling, bring the cream to the boil. Whisk the egg yolks and sugar together until light and creamy in colour. Pour one-third of the boiling cream onto the egg yolk mix and whisk until smooth. Whisk the remaining cream onto the chocolate and then combine the two mixtures until smooth. Fill the tart and bake at 110°C/225°F/gas mark ¹/₄ for 30–40 minutes or until the tart is set but with no colour.

To frost the redcurrants, simply brush the strands of currants with a little egg white and then coat with the sugar. Leave in a warm place overnight so that they become crisp and then use to garnish the tart.

**(Left) Bitter Chocolate Mousse, Crème Brûlée and Lemon Pots.**

# picnic on the lawn

Attractive Nantucket baskets, filled with interesting foods full of flavour are waiting for guests to carry them away for a picnic in the garden. Blankets, cushions, small tables and chairs are placed on the lawn, inviting guests to relax and enjoy the day. A bar is decorated and placed in a spot easily accessible for the guests to serve themselves. At the end of the afternoon when the bride and groom have left, the guests leave with their baskets as a memento of the happy day. This is a very good way of entertaining a large number of guests.

---

ADULTS' PICNIC

SERVES 50

*Square Rolls filled with Roasted Vegetables and Parmesan*

*Gravlax and Horseradish Cream Cheese Wrap*

*Miniature Chicken Pies*

*Home-made Potato Crisps*

*Chilli and Tomato Feta Salad*

*Cup Cake with Preserved Roses*

CHILDREN'S PICNIC

SERVES 15

*Square Rolls filled with Egg Mayonnaise*

*Miniature French Stick filled with Chicken Salad*

*Home-made Potato Crisps*

*Toffee Apples*

*Butter Popcorn*

*Clown Cookies*

*Crayons and Colouring Books*

---

## ADULTS' PICNIC

### SQUARE ROLLS FILLED WITH ROASTED VEGETABLES AND PARMESAN

*2 large aubergines*
*4 large courgettes*
*Extra virgin olive oil*
*50 square crusty rolls*
*200g (6¹/₂ oz) pesto sauce*
*13 red peppers, quartered, deseeded, roasted and peeled*
*250g (8¹/₂ oz) Reggiano Parmesan, shaved*
*Sea salt and freshly ground black pepper*
*Yellow ribbon*

Heat a chargrill plate. Thinly slice the aubergines and courgettes approximately 2mm (¹/₁₀in) thick, brush with olive oil and season. Chargrill until bar marks are visible, place on a tray and leave to cool. Cut the rolls in half lengthways, brush with pesto then layer with the aubergine, courgette, red pepper and Parmesan. Tie a yellow ribbon around the roll, to resemble a present.

### GRAVLAX AND HORSERADISH CREAM CHEESE WRAP

*1kg (2lb 2oz) cream cheese*
*120g (4oz) creamed horseradish*
*¹/₂ cup chives, chopped*
*13 spinach tortillas*
*2kg (4lb 4oz) gravlax, sliced*
*7 hard-boiled eggs, cut into 8 segments*
*250g (8¹/₂oz) capers*

In a bowl mix the cream cheese, horseradish and chives, then place into a container. Lay out the tortillas on a work surface and spread with the cream cheese. Cover one side with the gravlax. Place 4 egg segments and a few capers on each tortilla, roll up tightly with cling film and place onto a tray in the fridge. To serve, remove the cling film and cut each wrap into 4 segments on a diagonal cut. Wrap in waxed paper and tie with raffia.

### MINIATURE CHICKEN PIES

FOR THE FILLING:
*Extra virgin olive oil*
*25 skinless chicken breasts*
*1 glass of good port*
*2.5kg (5lb 4oz) mixed wild mushrooms, brushed and finely chopped*
*10 shallots, peeled and finely chopped*
*¹/₂ cup flat-leaf parsley, finely chopped*
*¹/₂ cup fresh sage, chopped*
*3 tablespoons fresh soft thyme leaves*

FOR THE PASTRY:
*2.5kg (5lb 4oz) plain flour*
*45g (1¹/₂oz) sea salt*
*600g (1lb 4oz) lard, cubed*
*600g (1lb 4oz) unsalted butter cubed*
*5 large free-range eggs, beaten*

*300ml (¹/₂ pint) milk*
*10 large free-range egg yolks, beaten*
*2.6 litres (3¹/₂ pints) rich brown chicken stock*
*25 leaves gelatine, soaked in cold water*
*Sea salt and freshly ground black pepper*

SPECIAL EQUIPMENT:
*50 x 7cm (2¹/₂ in) ring moulds*

TO MAKE THE FILLING:
Heat a large sauté pan with a little olive oil, seal the chicken breasts on all sides until golden. Season and place to one side. Deglaze the sauté pan with the port, and pour over the chicken. Leave to cool. When cold, slice each chicken breast into 4 lengthways. Cover and place in the fridge. Heat a large sauté pan with a little olive oil, sauté the

mushrooms, adding a few shallots at a time. Season, drain and place in a bowl; add the herbs and mix well.

Leave to cool. Place the ring moulds onto trays that will fit in the fridge. Layer the moulds starting with the mushrooms, chicken, and repeat until the moulds are full. Cover and place in the fridge.

TO MAKE THE PASTRY:
Sieve the flour and salt into a large bowl. Make a well in the middle, add the lard and butter

into the well and rub into flour until it resembles breadcrumbs. Add the eggs and 750ml (1 $^1$/$_2$ pints) cold water; mix well until it forms a dough. Turn out onto a floured cool work surface. Knead until smooth. Wrap in cling film and place in the fridge for 1 hour.

TO MAKE THE PIES:
Remove the pastry from the fridge. Place on a floured board, roll out 50 16cm (6$^1$/$_2$in) circles of pastry 4mm ($^1$/$_{10}$in) thick. Layer the pastry between non-stick paper on baking sheets and

**(Above) Adult's picnic baskets filled with homemade snacks and treats.**

place in the fridge. Roll out the remaining dough and cut out 50 6.5cm (2 $^1$/$_2$in) circles for the top. Store as for the large pastry discs.

Preheat the oven to 190°C/375°F/gas mark 5. Line baking sheets with nonstick baking parchment. Remove the chicken and the large pastry circles from the fridge. Place the pastry circles on a floured work surface. Place the ring mould in the centre of the pastry, remove the mould, place the smaller pastry disc on top. Add the milk to the beaten egg yolks and brush the pastry. Pull the sides of the pastry to the top of the chicken mixture. Brush the lip of the pastry with the egg glaze, and seal. Brush the pies all over with the egg glaze. Make a 1cm ($^1/_2$in) hole in the centre of each pie. Place on the prepared trays and bake in the oven until golden brown for 30–40 minutes.

Meanwhile, heat the stock in a large saucepan. When the stock has boiled, remove from the heat and leave for about 10 minutes. Add the soaked gelatine and whisk into the stock. Strain into jugs. Remove the pies from the oven and place on cooling racks. With a funnel, pour the heated stock into the centre of each pie. This will need to be topped up about three times, or until the stock is visible. Leave to cool. When cold, wrap in greaseproof paper and place in an airtight container in the fridge.

## HOME-MADE POTATO CRISPS

*10 large King Edward potatoes*
*250g (8$^1/_2$oz) unsalted butter*
*1 clove garlic*
*Sea salt and freshly ground black pepper*

*50 cellophane bags*
*Ribbon*

Preheat the oven to 200°C/400°F/gas mark 6. Line a few baking trays with some greaseproof paper. On a mandolin slice the potatoes to approximately 1mm thick; put the sliced potatoes in cold water to stop discoloration. Place the butter and garlic in a saucepan and slowly melt the butter. Remove from the heat and keep warm.

Take a medium-sized heart-shaped cutter and cut out hearts from the potato slices, pat dry with kitchen paper and place on the prepared baking trays. Brush with the garlic

butter, sprinkle with sea salt and freshly ground black pepper, cover with a piece of parchment paper and bake until crispy and golden. Remove and leave to cool. When cold, store in an airtight container in a cool place. To serve, place the crisps in cellophane bags, and tie with ribbon.

## CHILLI AND TOMATO FETA SALAD

*10 x 250g (8$^1/_2$oz) punnets small cherry*
  *tomatoes*
*4 red onions, peeled and finely sliced*
*5 red chillies, deseeded and finely shredded*
*1 cup basil, shredded*
*1 cup mint, shredded*
*1 cup coriander, shredded*
*450ml ($^3/_4$pint) lemon olive oil*
*Juice of 3 lemons*
*2kg (4lb 4oz) feta, cut into 1cm ($^1/_2$in) cubes*
*Sea salt and freshly ground black pepper*

Place all the ingredients, except the feta, in a large bowl, season, and mix well. Carefully mix in the feta in and spoon into little dishes.

## CUP CAKES WITH PRESERVED ROSES

FOR THE GARNISH:
*50 open roses, 2.5cm (1in) in diameter*
*100 mint leaves*
*2 large free-range egg whites*
*120g (4oz) caster sugar*
*Silica gel*

FOR THE ROSE WATER SYRUP:
*Petals from 3 large scented roses, washed*
  *and dried*
*100g (3$^1/_2$oz) caster sugar*

FOR THE CUP CAKES:
*720g (1lb 8oz) unsalted butter*

*720g (1lb 8oz) caster sugar*
*12 large free-range eggs, beaten*
*720g (1lb 8oz) self-raising flour, sifted*

FOR THE ICING:
*300g (10oz) white fondant icing (from a good*
  *pastry supply shop)*

SPECIAL EQUIPMENT:
*White cup cake paper cases*
*Muffin tins*

TO PRESERVE THE ROSES & MINT:
Do this two days before the wedding. Paint each rose and mint leaf with a little egg white and dip in the caster sugar. Leave in a warm place overnight to harden. Store in an airtight container with silica gel.

TO MAKE THE ROSE WATER SYRUP:
Place the ingredients into a large saucepan with 100ml (3$^1/_2$fl oz) water over a low heat, bring to a simmer and remove from the heat. Cover and leave to infuse for about 1 hour. When cold, strain into a jug.

TO MAKE THE CUP CAKES:
Preheat the oven to 180°C/350°F/gas mark 5. Place the baking cases into the muffin tins. Cream together the butter and sugar in an electric mixer until light and fluffy. Gradually add the beaten eggs. Do not allow to curdle. Fold in the flour. Spoon the mixture into the baking cases. Bake for about 20–30 minutes until well risen and golden brown. Remove from the oven, place the cakes onto cooling racks and drizzle each cake with the rose water syrup.

TO ICE THE CUP CAKES:
Carefully heat the fondant in a saucepan over a low heat. When it is liquid, spoon a little fondant over each cake, making sure they have a smooth, even coating. Leave uncovered to harden the icing. To serve, place a rose on the centre of each cake, and place in the basket.

# CHILDREN'S PICNIC

## SQUARE ROLLS FILLED WITH EGG MAYONNAISE

15 large free-range eggs, hard-boiled and
   shelled
200g (6¹/₂ oz) mayonnaise
2 punnets cress
15 square crusty rolls
200g (6¹/₂ oz) unsalted butter
Sea salt and freshly ground black pepper
Yellow ribbon

Grate the eggs into a bowl. Mix in the
mayonnaise and cress and season. Halve the
rolls, butter each side and fill with egg
mayonnaise. Tie with a ribbon.

## MINI FRENCH STICK FILLED WITH CHICKEN SALAD

Extra virgin olive oil
8 chicken breasts, skin removed
15 thin French sticks, approximately 16cm
   (6¹/₂ in) long
200g (6¹/₂ oz) unsalted butter
200g (6¹/₂ oz) mayonnaise
4 baby gem lettuces, washed and dried
Sea salt and freshly ground black pepper

Preheat the oven to 200°C/400°F/gas mark 6.
Heat a sauté pan with a little olive oil. Season
the chicken breasts and seal on both sides
until golden. Transfer to a roasting tray, place
into the oven and cook for 10 minutes. Remove
and leave to cool. When cold, thinly slice and
set aside.

Halve the French sticks, butter both sides
and spread with mayonnaise. Layer the
chicken and the lettuce and season.

## HOME-MADE POTATO CRISPS

Repeat the recipe for the Adults' Picnic, but
omit the garlic.

## TOFFEE APPLES

15 Lady apples
15 liquorice root (buy from health stores)
1kg (2lb 2oz) caster sugar

Wash, dry and remove the stalks from the
apples. Place a liquorice root into the base of
each apple. Set to one side. Place the sugar in
a heavy-bottomed saucepan with 120ml (4fl
oz) cold water. Over a low heat, melt the sugar,
increase the heat and cook to a temperature of
174°C/350°F or to a light caramel colour.
Remove from the heat. Cover your hand and
arm with a long oven glove, and dip each apple
into the caramel, making sure the apple is
completely covered and the caramel forms a
coating around the base of the liquorice root, to
seal the apple completely. Place on a baking
tray lined with silicon paper and leave to cool.
When cold, store in a cool place.

## BUTTER POPCORN

60g (2oz) butter
120g (4oz) popping corn

FOR THE CARAMEL:
120g (4oz) demerara sugar
30g (1oz) golden syrup
30g (1oz) unsalted butter
30ml (1fl oz) malt vinegar

Cellophane bags
Ribbon

Melt the butter in a heavy-bottomed saucepan
with a lid. Add the corn and replace the lid.

Shake continuously over a high heat until the
popping stops. Remove from the heat and
transfer to a tray to cool.

Place all the ingredients for the caramel in
a saucepan with 30ml (1fl oz) water and stir
over a high heat until all the ingredients have
dissolved. Leave to boil for 3 minutes or until
golden brown. Add the popcorn and stir until
thoroughly coated. Remove from pan and leave
to cool. Store in an airtight container in a cool
place. To serve, fill the cellophane bags with
the popcorn and tie with ribbon.

## CLOWN COOKIES

MAKES 20
240g (8oz) unsalted butter
400g (13oz) caster sugar
2 large free-range eggs
600g (1lb 4oz) plain flour
1 teaspoon salt
15ml (¹/₂ fl oz) vanilla essence
Zest of 2 large lemons

FOR THE ICING:
3 large free-range egg whites
600g (1lb 4oz) icing sugar
Juice of 1 large lemon
Various colours and sanding sugars

TO MAKE THE CLOWN COOKIES:
Preheat the oven to 170°C/325°F/gas mark 5.
Line a baking tray with nonstick baking
parchment paper or a silicon mat. Cream the
butter and caster sugar in an electric mixer
until light and fluffy. Add the eggs gradually
and beat until smooth. Carefully fold in the
remaining ingredients. Remove, place onto a
floured surface and knead until smooth. Cover
with cling film and rest in the fridge for 1 hour
or until firm.

Place the dough on a floured work surface
and roll out to 5mm (¹/₄in) thick. Cut out with a
clown cookie cutter and place on the tray. Bake
in the preheated oven for 15–20 minutes or

until golden brown. Remove from the oven and cool on a wire rack. When cold, store in an airtight container in a cool place.

TO MAKE THE ROYAL ICING:
Place the egg white and icing sugar in an electric mixer and beat until stiff. Add the lemon juice and beat until smooth. Colour as required and decorate as desired.

**(Above) Children's picnic baskets filled with home-made snacks and treats.**

# formal dinner

Our formal dinner for 20 people has been created for you to take time over and enjoy each course, perhaps with a dance in between. Linger over the delicious dessert and macaroons with a cold glass of pink champagne.

FIRST COURSE

*Quail and Foie Gras Salad with Truffle Dressing*

FISH COURSE

*Vichyssoise of Seafood with Caviar Cream*

MAIN COURSE

*Lamb Niçoise with Thyme and Black Olive Jus*

DESSERT

*Chocolate Top Hat*

*Pistachio Macaroons*

## QUAIL AND FOIE GRAS SALAD WITH TRUFFLE DRESSING

*Olive oil*
*2kg (4lb 4oz) mixed small wild mushrooms,*
*    cleaned*
*4 shallots, peeled and finely diced*
*1 tablespoon soft thyme leaves*
*10 quail's eggs, soft-boiled, peeled, placed in*
*    a container and covered with water*
*40 quail breasts, trimmed and bone removed*
*2kg (4lb 4oz) foie gras, cut into 20 slices,*
*    placed in a bowl and just covered with milk*
*40 baby leeks, blanched and chargrilled*
*500g (1lb 1oz) mixed salad leaves*
*120g (4oz) black truffle, finely shaved*
*Sea salt and freshly ground black pepper*

FOR THE DRESSING:
*3 tablespoons sweet white wine vinegar (such*
*    as Condimento Morbido)*
*4 tablespoons white truffle oil*
*2 tablespoons extra virgin olive oil*
*Sea salt and freshly ground black pepper*

Heat a large frying pan with a little oil, sauté a few mushrooms and shallots at a time, season. When all the mushrooms have been sautéed, mix with the thyme leaves and set aside.

Reheat the pan with a little more olive oil; season the quail breasts on both sides, pan-fry until golden brown and still slightly pink inside. Remove and keep warm.

**(Below) Quail and Foie Gras Salad with Truffle Dressing.**

Remove the foie gras from the milk and pat dry. Line a metal tray with kitchen paper. Reheat the pan to almost smoking hot. Season the foie gras, sear a few slices at a time for approximately 30 seconds on each side. Place on the lined tray and keep warm.

Mix all the dressing ingredients together. Drain and dry the quail's eggs and cut lengthways; thinly slice the quail breasts. Arrange all the salad in the centre of the plate and top with half a quail's egg. Drizzle the dressing over and around the salad.

## VICHYSSOISE OF SEAFOOD WITH CAVIAR CREAM

FOR THE SOUP:
2 tablespoons extra virgin olive oil
6 shallots, peeled and finely sliced
4 cloves garlic, peeled and crushed
1.2kg (2lb 8oz) white part of leeks, washed, dried and finely sliced
600g (1lb 4oz) Desirée potatoes, peeled and diced
6 litres (10½ pints) vegetable stock

800g (1lb 10oz) green part of the leeks, washed, dried and finely sliced
450ml (¾ pint) double cream

FOR THE SEAFOOD:
4 x 600g (1lb 4oz) lobsters, poached, meat removed and sliced
1kg (2lb 2oz) cooked squid rings
60 Mediterranean prawns, peeled and split lengthways
100 cooked mussels
40 medium scallops, poached and sliced widthways
1 cup dill
Sea salt and freshly ground black pepper

FOR THE GARNISH:
250g (8½oz) Sevruga caviar

Heat the olive oil in a frying pan. When hot add the shallots, garlic and white of the leek and sauté, but do not colour. Add the diced potatoes and vegetable stock, bring to the boil and simmer for 40 minutes. Add the green leeks, season and cook for a further 10 minutes. Remove from heat and leave to cool. Blend until smooth. Pass through a fine sieve into a container. Stir in the double cream, check the seasoning, cover and refrigerate.

To serve, layer the seafood and dill in the centre of each bowl, seasoning each layer. Carefully pour the soup around the seafood and place a spoonful of caviar on top.

## LAMB NIÇOISE WITH THYME AND BLACK OLIVE JUS

2 litres (3½ pints) extra virgin olive oil
60 small shallots, unpeeled
60 cloves garlic, unpeeled
60 red cherry vine tomatoes
20 baby aubergines, top and bottom removed
150g (5oz) unsalted butter
2kg (4lb 4oz) spinach, washed and stalks

removed
10 x 300g (10oz) lamb loins, trimmed
Sea salt and freshly ground black pepper

FOR THE SAUCE:
1.2 litres (2 pints) lamb jus
20 black olives, finely diced
5 plum tomatoes, peeled, deseeded and diced

Heat the olive oil in a flameproof casserole on a low heat. Carefully add the shallots and cook for 40 minutes. Once cooked, remove and place onto a roasting tray. Repeat with the garlic but this time for 30 minutes. (The garlic and shallots should be nice and soft.) Do the same with the cherry tomatoes for 2 minutes. Reserve the oil to use later in the recipe.

Take a sharp knife and criss-cross the top and bottom of the aubergine, place in a bowl, drizzle with a little of the oil and season. Heat a large pan with a little oil and sauté the aubergines on all sides until soft, then place on the roasting tray with the other vegetables.

Heat a large saucepan, add half the butter. When foaming add half the spinach and sauté until wilted. Season, place in a colander and drain. Repeat with the remaining spinach and leave to cool. Pick out 60 of the undamaged leaves and lay flat on a tray. With the remaining spinach, make 60 balls about 2.5cm (1in) across and wrap each ball with the reserved spinach leaves; place onto a metal tray. Cover with foil and place in the fridge.

Heat a little oil in a frying pan. Season the lamb. When the oil is hot, seal the lamb until brown on all sides, then place on a baking tray and set aside.

To serve, preheat the oven to 200°C/400°F/gas mark 6. In a saucepan bring the lamb jus to the boil, then simmer over a low heat. Place the lamb in the oven. After approximately 5 minutes, add the vegetables

**(Left) Vichyssoise of Seafood with Caviar Cream. (Right) Lamb Niçoise with Thyme and Black Olive Jus.**

and cook for a further 10 minutes. Remove the lamb and vegetables from the oven and keep warm. Slice each lamb loin into 4 and place 2 pieces in the centre of each warmed plate. Place 1 aubergine next to the lamb and arrange 3 of each of the vegetables around the lamb. Scatter black olives and diced tomato around the plate and drizzle with the jus.

### FOR THE GANACHE:

*300ml (1/2 pint) double cream*
*60ml (2fl oz) light corn syrup*
*375g (12 1/2 oz) bitter chocolate, chopped*
*450g (1lb) blackberries*

### FOR THE WOOD BARK AND DECORATION:

*Sheet of acetate 6 x 52cm (2 1/2 x 21in)*
*75g (2 1/2 oz) extra bitter chocolate*
*100g (3 1/2 oz) white chocolate*
*Wood-graining tool*
*Pansies, blown garden roses or any edible flowers*

### TO MAKE THE SPONGE:

Preheat the oven to 200°C/400°F/gas mark 6. Grease and line a 12cm (5in) round, 8cm (3 1/2 in) deep cake tin with nonstick baking paper.

Place the eggs and sugar together in an electric mixer and whisk until doubled in volume. Meanwhile, place the butter in a heavy saucepan over a medium heat to melt. Sift the flour and cocoa powder into a bowl. When the egg mixture is ready, carefully fold in the flour/cocoa mix, and rapidly stir in the melted butter. Pour into the prepared cake tin. Bake for 20–30 minutes or until springy to the touch. Remove from the oven. Leave to cool for about 5 minutes, then turn out onto a cooling rack. When cold, store in an airtight container in a cool place or place in the freezer.

### TO MAKE THE SYRUP:

Place the ingredients in a saucepan with 90ml (3 1/2 fl oz) cold water and bring to the boil. Leave to cool. When cold, store in an airtight container in the fridge.

### TO MAKE THE GANACHE:

Bring the cream and syrup to the boil in a heavy-bottomed saucepan over a high heat. Pour onto the chocolate and stir until smooth.

### TO ASSEMBLE:

Slice the sponge into three widthways. Soak each layer in the syrup and spread with a little ganache. Put half the blackberries onto the bottom layer and cover with more ganache; repeat with the second layer and finish with the final piece of sponge on top. Smooth the remaining ganache over the top and sides of the cake. Place the cake on a stand.

### TO MAKE THE BARK AND FINISH THE CAKE:

Cut one strip of acetate the circumference of the cake. Melt the bitter and white chocolates over water in two separate pans. Spread the acetate with the bitter chocolate with a wood-graining tool and leave to set. Spread the white chocolate evenly over bitter chocolate and wrap the strip around the cake. When set, peel off the acetate and cover the top of the cake with flowers.

**From left to right: Heart Cake, Mini Square Meringue Cake, Chocolate Wood Cake, Mini Croquembouche and Carrot Cake.**

# HEART CAKE

This recipe is for a delicate pink romantic heart decorated with lace icing and fresh red roses.

FOR THE SPONGE:

*6 large free-range eggs, separated*
*135g (4½oz) caster sugar*
*125g (4½oz) ground almonds*
*125g (4½oz) ground hazelnuts*
*75g (2½oz) plain flour, sieved*

FOR THE ICING:

*500g (1lb 1oz) packet regal icing*
*3 drops red food colouring*
*120g (4oz) icing sugar*
*1 free-range egg white*

TO DECORATE:

*Pink ribbon and Red roses*

Grease and line a 15 x 12 x 8cm (6 x 5 x 3½ in) heart-shaped cake tin with nonstick baking paper. Preheat the oven to 180°C/350°F/gas mark 5.

In an electric mixer whisk the egg yolks and 75g (2½oz) of the sugar until doubled in volume and light and creamy, then carefully fold in the ground nuts and flour. In a separate mixer, whisk the egg whites to peaks then slowly add the remaining sugar and whisk until stiff, then carefully fold into the nut mixture. Pour into the prepared tin. Bake for 20–30 minutes or until springy to the touch. Remove

from oven and cool. After about 5 minutes,
turn onto a cooling rack. When cold, wrap in
nonstick paper and store in an airtight
container in a cool place or freeze.

TO MAKE THE ICING:

Remove the regal icing from the packet.
Sprinkle a cool work surface with a little icing
sugar. Knead the icing into a flat ball with a
slight hollow in the centre. Drip the food
colouring into the centre and knead until the
colour is evenly distributed throughout the
icing. There must be no streaks. Roll out to
5mm (¼ in) thickness. Cover the cake and trim
off excess. Tie the ribbon around the base.
Beat the icing sugar into the egg white until
stiff, then pipe the desired pattern on top.

TO SERVE:

Place the cake on a stand and decorate with
red roses.

# MINI CROQUEMBOUCHE

A miniature version of the large cake featured
on page 162.

FOR THE CHOUX PASTRY:

*200g (6½ oz) unsalted butter*
*1 teaspoon salt*
*1 teaspoon caster sugar*
*400g (13oz) plain flour*
*10 large free-range eggs, plus 1 egg to glaze*

FOR THE NOUGATINE:

*250g (8½ oz) fondant icing*
*30g (1oz) flaked almonds*

FOR THE PASTRY CREAM:

*600ml (1 pint) milk*
*600ml (1 pint) double cream*
*3 vanilla pods*
*12 free-range egg yolks*
*250g (8½ oz) caster sugar*
*180g (6oz) plain flour*

FOR THE CARAMEL:

*750g (1lb 8oz) caster sugar*

TO MAKE THE CHOUX PASTRY:

Preheat the oven to 190°C/375°F/gas mark 5.
Line baking trays with nonstick baking paper or
silicon mats.

Place 500ml (16fl oz) water, the butter,
salt and sugar in a large heavy-bottomed
saucepan. Over a gentle heat, stir until the
mixture is boiling. Add the flour and cook until
the paste forms a dough in the centre of the
saucepan and has a shiny texture. Remove
from the heat and put into an electric food
mixer fitted with a paddle. Gradually beat in the
10 eggs, one at a time.

When all the eggs are incorporated, place
the mixture into a piping bag fitted with a 2cm
(¾ in) nozzle. Pipe balls no bigger than 2cm
(¾ in) in diameter onto the trays. Place the
trays in the oven and bake for 15 minutes until
the pastry is well risen and golden brown.
Reduce the heat to 160°C/325°F/gas mark 4
and cook for a further 15–20 minutes until the

**(Above) Mini Croquembouche.**

choux balls are dry to the touch when broken
in half. Remove from the oven and leave to
cool. When cold, store in airtight containers in
a cool place or freeze.

TO MAKE THE NOUGATINE DISC:

Preheat the oven to 180°C/350°F/gas mark 5.
Line a baking tray with nonstick baking paper,
and prepare a second tray with nonstick baking
paper with a greased 25cm (10in) flan ring in
the centre.

Place the fondant icing in a small
saucepan over a medium heat and stir until
liquid. Leave on the heat and bring to a
caramel; it is important not to stir the caramel
at this stage as it will crystallise. Pour onto the
lined tray and scatter over the flaked almonds.
Leave until cold. When cold, break the caramel
into small pieces and place in a food processor
and blend to a fine powder. Sprinkle a thick,
even layer of the nougatine in the ring. Place in
the oven and cook until the sugar has dissolved

(about 10 minutes). Remove from the oven and leave for about 10 minutes, then remove the ring. When cold, store in an airtight container in a cool place.

## TO MAKE THE PASTRY CREAM:
Bring the milk, cream and vanilla pods to the boil in a heavy-bottomed saucepan. Meanwhile, whisk together the egg yolks, sugar and flour in an electric mixer until smooth. Pour the boiling liquid onto the yolks and whisk until smooth. Return to the heat and whisk for a further 5 minutes or until the pastry cream boils. Remove from the pan and place a disc of damp greaseproof paper on top to prevent a skin forming. Leave to cool. When cold, cover with cling film and refrigerate.

## TO FILL THE CHOUX BALLS:
Make a hole in the flat side of the choux balls. Place the pastry cream in a piping bag and fill each choux ball with the cream. Leave in a cool place.

## TO MAKE THE CARAMEL:
Place the sugar in a heavy-bottomed saucepan and just cover with water. When the sugar has dissolved, increase the heat and cook the sugar to a dark caramel. Remove from the heat.

## TO ASSEMBLE:
Place the nougatine disc on a cake stand. Take the choux balls and dip the rounded side into the caramel and use to stick to the base. Continue doing this until a pyramid is formed. Top with spun sugar.

# MINI SQUARE MERINGUE CAKE

This is one of my favourites as I love meringue in any shape or form.

FOR THE SYRUP:
*120g (4oz) caster sugar*
*Zest and juice of 1 large lime*

FOR THE SPONGE:
*8 free-range eggs*
*300g (10oz) caster sugar*
*375g (12¹/₂ oz) plain flour, sieved*

FOR THE FILLING:
*500ml (³/₄ pint) double cream*
*30g (1oz) icing sugar*
*1 vanilla pod, halved and deseeded*
*1 punnet strawberries*
*1 punnet raspberries*
*1 punnet blackberries*

FOR THE MERINGUE:
*8 large free-range egg whites*
*400g (13oz) caster sugar*

## TO MAKE THE SYRUP:
Place the ingredients in a saucepan with 120ml (¹/₄ pint) water and bring to the boil. Remove and leave to cool. When cold, strain and place in an airtight container in the fridge.

## TO MAKE THE SPONGE:
Preheat the oven to 200°C/400°F/gas mark 6. Grease and line a 12cm (5in) square cake tin.

In an electric mixer whisk the eggs and sugar together until light and creamy and doubled in volume. Carefully fold in the flour and pour into the prepared cake tin. Bake for 20–30 minutes or until springy to the touch. Remove and leave for about 5 minutes, then turn out onto a cooling rack. When cold, wrap in greaseproof paper, place in an airtight container and leave in a cool place or in the freezer.

## TO MAKE THE FILLING:
Whisk the cream, icing sugar and vanilla together until thickened. Place in a covered bowl in the fridge.

## TO MAKE THE MERINGUE:
Whisk the egg whites with 30g (1oz) sugar until stiff. Slowly add the remaining sugar and whisk until thick and glossy.

## TO ASSEMBLE:
Slice the sponge into three layers. Drizzle the syrup over each layer. Spread one-third of the cream over the first layer and fill with half the fruit. Repeat and top with final layer of sponge. Cover the top and sides with the remaining cream. Fill a piping bag fitted with a 1cm (¹/₂ in) nozzle with the meringue. Starting at the base of the cake, pipe 2cm (³/₄in) high spikes to cover the complete cake and glaze with a blow torch. Place on a cake stand.

# LEMON PARCEL CAKE

This is the perfect cake for a small wedding party. Here Vince O'Toole has made the prettiest yellow and white sugar ribbon. It takes years of experience to be able to make one, but you could buy striped ribbon from a specialist ribbon store.

FOR THE SYRUP:
*300g (10oz) sugar*
*Zest of 4 lemons*

FOR THE SPONGE:
*250g (8¹/₂ oz) unsalted butter*
*250g (8¹/₂ oz) caster sugar*
*5 large free-range eggs*
*250g (8¹/₂ oz) plain flour*
*15g (¹/₂ oz) baking powder*
*Zest of 5 lemons*

FOR THE LEMON CURD:
*250g (8¹/₂ oz) unsalted butter, cubed*
*250g (8¹/₂ oz) caster sugar*
*Juice of 5 lemons*
*8 large free-range eggs*

FOR THE ICING:
*750g (1lb 10oz) packet regal icing*
*Icing sugar, for dusting*
*3 drops yellow food colouring*

## TRADITIONAL WEDDING CAKE SERVES 150

A recipe by Jane Grafton, our ex-pastry chef.

FOR THE WEDDING CAKE:

*3kg (6lb 4oz) currants*
*3kg (6lb 4oz) sultanas*
*2kg (4lb 2oz) raisins*
*750g (1lb 9oz) glacé cherries, quartered*
*750g (1lb 9oz) mixed peel*
*1kg 500g (3lb 2oz) butter*
*1kg 500g (3lb 2oz) soft dark brown sugar*
*25 eggs, beaten*
*1kg 500g (3lb 2oz) plain flour*
*large pinch of salt*
*large pinch of nutmeg*
*120g (4oz) mixed spice*
*Zest and juice of 4 lemons*
*200g (6oz) rum or brandy*
*500g (1lb 1oz) flaked almonds*
*Extra rum or brandy to soak the cooked*
  *cakes*

EQUIPMENT:

*Cake tins:*
*1 x 30cm (12in) diameter tin*
*1 x 25cm (10in) diameter tin*
*1 x 15cm (6in) diameter tin*
*Parchment paper*

FOR THE ALMOND PASTE

*Allow 1.5kg (3lb 2oz) almond paste for the*
  *30cm (12in) cake*
*1.5kg (2lb 10oz) for the 25cm (10in) cake*
*750g (1lb 9oz) for the 15cm (6in) cake*
*Boiled apricot jam for helping the almond paste*
  *adhere to the cake*
*Icing sugar for dusting*

EQUIPMENT

*Rolling pin*
*Pastry brush*
*Palette knife*
*Cake boards:*
*1x 40cm (16in) diameter*
*1x 35cm (14in) diameter*

TO MAKE THE SYRUP:

Place the ingredients into a saucepan with 300ml (1/2 pint) water and bring to the boil. Remove and leave to cool. When cold, strain and place in an airtight container in the fridge.

TO MAKE THE SPONGE:

Preheat the oven to 180°C/350°F/gas mark 5. Line a 20cm (8in) square, 8cm (3 1/2 in) deep tin with nonstick baking parchment. In an electric mixer beat the butter and sugar together until light and fluffy. Gradually beat in the eggs, then fold in the flour, baking powder and zest. Bake for 30–40 minutes or until golden and springy to touch. Remove from the oven. After about 5 minutes turn onto a cooling rack. When cold, wrap in greaseproof paper and store in an airtight container in a cool place or in the freezer.

TO MAKE THE LEMON CURD:

Whisk together the butter and sugar in a small saucepan over a low heat until smooth and glossy. Whisk in the lemon juice and then the eggs, return to the heat and whisk until thickened. Pass through a fine conical sieve into a bowl. Cover with wet greaseproof or nonstick paper to prevent a skin forming and leave to cool. When cold, cover with cling film and place in the fridge.

TO FILL THE CAKE:

Cut the cake into three lengthways, drizzle with the syrup and spread each layer with the lemon curd. Cover and place in the fridge.

TO MAKE THE ICING AND FINISH THE CAKE:

Remove the icing from the packet and place on a work surface dusted with icing sugar. Knead to a smooth ball with a slight hollow in the centre. Drop the food colouring into the centre and knead until all the colour is mixed and there are no streaks. Roll out to 5mm (1/4 in) thick, cover the cake with the icing and trim off the excess. Finish with a yellow and white ribbon.

*1x 30cm (12in) diameter*

## FOR THE ROYAL ICING
*3 egg whites*
*500g (1lb 4oz) icing sugar*
*1 teaspoon glycerine*

## EQUIPMENT
*Cake turntable*
*Palette knife*
*Metal ruler, approximately 40cm (16in)*
*Pastry scraper*

## TO MAKE THE FRUIT CAKE
The night before cooking, mix together the currants, sultanas, raisins, cherries and mixed peel. Then add the zest and juice of the lemons and the rum or brandy. Combine well and then leave covered, in a cool place.

Grease and line the cake tins, making sure that the sides are lined with at least two layers of paper. This is to ensure the outside of the cake does not colour too much during cooking.

Preheat the oven to 160°C/320°F/gas mark 3.

Cream together the butter and sugar, until light. Gradually add the beaten egg, mixing well between each addition.

Sieve together the flour, salt, nutmeg and mixed spice, and fold into the mixture.

Finally fold in the soaked fruit and the flaked almonds. Divide the mixture between the cake tins and bake for approximately 4 hours, 2 hours and 1 hour respectively. Insert a skewer into the centre of each cake, and when it comes out clean, the cake is cooked.

Allow to cool in the tins, on a cooling rack, and then turn them out. When completely cold, wrap in fresh parchment paper and cling film.

The cakes are best made three months in advance, and stored in a cool dry place.

Once or twice before decorating your cakes unwrap them and feed with a little extra rum or brandy. This will ensure a moist cake.

Do not use sherry or any other fortified wine as this will cause fermentation while being stored.

## TO MAKE THE ALMOND PASTE
Brush the top of the cake with boiled apricot jam, and roll out a piece of almond paste to cover the top. Turn the cake over onto the paste, trim away any excess, and smooth with a palette knife. Turn the cake over again and place into the centre of the cake board.

Roll out another piece of paste in a long strip, and trim to fit the depth of the cake. Brush the sides of the cake with more jam, and place on the strip of paste. Press lightly, but try to avoid making any indentations, as this will show when icing the cake.

Allow the cake to dry for 24 hours before icing. Otherwise the oils from the almonds will show through and spoil the effect of the finished cake.

## TO MAKE THE ICING
To ice and decorate a three-tier wedding cake you will need approximately 4 batches of the above recipe.

Place the egg whites in a mixing bowl. Gradually stir in the icing sugar, mixing to a smooth paste. Add the glycerine and beat the icing until it reaches a similar consistency to a stiff meringue. Store in a sealed container or a bowl covered with a damp cloth until required.

The glycerine is added so that the icing will not set too hard. This ingredient can be left out when making the royal icing for any decoration on the cake.

To ensure the best results all the equipment must be free from any grease, so rinse well with very hot water before commencing.

## TO FINISH THE CAKE
Place the cake on the turntable. Using a palette knife spread some of the royal icing evenly onto the top. Remove the cake from the turntable and put on a flat surface. Place the metal ruler, at a 45-degree angle, on the side of the cake furthest away. Draw the ruler slowly and evenly towards you, leaving a layer of icing on the cake. Remove any icing from the sides in a downward motion, with a knife or pastry scraper. Allow the top to dry completely before icing the sides.

To ice the sides, again place the cake onto the turntable. With a palette knife in a vertical position, spread the icing onto the cake. Using a scraper, place the edge against the side of the cake. Rotate the cake in one movement, if possible, keeping the scraper stationary. Remove any excess icing on the top; this will ensure that the edges of the cake are smooth.

Allow to dry before continuing with the layers. As described, the technique is to ice the top and sides alternately, allowing each coat to dry before applying the next one. It is recommended that the cake should have 4 coats on the top and 3 coats on the sides.

**(Left) Lemon Parcel Cake.**
**(Below) Traditional Wedding Cake.**

# Author's Acknowledgements

In writing and creating *Weddings*, I relied on the support and help of many people. I would like to thank the following:

My staff, without whose professionalism and dedication our weddings would not be perfect. Richard Cubbin, Dave Withers and Paul North for their creativity, and for testing recipes and preparing food for photography.

Ming Veevers Carter, Lizzie and Justine for the most wonderful flowers, bouquets, ideas and kindness. Detta Phillips for her lovely bouquets and rich roses.

Helen Woodhall, my editor, who has made this project effortless and creative.

Pippin Britz, for her help, advice, creativity and energy in bringing my visions and ideas to life.

Tim Winter and Jo Fairclough for making the days of photography great fun.

Bryan and Nanette Forbes for their encouragement and support in writing this book, and for use of their beautiful lake and gardens for our summer wedding by a lake.

Joan White for reading and correcting my text.

Special thanks for the gracious generosity of the following companies and friends:

Graham, Terry and Sophie of Jones Hire for the loan of their china, glassware, cutlery, linen, chairs and tables. Annie and William Melon of Top Table who also loaned their beautiful china, cutlery and glassware. Maryse Boxer for the pretty glasses and china. The Wedding Shop for our brides' and bridesmaids' dresses and accessories. Kara Kara for the stunningly wrapped presents and frosted sake glasses. Theo Fennell for advice and magnificent rings. Guinevere Antiques for glasses, cutlery and linen. Sarah White for her encouragement and tablecloths. Gib Edge for arranging the pretty Saxon Church and trap.

The Rev. Frank Mercurio for his advice on weddings in the Church of England. Father Michael for information on marriage in the Roman Catholic Church. The secretary of the St. Johns Wood Synagogue for information on Jewish Weddings.

Derek Thompson and Tom Flaherty for valuable advice on hair and makeup for brides. Marc Staines for information about photography and videos

Last but not least my friends and customers, whose wedding photos grace the end papers.

## PHOTOGRAPHIC ACKNOWLEDGEMENTS
The publisher would like to thank the following for their permission for reproducing the images on the following pages: pages 54–55 Getty Images/Telegraph; page 59 Chuck Fishman/Image Bank; page 62 Sally Griffyn; page 64 James Stafford; page 65 Super Stock; page 71 Glamis Castle; page 75 Super Stock; page 76 Emily Stoner; page 98 The Bridal Design Room Ltd.; page 109 Journal Für Die Frau/Camera Press.

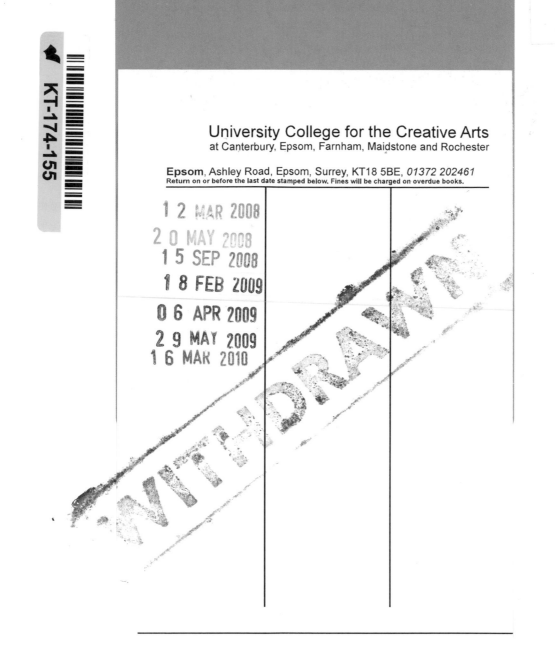

09 08 07 06 05    5 4 3 2 1

Library of Congress Cataloging-in-Publication Data

Simmons, Christopher.
  Logo lab : featuring 18 case studies that demonstrate identity creation from concept to completion / by Christopher Simmons.-- 1st ed.
      p. cm.
  ISBN 1-58180-549-7 (pbk. with flaps : alk. paper)
  1.  Logography--Design--Case studies. 2.  Commercial art--Case studies.  I. Title.
  NC1002.L63S55 2005
  741.6--dc22
                                    2005000757

Edited by: Amy Schell
Designed by: Lisa Buchanan-Kuhn, Karla Baker
Production coordinated by: Kristen Heller
Photographer: Hal Barkan

The credits on page 142 constitute an extension of this copyright page.

## DEDICATION
For my students.

## ACKNOWLEDGMENTS
As with all creative endeavors, the result is a product of combined efforts, passions and perspectives. In some sense, every interaction, conversation, argument and observation has contributed to the substance of this book. There are, however, a number of individuals without whom it simply would not be. Special thanks are owed to the following: To Clare Warmke for giving me a chance, with extra thanks to Amy Schell for giving me many more than I deserved; my family, especially my parents, from whence all things wise and good flow in my direction; my teachers, especially Doug Akagi, because we can never thank them enough; Cinthia and Craig, who make all things better; and to each of the contributors, and David Turner, for taking the time and effort to help make this book different. And finally, the deepest, most profound and enduring thanks to Amelie, to whom I really ought to have dedicated this book but instead have dedicated all else.

## ABOUT THE AUTHOR
Christopher Simmons is a designer, writer and educator. Previously a principal at Alterpop, in 2004 Christopher left the firm he redefined to launch his own design office, affectionately named MINE. Christopher developed and teaches a course entitled Identity Design at the California College of the Arts (formerly CCAC) and also at the Academy of Art University in San Francisco. He has lectured on design issues at Sonoma State University, University of California Santa Cruz, California Polytechnic State University and for the American Institute of Graphic Arts (AIGA) and the Western Art Directors Club (WADC). Christopher is the president of the San Francisco chapter of the AIGA, whose mission it is to advance excellence in the craft and practice of design. His work is consistently chosen by respected competitions, books and periodicals as representative of bold, innovative and effective design.

# FOREWORD

*"I am a designer because design is challenging and unpredictable. I am a designer because I think there's nothing as interesting as a blank sheet of paper. I'm a designer because I love designing."*

Why are so many graphic design books too boring to actually read? We look at the pictures, scan the captions and skip the text. Is it because graphic design itself is boring?

A couple of years ago I saw a presentation by Bill Cahan in which he showed a video of one of his employees at work. Apart from the occasional mouse click or tilt of the head, the person was completely motionless, staring at a computer screen. This, he said, was the life of a designer. Of course he was having some fun at his own expense and deliberately underplaying the real story. The real story was going on inside that designer's head.

A few months later I asked David Baker, a business consultant, to take a look at our business. He gave us a lot of useful advice, and on one point he was adamant: "You must have your own design process, and preferably you should trademark it." The reason, he said, was that clients generally couldn't tell good design from bad, but they could understand process. A trademarked process smelled of B.S. to us (it was something our competitors did) so we ignored his advice. We were missing

the point. People want to be told a story. Stories are interesting, engaging … convincing. We already had our own design process; it was just a story we weren't telling very well. As our storytelling improved, so did our bottom line. David was right.

This book unearths the real stories: What went on inside each designer's head as he or she struggled with the demanding task of designing a logo? It does what many designers do badly—it brings the design process to life in an engaging and personal way. I didn't get into this business because I like sitting at a computer all day or because I want to "own a design process." I am a designer because design is challenging and unpredictable. I am a designer because I think there's nothing as interesting as a blank sheet of paper. I'm a designer because I love designing. The stories in this book go a long way toward explaining not only how designers work but why.

There's a story about Art Chantry designing dozens of logos for a single client because he thinks logos are stupid.

He believes creativity is a form of obsessive-compulsive disorder. Read his story and you'll understand why. There's a story about Elixir Design taking a weary cliché and giving it new dimension and meaning. The story of Mires Brands' work for Taylor Guitars is an ode to craftsmanship. Werner Design Werks' story is about transforming paper into an emotional connection between children and their grandparents. The stories are as different as the logos themselves and yet there are striking similarities. Each reflects the designer's particular sensibility while illustrating the challenges we all face. If you're interested in logo design and what makes logo designers tick, here's a book you'll actually read, enjoy and remember.

So the good news is that graphic design really is pretty interesting. To me, that will always be a story worth telling.

**DAVID TURNER**
**Turner Duckworth**
**San Francisco & London**

**Client:** Taylor Guitars      **Creative Director:** Scott Mires
**Design Firm:** Mires Brands      **Designers:** Miguel Perez, Gale Spitzley

This is one of those stories designers dream of. For reasons wholly unrelated to the writing of this book, I had occasion to buy a guitar recently. I was shopping for a gift and, not knowing a thing about guitars, headed down to a local music shop and started browsing. Among the Fenders, Gibsons and Martins, one instrument in particular caught my eye. It was a Taylor Big Baby, its elegant logotype smiling at me from atop the peg head. I bought it. I would learn later that my purchase was a sound one and that Taylor makes some of the best guitars in the business, but I was already sold. The beautifully proportioned instrument, hewn of Sitka spruce and Big Leaf maple, was indisputably a thing of beauty, but it was the subtle typographic craftsmanship of the logo that confirmed to me that this was a company committed to quality. Such is the power of design.

Scott Mires, a principal at Mires Brands and creative director on the Taylor project, is a twenty-year veteran of the design industry and a guitar player himself (an interest he developed in working with Taylor). He remembers when Taylor was a small and struggling brand, one that was sold through word of mouth in independent shops to a small but loyal fan base. Scott can tell you everything you'd want to know about the guitar maker, how

The genetic link between the original logo and its modern incarnation is evident, but the revitalized version embodies the grace and elegance of a modern brand. No longer just a maker of quality guitars, Taylor has become a lifestyle brand. It is the Harley-Davidson of the guitar industry.

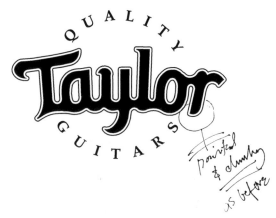

## PICK ME UP:

A hangtag in the shape of an oversized guitar pick resurrects the client's early notion of referencing familiar and iconic shapes in the identity.

their instruments are built and how both the company and its customers feel about their products. He can educate you on the process of building a Taylor guitar—what parts of it are machine made and what elements are finished by hand. It's a process he describes as fastidious, intricate and as being a careful and deliberate balance between craftsmanship and technology— terms that are equally applicable to the elegantly understated logotype that also manages to be boldly assertive.

It's the equilibrium struck by this dichotomy that the logo successfully captures. For a company like Taylor, with traditional roots and commitment to exploring innovative applications of technology, it strikes the right chord. "They had outgrown their old logo," Scott says candidly. "They needed a look that matched the quality of their guitars." Bob Taylor, president and founder of Taylor

Guitars, puts it more bluntly. "Our old logo was amateurish," he says. "It was something we thought up ourselves years ago and just never paid much attention to." The company's business had grown, and Bob and partner Kurt Listug realized that it was time to grow the brand as well. On a referral from their ad agency, Bob contacted Mires Brands to redesign their catalog and letterhead—a decision that lead to a ten-year (and ongoing) partnership between the two creative companies. In that time, Mires has completely revitalized the Taylor brand, creating an elegant new look and a sophisticated new feel that permeates every aspect of their communications. At the heart of it all is the logo.

The original logo, a distinctive but awkward hand-lettered script, was already well established in the hearts and minds of Taylor's loyal customer base. "The most sellable thing is the Taylor name," Scott

explains, "but in many ways Taylor is also somewhat generic because so many other products share that name. We wanted to somehow bring 'guitars' into it and at the same time make it more corporate. That was really the challenge." Although the existing logo was only "half done" as Scott puts it, both Taylor and Mires agreed from the outset that its look should be preserved but refined into a tighter, more crafted mark. "I'm a tweak-head," Bob Taylor confesses. "I'm someone who believes that tweaking a thing until it's right is more creative than tossing everything out and starting over." Scott Mires possesses a similar attitude. "For us it's always about 'How can we optimize what we have? How can make this better?'" But Scott also warns that clients don't want things to just look better. "They want measurable reasons why to change," he explains. For Scott and designer Miguel

# TAYLOR'S 2004 CATALOG:

Mires Brands has continued to design Taylor's catalog since their first assignment a decade ago, evolving and pushing the look to keep Taylor Guitars a strong and progressive brand.

# THE MAN BEHIND THE NAME:

Every certificate is signed by Bob Taylor himself—expressing Taylor's commitment to quality.

Perez, who has created more than half of the logos in the Mires portfolio, the question was about communicating what Taylor was all about and making sure the mark could be successfully applied across a broad range of media.

Mires began the project as they do all identity projects: embarking on a discovery phase to assess the competition and then find a unique position for their client within that space. "At this phase we're looking really, really roughly," Scott says. "We're collecting research and roughing out some directions. The client had this idea that maybe the logo should be in the shape of a peg head, so we looked at that as well as a range of our own ideas. Typically we're working in thumbnails; we try to stay away from the computer at first so we really are just talking about the idea."

After completing the discovery they move into a conceptual phase where again the team works loosely. Scott typically uses thumbnails at this stage as well, and although everyone in the office works a little differently, he says they're all trying to crack the same idea: in this case, "How do we say this is a guitar company? How do we say this is a *great* guitar company?" Once Scott is satisfied with the range of exploration (in this case about a dozen viable directions, though for some projects he'll show many times that), he presents the thumbnails to the client. "Over the years in working with Taylor we've developed a very close relationship," Scott says. "A lot of that grew out of them seeing some thumbnails and saying, 'So this is what I'm paying for? It seems so simple. It seems so rough.' And then when they saw the finished product they said, 'Wow. Now I get it.' So now when they see thumbnails they see through to the ideas. They realize that it's going to end in an

execution and an implementation, of course, but that it starts with a concept. That's a really fulfilling part for a client to be involved in. We could talk about the form and say, 'Okay, Taylor, we're going use Weiss as your font,' and that wouldn't mean a whole lot to them. But when we say, 'There's going to be consistency of typography no matter what type of application you're creating, and that consistency is going to make people see Taylor Guitars,' then we're talking about an idea. They get that."

It helped to be working with a creative company. As Bob Taylor points out, they're designers, too. Bob's designer eye for detail was equally keen when it came to the logo. "Bob saw the returns and the negative areas that most clients would never notice. To him those mean something, and we would discuss why we were doing certain things." Scott specifically

# THE WEB SITE:

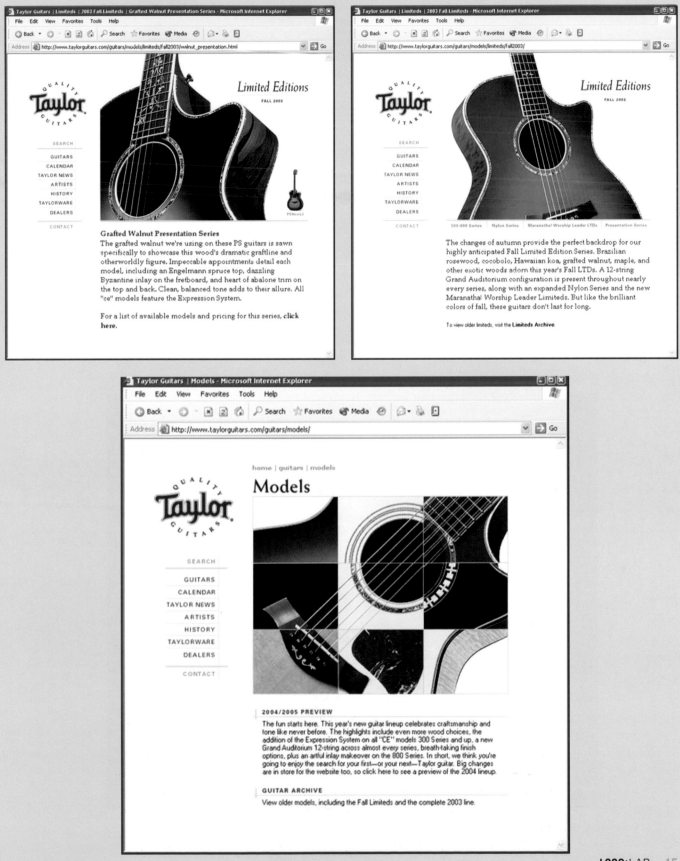

remembers Bob looking at how they were handling the *r* and how the descender on the *y* dipped down. While some designers shy away from input on that level, at Mires it's an important part of the process. When a client isn't happy with an aspect of the design, Scott reminds himself that they're coming from a position of knowing their market. His position in those instances is to take that input and use it to make the project better. It works the same way within the Mires office. There aren't any walls at Mires Brands, and while small teams are assigned to work on each project, other designers are encouraged to provide informal input throughout the process. "It's not always a creative director

saying, 'Do this,'" Scott says. "The ideas can come from anywhere."

That level of collaboration continued through the development and refinement phases, as Mires undertook the process of tweaking and honing every aspect of the logotype. "Miguel is the king of tweaking," Scott says of the company's lead logo designer. His work is evident here. Because the essential form of the logotype was to remain the same, the process became an exercise in finessing every detail of the letterforms, then massaging each of those elements into an exquisite whole. The curved baseline on which the logo sits was refined to a more graceful arc. The shape and proportion of each let-

terform were carefully reexamined and modified (most notably the *a* and the *r*). The letter spacing was closed up and the character weight increased to give the logo a denser, more emblematic feel. A stroke was added that both softens and grounds the logo against a variety of media, and finally the logo was embraced with the tag line "quality guitars" to solidify Taylor's position in the consumer's eye. The result is a look that Bob Taylor describes with satisfaction as being unique but familiar— the perfect embodiment of the growing Taylor brand.

*"Because the essential form of the logotype was to remain the same, the process became an exercise in finessing every detail of the letter-forms, then massaging each of those elements into an exquisite whole."*

## DISTINCTIVE IN SO MANY WAYS:

T

The revitalized logo was carefully drawn with a view toward broad implementation. Whether blind embossed, lit up in neon or embroidered on cap, polo or gig bag, the mark is an undeniable expression of quality.

In
it
n

P
c
b
k
c

# VARIATIONS ON THE THEME:

These alternate logos are meant to deliver flexible solutions to the client. Left, the logo for large format use. Right, the secondary logo uses a horizontal orientation.

among these whimsical objects that is both complex and simple, appealing simultaneously to the emotion of grandparents and the creative perception of children. There is an entire narrative told in the moment it takes to observe this mark. Every detail reveals a piece of the story: The larger, elder bird grounds the entire scene—it has feet but no wings—while the smaller bird completes the generational metaphor—with wings but no feet—invigorating the scene with young energy as it hovers above the type. Through their gaze they greet each other

with knowing emotion, wrought more from the viewer's own experience than the simple circles that stand in for eyes. Which of the two is the receiver is also left skillfully ambiguous, allowing each viewer to place him or herself in the scene as he or she sees fit. The type recalls the cursive we were taught in school, reinforcing again the physical act of writing. In sum, the mark is a sweet and touching pantomime, performed in the familiar language of our childhoods, through the whimsical hand of design.

## CATALOG AND PACKAGING:

Sandstrom's logotype is links the company's well known, well worn One Star and All Star shoe brands into a cohesive product line. Packaging details reference the shoes' construction—and the company's heritage.

# WHAT'S OLD IS NEW AGAIN:

An early photo of Chuck Taylor serves as both a literal and metaphorical backdrop for Sandstrom's twenty-first century iteration of the Converse logotype. Past and present are inexorably linked. (Logo buffs, can you identify the famous *F* on Chuck's jersey?)

It's really a case of two talented teams working together."

From that collaboration came an identity whose legitimacy is one that harmonizes with all of their current products. It doesn't matter if it's the most advanced shoe or the oldest canvas hightop in the box, this logo works for both."

The mark itself is indeed a remarkably restrained and sensitive solution, and a result that is perhaps more timeless than the original.

*Postscript: Shortly after completing this chapter I happened into a shoe store that was still stocking both boxes. If there was ever an argument for the power of design to articulate a brand, this was it. Side by side the identical product spoke with two different voices: One, the ultra-thin, ultimately interim redesign in white type on a blue background, at best made a tentative gesture for my attention. The other, Sandstrom's robust and confident logotype in cream lettering on an all-black box punctuated with two silver grommets, had the clerk searching for my size. You might call me a sucker for design, but isn't that the point?*

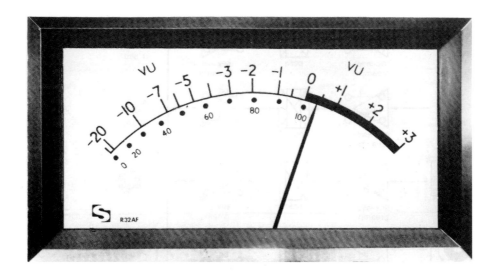

VU (Volume Unit) meters display the average volume level of an audio signal. Dan's logo is stripped of its extraneous elements, transforming the mundane object into a sleek and stylish metaphor.

spoke with the guys at CineSound, they seemed to be leaning toward more literal and diagrammatic ideas." Dan was faced with his first challenge—not how to reconcile divergent aesthetic inclinations but identifying the true client and command structure within the context of the project. Alternately dealing with the owner and the owner's art director friend and representative, Dan was receiving conflicting information. He elected to focus on the owner's preferences and began developing marks that reflected his vision. As he did so, Dan found that his personal interest in music, combined with his technical background in electronics, helped him zero in on possible concepts for the mark. "From the outset, the VU meter seemed like an obvious concept," he says. "It's easily identified with what they do, even if you don't know exactly what a VU meter does." Among Dan's initial sketches are both dig-

ital and analog versions of the feedback device, both of which he presented in the first round. "The owner liked the VU meter idea right away," he remembers, "but then came the problem of refining it." In particular, the client wanted to move away from red (the color they were using in their existing materials) and instead requested that the color be changed to blue. "He told me they were sick of red," says Dan, "but blue just didn't make sense with the concept they had chosen." It is, of course, the classic problem of balancing a design's formal qualities and the need to effectively communicate its message. In logo design this struggle is often manifest in the debate over color. Years ago there was a building campaign for the Art Gallery of Nova Scotia that included "I Heart Art" bumper stickers. The red heart raised the ire of the Progressive Conservative Party of Nova Scotia as

being a "liberal" color. As the party in power, they wanted the heart to be blue. More recently, I was working on an identity for a school whose color requirements stated that the logo include neither red nor blue ("gang colors"), while simultaneously creating a mark for an event commemorating 9/11, in which case the client required the inclusion of both. Color can be an emotional touchstone for many people. A client once stormed out of a meeting denouncing my use of yellow. Apple used six colors to battle Big Blue, and UPS built an entire campaign asking, "What can brown do for you?"

The debate over red vs. blue took two presentations to resolve. "I think the process was made more complicated because I was a student," says Dan. "It was difficult for them to trust me on a lot of issues because I was young and inexperienced. I would tell them something and

# THE BEGINNING OF AN IDEA:

By his own admission, Dan doesn't sketch as much as he should. In this case, however, these were all he needed to spark his initial concept.

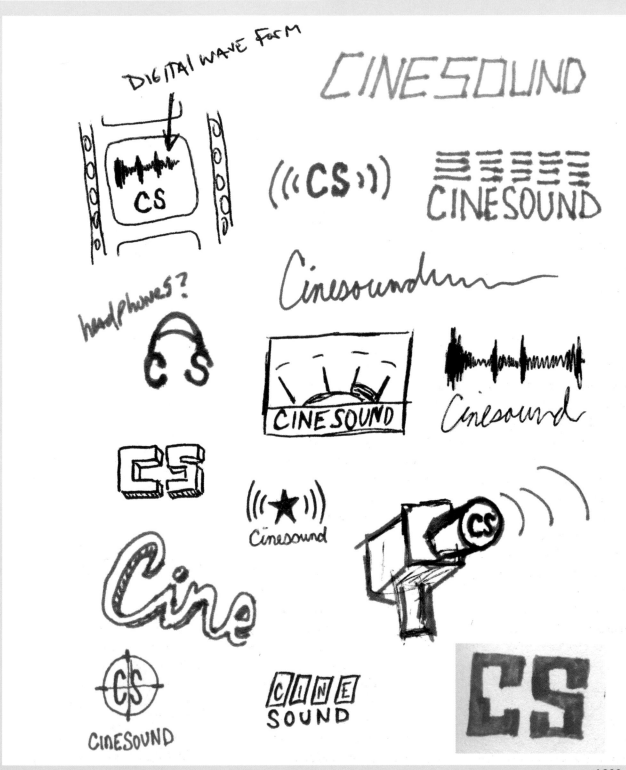

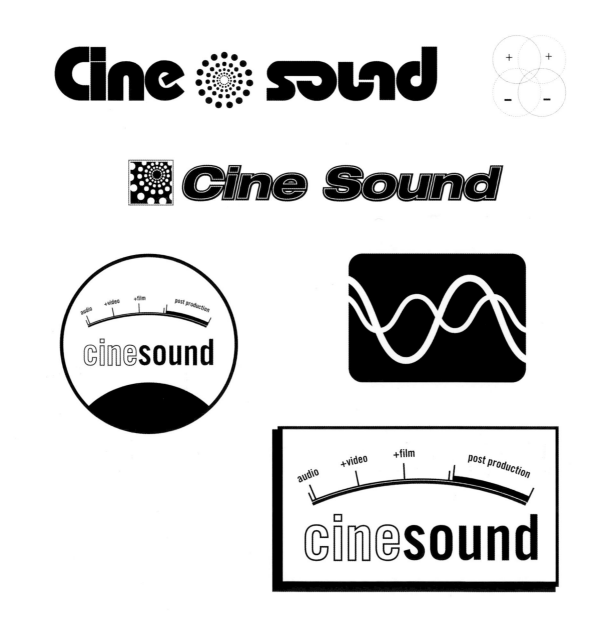

Most of Dan's early ideas in this, his first presentation, centered on the VU meter concept. There was early concern about the analog version portraying the company as old-fashioned or behind the technology curve, but those fears were assuaged by the fact that the analog version was far more recognizable, memorable and—by allowing for the company's descriptor to be integrated with the mark—ultimately more meaningful.

As you can see, the blue version just doesn't have the impact or authenticity of its incarnadine counterparts. And where authenticity is concerned, the use of Clarendon makes this logo look more like a mark for a fifties hi-fi set than a serious sound editing studio. In the end, Helvetica was a quietly appropriate choice.

N G I
COMMUNICATIONS

Early design explorations. At NOON, designers are encouraged to sketch as freely as possible. In the early stages ideas are considered for what they mean, not how they look.

 COMMUNICATIONS

NGI : COMMUNICATIONS

 COMMUNICATIONS

 NGI COMMUNICATION

 NGI COMMUNICATIONS

 NGI COMMUNICATIONS

NGI COMMUNICATIOI

 COMMUNICATIONS

 NGI COMMUNICATIONS

NGI COMMUNICATIONS

 NGI COMMUNICATIONS

 NGI COMMUNICATIONS

NGI  COMMUNICATIONS

 NGI COMMUNICATIONS

 NGI COMMUNICATIONS

# EARLY FAVORITES:

Two directions emerged as possible finalists. Left, an abstract symbol resembling musical notes and representing the idea as both a technical and fluid discipline. Right, NGI in Morse code.

does their own exploration. Hopefully they're trying to resolve one of the issues or adjectives we discussed, but they're free to go off on their own tangents as well." By not limiting her designers, Cinthia feels they produce richer solutions, and in the process experience a greater sense of ownership of the result. It was through some tangential exploration that one of the designers came up with the idea of using Braille.

"Immediately everyone was like, 'Oooh, cool, Braille,'" she laughs, "and we had all these fantasies about blind embossing and die cutting and all that. Of course once we got that out of our system we realized that it didn't really mean anything in terms of Nikki's business." But the Braille idea set the designers thinking about other visual communication systems, and it wasn't long before somebody else brought up Morse code. Cinthia rec-

ognized the purity of the concept immediately. To her, it represented the very essence of Nikki's work. It was simultaneously bold and subtle, obvious in form but obscure in meaning, the kind of logo that challenges the viewer to read and interpret in a way that parallels the work of a good writer. Moreover, it was a tremendously flexible identity, one that could easily grow and evolve with Nikki's business.

"To me it's not about producing that perfect icon" says Cinthia. "That's not what a logo is necessarily about. Someone once told me that a great logo is one that can be successfully implemented." In other words, you have to stop thinking about the logo as an object and consider it in the context of a larger system. Because NOON does a lot of print work, they have an abiding appreciation of the physical implementation of ideas. "I always

look at a logo as part of a business system," says Cinthia, who also says that at a minimum she will design a business card as part of the logo design process. "Clients always ask me, 'Will it cost more?' and I say, 'Well no, because I need to do it anyway so I know that it works, otherwise it's going to suck for you later and I'm going to feel bad.'" To avoid such regret, she also makes sure to blow every identity the studio designs up to monumental scale. "Haven't you ever seen one of your logos on a billboard or someplace and just wanted to shoot yourself?" she asks. "You always have to anticipate how it might be used. Why is Nike so successful? It's not a great icon, but it's implemented brilliantly. It's all about the execution."

"I think that's an important aspect of identity that a lot of people overlook," says Cinthia. "It really isn't about the mark as much as how you use it and how peo-

# THE COLOR OF LANGUAGE:

# GIVING CREDIT TO THE AUDIENCE:

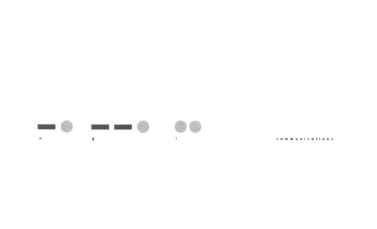

With the concept locked down, Cinthia confesses that they tried to "chic it up a bit" through the application of color. As attractive as some of the explorations are, it was ultimately decided that a system as basic as Morse code was best expressed in black and white.

Not sure that anyone would really understand the code, NOON looked at including a key to allow people to decipher its meaning. In the end they decided not to dumb down the concept but allow the viewer to engage the logo on his or her own level.

ple relate to it." She also asserts that logos don't need to be exclusive in the way most designers are trained to think they should. Morse code, for example, is just another alphabet, one free of distinction and embellishment. "No one owns it," says Cinthia. "Everyone can use it as long as they know it—that's the concept. One of the best things about this logo is that anyone can have it, you can go out tomorrow and put your initials in Morse code and that's just fine. It's about communication and connection, not about ownership and exclusivity." It's a solution that she says she would never entertain for a corporate client. "They'd think I was on crack," she

laughs, "but Nikki was prepared to give us a lot more freedom to really do something meaningful for her."

Designers often dream of projects in which they're given free reign, but Cinthia cautions that they're much harder than those that may seem more limiting. "It's tempting to start dumping all those ideas that you've always wanted to try (like using Braille) into those kinds of projects," she says, "because you know this is your one chance to get away with it. In the end, though, your instincts kick in and you come back to what you're supposed to do. That's when you realize that you're not a totally psycho designer, that

you don't need a client to keep you in check. If you're really a good designer you can do that for yourself. Discipline is as important as creativity."

The austere NGI logotype is a study in the art of disciplined design. It is in essence as basic a monogram as can be imagined. Its rhythmic dots and dashes telegraph a subtle comment on the overlooked utility of communication and create a lingering relationship between message and receiver. Conceived in an atmosphere of total creative freedom, it is courageously the very least it can be.

F

Ta
Fil
for

a
Fi
at
Al
be
ta
in
"
ag
p
d

fu
d
b
c
t
s
t
c
l
a

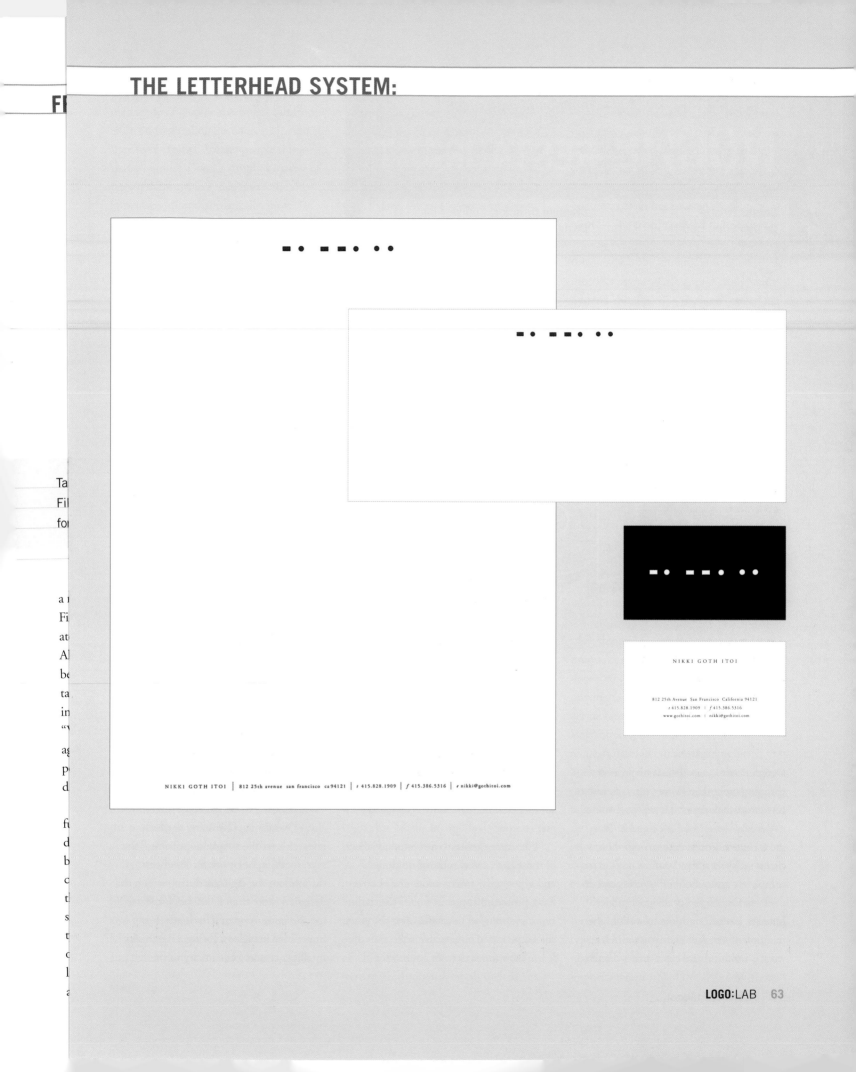

NIKKI GOTH ITOI | 812 25th avenue san francisco ca 94121 | t 415.828.1909 | f 415.386.5316 | e nikki@gothitoi.com

NIKKI GOTH ITOI

812 25th Avenue San Francisco California 94121
t 415.828.1909 | f 415.386.5316
www.gothitoi.com | nikki@gothitoi.com

When trying to make work look like it wasn't created on the computer, sometimes it's best not to use one at first. The designers twisted expressive characters from bent wire first, then created a computer-drawn script based on the bent-wire experiments.

needed release after a decade of economic depression. In many respects Noche was borne in circumstances that parallel those times. It is an oasis to which people can escape for an evening of carefree living. In the tradition that gave rise to the Copacabana, Louise Fili's Noche logo declares this a New York destination and the new Great American Nightclub.

# BUSINESS CARD OR LOGO?

The final logo is actually the full image you see here, so on business cards and postcards the identity is featured at full scale, making it less like an individual symbol and more of a complete identity experience.

think about it. And the thinking process is not conscious. It's an unconscious or a subconscious mosh. It's nonlinear, things happen randomly and this is the magic that is called human thought.

**CCHS: So where do you find distraction?**
**AC:** *For years what I did was I listened to music when I worked. I would put on a record, and the game was, I had this wall full of records. I had everything from sound effects to punk rock to opera in there, and a lot of it was crap. Polka music. Garbage. And I would pull this record off the shelf and I'd put it on the turntable (these were LP's) and I'd have to listen to one side of the record. And because of my interest in creative thought and stuff, I'd be sitting there trying to listen to the record and figure out what I'm listening to and how to come up with these ideas and how the music is interlocking and I'm looking at it and I'm thinking*

about that. In the meantime, the ideas would come through my hands. They'd come right on out. It's like I'm driving that car. Instead of driving a car, I'm listening to a record while I'm working on that design. And I began to realize that's what it was about—relaxation and letting go of control.

*Now I listen to talk radio when I work. Because I listen to what people are saying and I'm thinking about it. What you need to do is get that part of your thinking that's in the way and trust your mind to let it flow out of you. And it is really hard to describe. It is a very abstract concept, but it's actually a very physical process.*

**CCHS: It's funny, I have to listen to talk radio to go to sleep, just because I have so many ideas going on—**
**AC:** *Oh, shutting off, that's just as important. I used to drink ... I had to quit drinking years ago. A lot of the drinking process for*

me was just getting my mind to stop thinking. You know, they're finding out that obsessive-compulsive disorders like alcoholism, and depression and mania actually happen in a certain part of the brain and involve certain amino acids and certain chemical reactions. It's exactly the same part of the brain and the same amino acids and same chemical reactions that make up the creative parts of the brain. Creativity is a type of obsessive-compulsive disorder. The whole idea of the crazy artist is a reality ... The guy from Saturn, at least he's honest about the fact that he's crazy.

**CCHS: Well that might be a good note to end this on...**
**AC:** *Yeah. I think so.*

INSPECTORA

ESTRUS

No.3

ALSO AVAILABLE IN STEREO
HIGH FIDELITY

# THE POWER OF CHOICE:

These are just some of the more than six hundred sketches Jeff received from the six designers working on the project. From rough to refined, resolved and ill conceived, all are given consideration in the early stages. Here you can see circled the directions that Jeff felt showed promise.

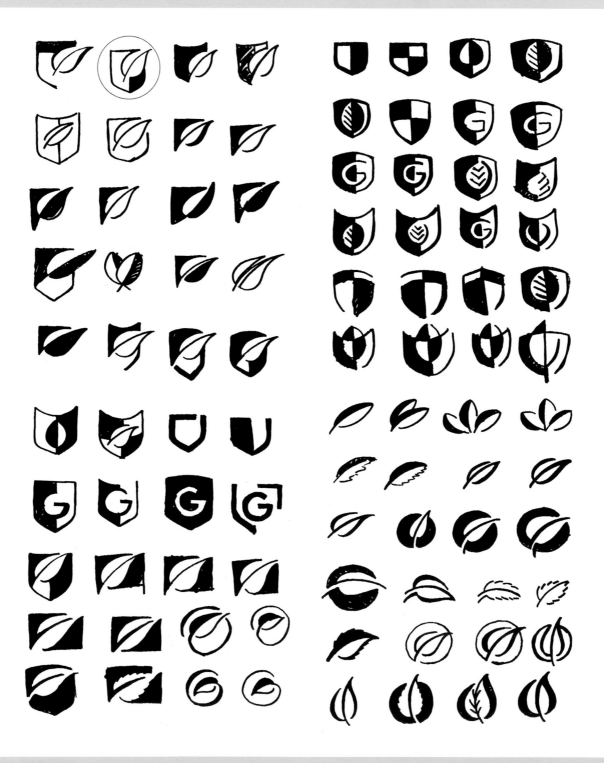

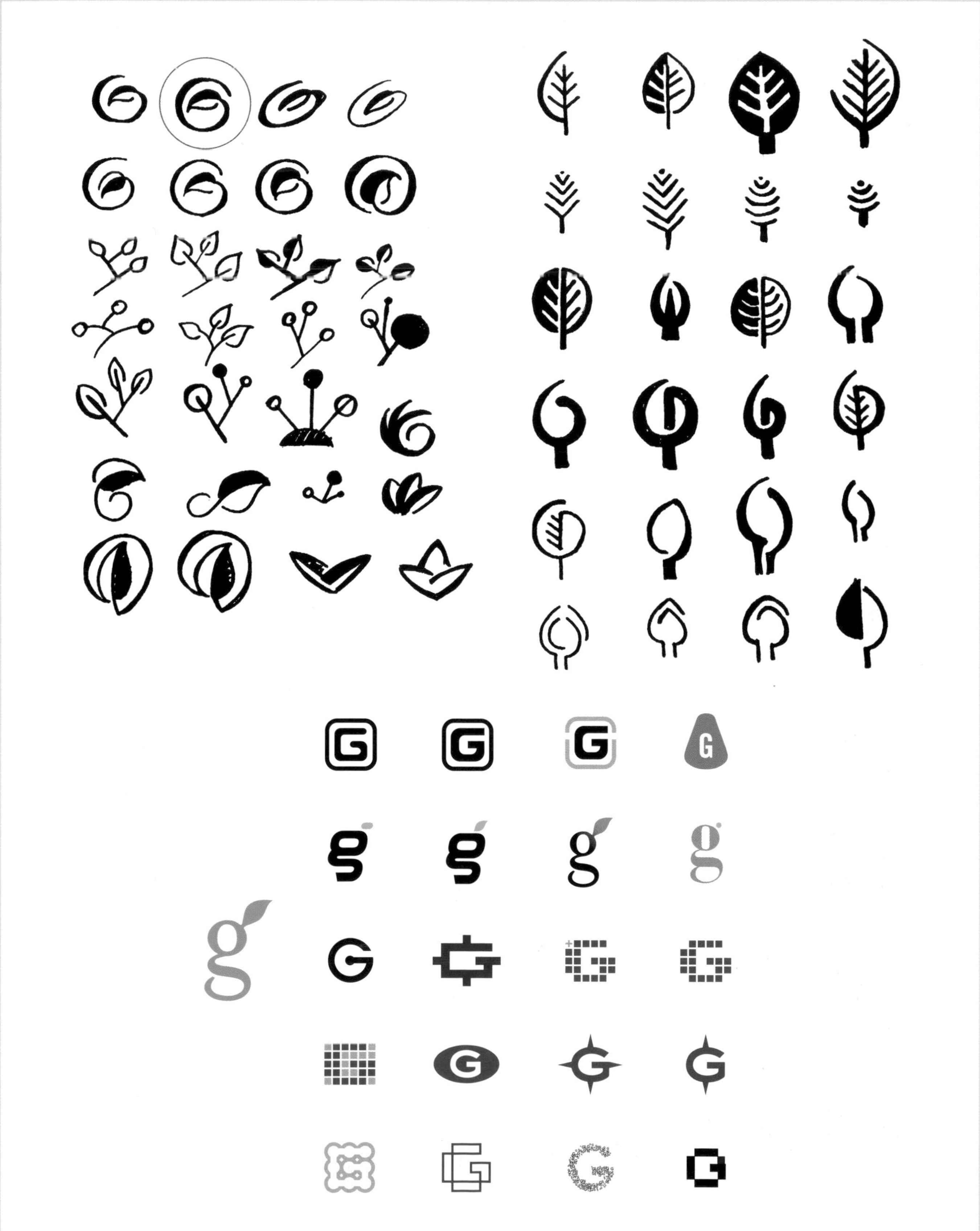

6. The recommendation that both symbols and wordmarks be explored as options.

Jeff's creative platform was just eight pages, including three pages of exhibits. Most of the writing was in point form. In contrast, I recently worked on an identity project that featured a sixty-page creative brief of dense prose. While there is no single formula to dictate the extent to which the platform is articulated, Jeff has very specific reasons for setting up his projects the way he does. "I want to target our creative direction as much as possible," he explains, "but at the same time I don't literal and someone else specifically because their work is a little more 'out there.' That way we get a broad range of thinking. If you have a bunch of designers in house then you really only ever have one team, and you get the same stuff over and over again." Jeff also says that everyone he works with has a different working method. "They're working from wherever they're working—here, Canada, Chicago, New York, wherever—and they're working however they're comfortable. I work with one designer who just scribbles things down on paper and faxes it in, and that's fine for me. I don't care. I'm looking "Just like we did at Landor," he says. He begins by editing out anything that is clearly off the mark, and then culls through the rest to narrow the field to fifteen to twenty potential directions. Jeff more seriously scrutinizes the short-listed directions until only three to five of the best candidates remain. When necessary, he may ask for an additional round of exploration with more focused direction. The finalists then undergo the requisite tweaks before being presented to the client. The refinements are usually performed by one of the in-house designers, but sometimes the person who created the

## "There are a lot of great print designers who just don't get identity—the people I use are people who do."

want to limit the designers—they need to be free to explore a wide range of approaches." To facilitate this, Jeff's briefs deal with broad concepts under which he organizes several specific attributes, any one of which can be the hinge on which the identity swings.

When Jeff speaks of designers, it should be noted that he only has two full-time employees. The rest he contracts on a project basis. "I have a group of about ten different designers that I like to work with. They're all really talented in developing ID," he says, adding that identity is the most difficult thing to do in design. "It's difficult because it is so conceptual and you have to tell a really strong story very quickly. If you're not someone who's really into designing identity, you're not going to have a clue how to do that. There are a lot of great print designers who just don't get identity—the people I use are people who do."

Jeff assembles his design team by bringing in as many designers as the budget will bear. "What I like about the way we're structured is that I can build a team that is most suited to the project. I might pick someone because they're very for the idea. Other people work on the computer in full color and that's fine, too. The people that I'm using are all gifted, they're all excellent, and I let them work however they need to give me their best thinking."

For Gilead, which had a healthy budget, Jeff had six designers work on the project. Two were in-house, with four others contributing an outside perspective. It's a proven structure that he makes no secret of when pitching to his clients. "I tell them, 'Here's your team: you get me, you get this person and this is their background and this is why they're great at naming or strategy. We're going to use these designers, and here's why they're all great for this project for different reasons, and so on,'" he explains. On rare occasions, Jeff does encounter some skepticism about his working methodology, mostly from clients who are used to working with larger offices. "In those instances, it's just too bad," he shrugs. "This is how I work. I've been doing this for twenty-five years, and it's just how I work."

Once all the sketches are in (usually after about a week or so), Jeff puts everything up on the wall for consideration. mark will make the tweaks. "It all depends on budget, time and talent," says Jeff. But regardless of who hones the design to its final form, Jeff works very closely with them. Having given his design team the freedom to explore a wide range of concepts, once the directions are selected the task becomes very specific. "I'm basically standing over shoulders at that point," says Jeff. "I'm working very closely with the designer to take the logo exactly where I want it to go."

For Gilead, Jeff reviewed over six hundred first-round sketches. "It's overwhelming," he says, "and it's our responsibility as designers to give the client a limited number of the best directions that also cover the broadest range of their communications attributes." He also cautions that it is never about looking cool. "You can't say that to a CEO, they don't want to hear it. Everything has to have thinking behind it. If we show a mark in color—even though it may be hypothetical—we have to be able to articulate a rationale for that color choice." In other words, Jeff talks to his clients about ideas, not design.

Jeff's strategy generally includes one direction that is conceptually close the

## TYPEMARK SKETCHES:

# REFINING THE CONCEPT:

Version 1                     Version 2                     Version 3

A shield, representing safety and protection, is combined with
a leaf, directly referencing the origins of the company's name.
The basic concept went through several revisions as Jeff and
the designer worked by phone and fax to develop a dozen
slightly different versions of the mark.

existing identity. While this is often the
weakest direction, especially for a company trying to signal growth or change, it
eases them into the process. This usually
gives the client something to reject, and
they end up pushing themselves to accept
a more courageous and effective solution.
Of course, there is always the risk that
they'll love it. Of the five marks that Jeff
presented, the first four were roundly
rejected. "John Martin, Gilead's president
and CEO, knew what he was looking at,"
says Jeff, "and he knew what we were talking about. His clarity and focus helped
move the process along swiftly." As an
example, Jeff cites one direction that,
going in, he thought was particularly
beautiful and well suited to Gilead's busi-

ness. John agreed but countered that the
beauty of the mark didn't appropriately
represent the gravity of the company's
products. "If you're taking drugs from
Gilead, it's basically an alternative to
dying," John told Jeff. "You have AIDS,
cancer … this direction doesn't convey the
severity of what we do." When John saw
the fifth and final mark, however, he was
totally blown away, declaring to Jeff,
"That's our logo. That's the one."

So impressed was the CEO by the
meaning and rendering of the mark that
he gave his approval there and then. Marcus Associates explored some alternate
type options but ultimately kept it as it
was presented.

# GRAPHIC STANDARDS:

As part of any major branding project, graphic standards are included to ensure the consistent and appropriate implementation of the identity.

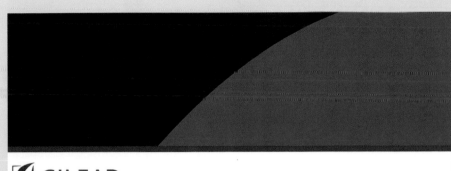

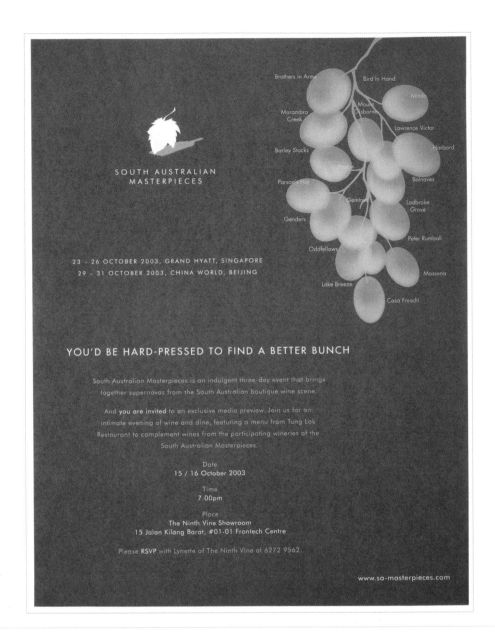

SOUTH AUSTRALIAN
MASTERPIECES

23 – 26 OCTOBER 2003, GRAND HYATT, SINGAPORE
29 – 31 OCTOBER 2003, CHINA WORLD, BEIJING

**YOU'D BE HARD-PRESSED TO FIND A BETTER BUNCH**

South Australian Masterpieces is an indulgent three-day event that brings
together supernovas from the South Australian boutique wine scene.

And **you are invited** to an exclusive media preview. Join us for an
intimate evening of wine and dine, featuring a menu from Tung Lok
Restaurant to complement wines from the participating wineries of the
South Australian Masterpieces.

Date
15 / 16 October 2003

Time
7.00pm

Place
The Ninth Vine Showroom
15 Jalan Kilang Barat, #01-01 Frontech Centre

Please **RSVP** with Lynette of The Ninth Vine at 6272 9562.

www.sa-masterpieces.com

This is the press release used by
Ninth Vine (before the logo was
finalized).

a tidy solution that at once speaks of vision, process and potential while managing to present industry clichés in a fresh light. The client had an immediate affinity for this direction, so much so that they used the concept sketch in their first press releases. "At that point, they had considered the logo approved and started running with it," marvels Karen, "so the early presentations to sponsors were using a concept version of the logo!"

Despite the client's apparent contentment with the mark, Karen and her team continued to tweak the logo, addressing its color, form and typography. The leaf was reinterpreted in a more stylized depiction, with a more extreme perspective to add greater dimension and movement to the design. In the final version, the leaf appears to have more volume and therefore a more assertive presence. Its mass helps give it definition, helping it appear to float off the page. The color evolved

from the original bright Australian green to a more sophisticated turquoise. Typographically, the shift from serif to sans serif moved the identity into a more contemporary context. It retains a refined sense of tradition but establishes itself as a relevant authority moving forward. When the tweaks were complete, Karen presented the refined mark to the client. "I asked them, 'Please use this new and improved logo instead.'" And they did.

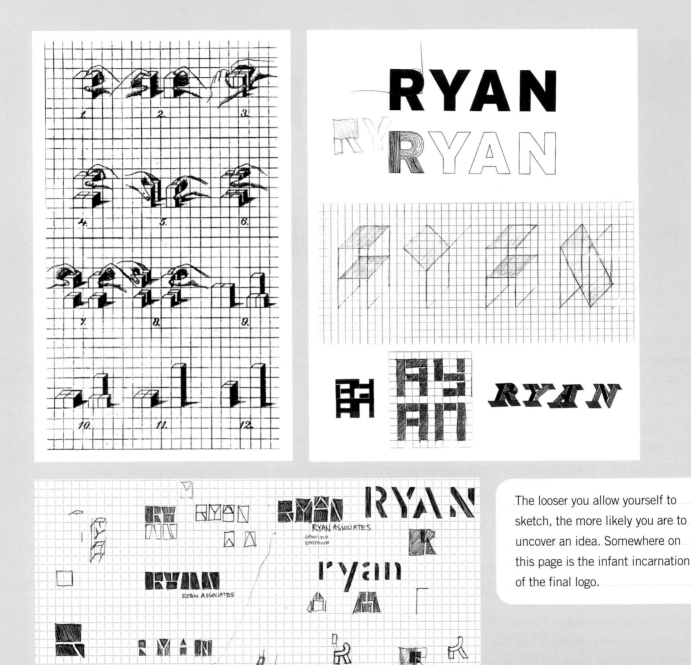

The looser you allow yourself to sketch, the more likely you are to uncover an idea. Somewhere on this page is the infant incarnation of the final logo.

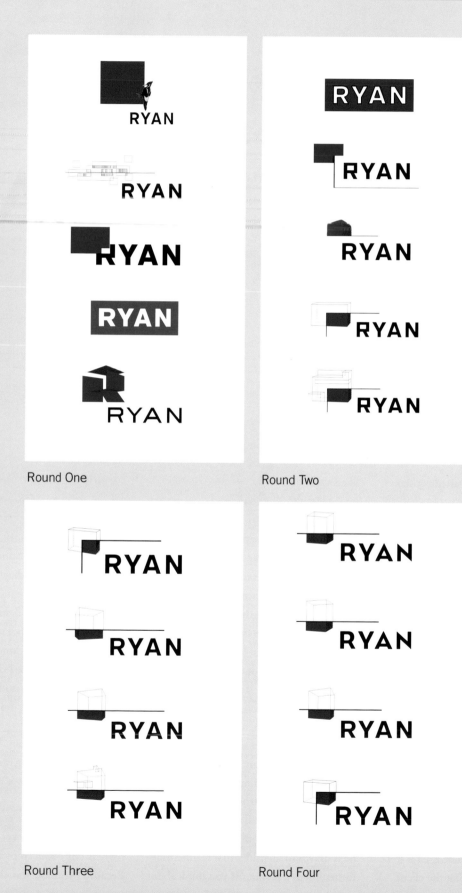

Round One

Round Two

Round Three

Round Four

## EARLY DIRECTIONS:

Cowboys, cattlebrands, the Lone Star, and the open road inform these early directions for the team logo.

epic, larger–than-life image of the freedom of the untamed frontier, even in the most stalwart of hearts. It represents the pride and heritage that is so much a part of the people of Texas." Focused on that spirit, Mark went about the task of designing the team's logo, but to him it was more than just a team identity. "I wanted to create a symbol of the Lone Star State for the people of Texas," says Mark. "I knew from living and visiting there how important the state flag was to Texans. I think I always knew I would incorporate the state colors and the star." Because of Texas' storied heritage, Mark also felt the colors should be "dirty"—as if they had been through battle. Even with these preconceptions, Mark was trying to solve a design problem for his client. Their job brief required that he show a range of thinking, so he committed himself to exploring a range of solutions.

**April 11, 2000**

Mark sends his first pencil sketches to the NFL for review. "I like to draw," he says. "I sketch everything first, then I draw it on the computer. Even after the computer file is really tight, I will print out the design and redraw it to resolve curves or quickly try a different idea. Then I redraw them on the computer."

**April 19, 2000**

Mark sends five logo directions, based on his sketches and client feedback, to the NFL for review. As part of his presentation he writes, "Houston and Texas overall have a deep-rooted history with football and the purity of the game. The following designs get back to the real football: its roots, pride, integrity, honor. The simplicity of these designs is their strength and virtue." The presentation also includes historical images of early football heroes, pictures of family

and snapshots from his trip to Texas, including a shot of the open road and a fifty-foot Texas flag billowing in the republic's big sky. The designs are shown in the dirty red, white and blue he first envisioned. They include a cattle brand, a highway sign, a rodeo rider, the state of Texas and a simple lone star. Each is shown in the context of a uniform and helmet as well as some simple merchandising applications. "When I'm working on a project I always remind myself that it's not about me," Mark explains. "The work I do for the NFL is important, but it's a small part of a huge undertaking. The biggest part of the whole equation is the fans. I always try to ask myself, 'How is a fan going to use this?' So while I always do a helmet or uniform for the team, right alongside that I try to show a T-shirt or a hat or some other kind of merchandise that a fan might wear."

## REFINEMENTS:

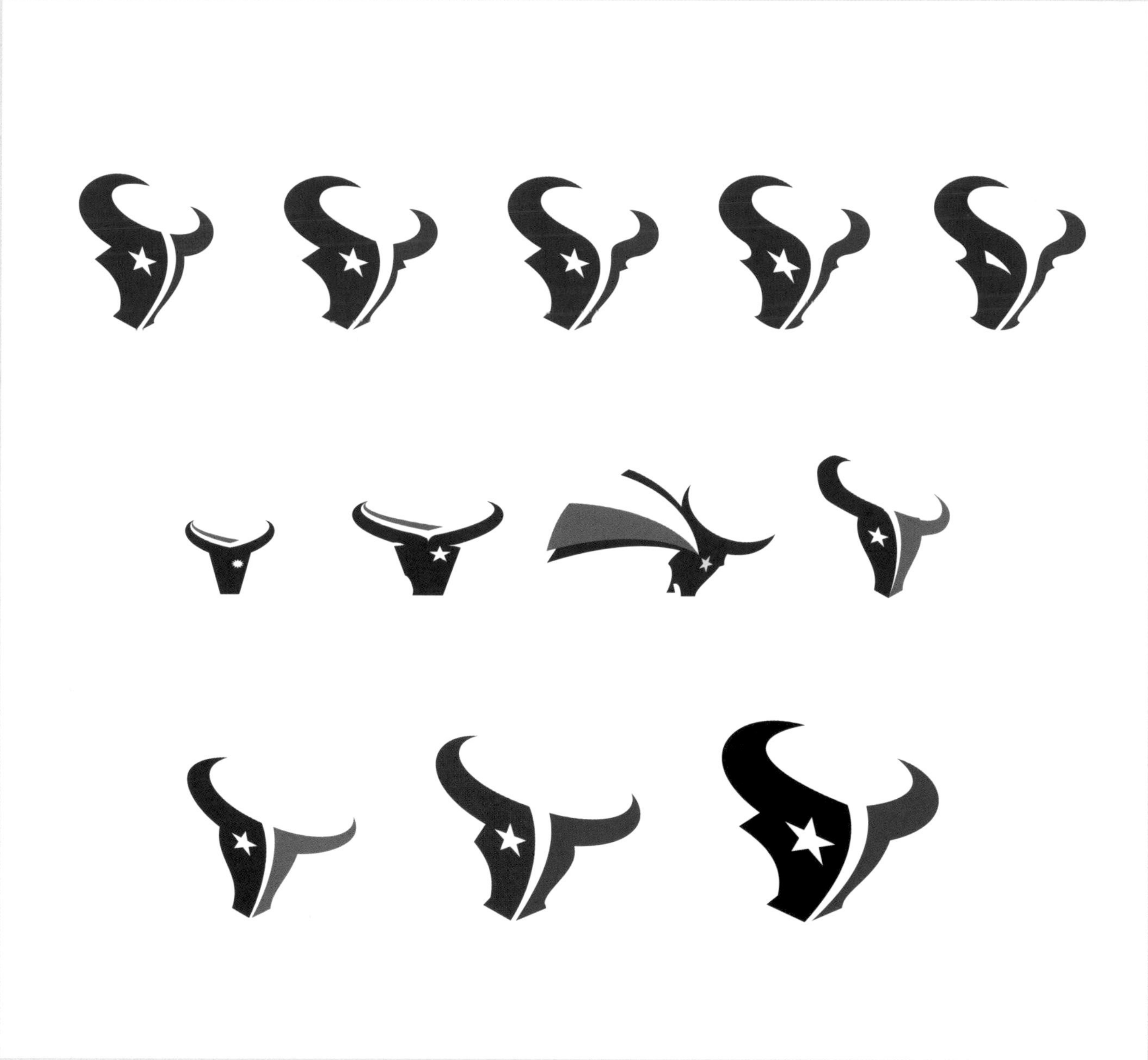

# QUEER EYE FOR THE STRAIGHT GUY

**Client:** Scout Productions     **Designer:** Adam Larson
**Design Firm:** Shrine Design

Through the glory of the Internet I stumbled upon shrine-design.com a good while before I even thought of writing this book. I'd never heard of it or its creator, Adam Larson, and the first thing I wondered was why? If you were to throw a dart at his web site you'd do some real damage to your monitor, but you'd also be guaranteed of hitting something totally cool. If you really must, you may go there now. If you do,

take some time to check out his wonderfully original illustrations, but be sure to come back and read about how he became involved with the Queer Eye for the Straight Guy logo.

An associate design director at advertising behemoth Arnold Worldwide's Boston office, Adam designs and oversees a variety of projects, ranging from print work for Marshall Field's to products, print and

interactive work for the visually and conceptually arresting anti-tobacco "truth" campaign. On the day we talk he's interrupted twice by designers who need his input on one of the fifteen jobs he's overseeing for celebrity cruises. Adam is thirty. Shrine Design is something he does in his spare time.

When I first saw the Queer Eye logo on Adam's site the show wasn't even on

# ADAM OVER-DELIVERS:

A first round of broad exploration had Adam looking a range of solutions, most of which included either a literal or abstract depiction of an eye or some reference to the letter Q. You can see the early incarnation of the now ubiquitous Queer Eye glasses in this first round as well.

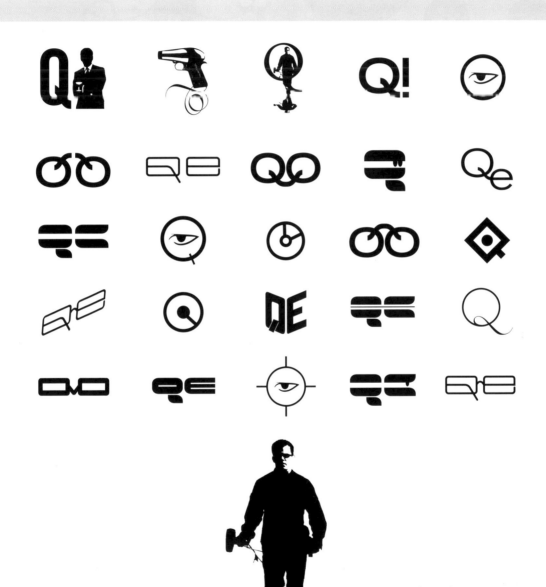

At the client's request, Adam experimented with creating a grungier logotype. But the fab five are more Hugo Boss than Joey Ramone, and this tangent was soon abandoned.

the show," Adam explains. "There was this idea that they might come out with a line of beauty products or fashion accessories. They even talked about having a Queer Eye-approved table at Barney's." Adam, perhaps trained by his job in the advertising industry to over-deliver, proceeded to mock up several of these scenarios for the show's producers. "I went totally overboard at that point," he laughs. "I mocked up the logo on T-shirts, watches, eyeglasses, embroidered jackets, beauty products, even a line of Vespas! It was sick."

With the logo approved (and applied over a comprehensive range of media), Adam moved on to address the type lock-up. "I really wanted them to abbreviate it to just Queer Eye since that's what I knew everyone would call it anyway, but at that point the producers were working with Bravo and the network felt strongly about

keeping the original title." Adam's solution was to emphasize Queer Eye by making that portion of the logotype distinctive—"queer," to use Adam's term—while letting the rest of the title recede through its simplicity. "The simple sans serif was straight and solid and kind of nondescript compared to the funkier Queer Eye," he says, "and it was all lower case. Bravo ended up changing that." Because the title is so long and has so much variation within itself—and because of the logo was developed independently of the typeface—the two don't ever live harmoniously with one another. "I looked at integrating the two, but they just weren't intended that way," says Adam. "If you notice, they always use just one or the other. If the title were simpler, it wouldn't be such an issue. The funny thing is, a lot of the time they just call the show Queer Eye anyway."

What at first seemed like a dubious opportunity to create a logo for a long-shot television pilot ended up going further than Adam ever imagined. The show, in case you haven't heard, is a runaway success, with international imitators, and now a version for women, Queer Eye for the Straight Girl. The show has won an Emmy, been featured in an American Express commercial and shows no sign of slowing down. Adam got his 300 percent bonus, but the real thrill is seeing his name in the television credits after the show.

With the final logo approved, Adam started looking at possible type lockups. There was some attempt to integrate the type and symbol, but the most successful versions treat the type as a separate but related entity. Below, the final approved type treatment.

# GETTING FROM THERE TO HERE:

| Zipfel |
| Kopfform |
| Kulleraugen |
| Handform |
| Naive Sachdarstellung |
| Knuffige Grundformen |
| Lineare Grundformen |

The essential details of a sample character's design attributes were first identified. Each element would be reinterpreted in a more contemporary form.

specific positioning toward a defined target group. Instead, the positioning could be described as providing "quality information and entertainment for the complete spectrum of the German population." With such a broadly identified audience, Rüdiger sought to narrow his focus somewhat. "Two target groups were considered crucial to the acceptance and success of the cartoon characters," he says. "First, the younger audience was of specific focus since the Mainzelmännchen are mainly featured in short clips between each commercial during the commercial blocks before 8:00 P.M. The other important group was twenty-five to forty-five-year olds who had a strong nostalgic connection to the characters." For several generations of Germans weaned on one of two nationalized television stations, the characters had become synonymous with entertainment. For many, the

Mainzelmännchen had become a romantic symbol for a less hectic, less profane and less commercial media culture. Rüdiger intended to honor those associations.

The designers began by examining what was essential about the existing characters, dividing their studies between figure and face. They resolved to keep as many conventions as possible so the cartoons would retain their innate character. Definitive characteristics of the character renderings such as pose, proportion, the four-fingered hand, simplicity of expression, etc. were preserved, albeit with a renewed sense of style. The line work was updated to a more precise system of tapered curves and deliberate angles. The one-piece coveralls were replaced with a more contemporary two-piece ensemble, and the colors were updated to more vibrant variations of their muted predecessors. Shadow details helped give the char-

acter a more dynamic and dimensional appearance. In short, the renderings were brought from their hand-drawn roots into the digital age.

The entire character redesign process spanned three presentations, each involving different scales of modification: mild, medium and advanced. Eventually, Simon & Goetz focused on two alternatives and finally decided to resolve only the most advanced redesign. Once the characters were developed, the team proceeded to develop accessories and environments for the station's new mascots. Together, these formed the visual language that would inform the larger branding initiative. The development of the branding concept followed a similar process. "In retrospect," says Rüdiger, "it is quite hard to say how many presentations we actually made. For each phase, I would assume we held three

# TYPE SKETCHES:

Mainzelmännchen

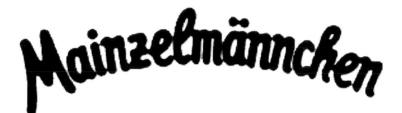

This is the original text style.

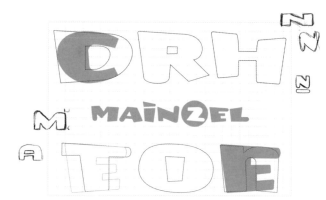

ORH
MAINZEL
TOE
A B C D E F G H I J K L M
N O P Q R S T U V W X Y Z
. , : ; - / ( ) ! ? %
1 2 3 4 5 6 7 8 9 0
ANTON BERTI CONNI
DET EDI FRITZCHEN
MAINZEL
MAINZEL
MAINZEL
MAINZEL
MAINZEL
MAINZEL
MAINZEL
MAINZEL
MAINZEL

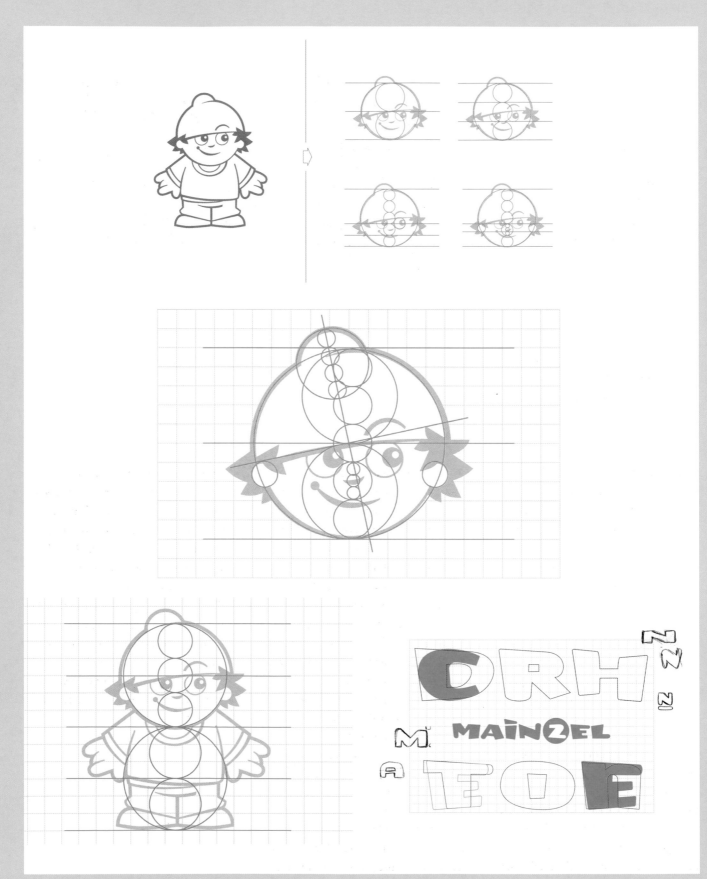

# MILD, MEDIUM AND ENHANCED:

Subtle shifts in line weight, color, and shadow radically alter the aesthetic quality of the characters, without reinventing their essential personality.

presentations until we got the final go for the actual graphic concept."

From the beginning, Rüdiger says the designers focused on developing a brand image that reflected the visual quality of existing premium products in the field of cartoon-license products. "Our inspiration was clearly driven by a technical and analytical filtering out of the timeless formal stereotypes of successful cartoon styles," explains Rüdiger. "The corresponding brand elements combine with the specific stylistic elements of character design, which together create the overall identity."

Creating the logotype required a more radical departure from the past than did the character redesign. Simon & Goetz actually developed an entire alphabet to complement the characters and then used that font to craft the logotype. The redesigned typeface retains some of undulating character of the original script but is

instead represented in irregular (but carefully considered) block capitals. The result is a playful and animated logotype that perfectly complements the newly created characters. The optimistic and curious face of a single of these characters engages the viewer with a knowing smile and cocked eye that seems to acknowledge both its past and present in a single succinct expression. The face is set against a circular field of orange, which visually connects with the reversed out Z in Mainzel. That Z, of course, is deliberately interchangeable with the numeral 2—a reference to the parent ZDF brand (remember that ZDF stands for Second German Television). The revised ZDF logo follows a similar logic and is tucked discretely in the upper-right corner.

From the first briefing through final development and creation of the design manual, the entire process took Simon &

Goetz approximately ten months. Throughout it all, Rüdiger's commitment to a systematic design process kept the project focused and on track. What could have been an emotional and highly subjective exercise was instead informed by thoughtful analysis, strategic consensus building and thorough (but appropriately limited) exploration. A long-standing and well-nurtured client relationship not only led to the project in the first place but also established an atmosphere of mutual trust and respect that supported its successful conclusion.

Type and image can lock up in infinite combinations. These are some of the playful solutions Rüdiger explored before settling on the less trendy final design.

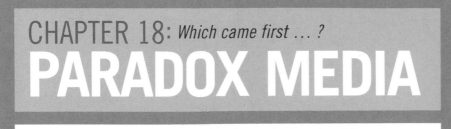

# CHAPTER 18: *Which came first ... ?*
# PARADOX MEDIA

**Client:** Paradox Media          **Designer:** Christopher Simmons
**Design Firm:** MINE™

Every once in a while you're given a gift. Sometimes it's a dream client, sometimes it's an opportunity to work in a new or exciting industry and sometimes it's a design problem for which the solution is inherently built-in. Such was the case with my Paradox logo.

I went to high school with a guy named Justin Katz. Together we founded an environmental club, produced and distributed an underground magazine laced with raunchy humor and political satire, pulled a few pranks and organized a school-wide walkout protesting the first Gulf War. Such was our high school bond. When we graduated, it made the local paper. Justin went on to the University of California San Diego and I (eventually) to the California College of the Arts (now CCA). For ten years or more, we pretty much lost touch until a chance meeting in an organic grocery store reunited us. By then, Justin had his own musical ensemble and had recently formed a production and promotion company called Paradox Media. I was working as a designer and teaching at CCA. We caught up over drinks a few times and quickly fell back into our collaborative ways. Justin gave me a handful of unlabeled CDs of his music for my class to listen to and interpret in a packaging design, agreeing to come to the final critique for a surprise

## EARLY EXPLORATIONS:

What is the nature of paradox? These first explorations are crude attempts to commit fleeting ideas to a physical form. Inspired by M.C. Escher, the self-consuming ouroboros and basic mathematical impossibility, each of these ideas took a backseat to the more succinct, efficient and friendly metaphor of the classic chicken vs. egg conundrum.

"real-world" evaluation. As it turned out, the surprise was on me—Justin showed up with his full band and gave us (and the entire school) a command performance. "I owe you for that," I told him. "Let me know if there is ever anything I can do."

"How about a logo," he replied. "Can you do that?"

Since that is what I do, I answered in the affirmative, and we agreed to meet the following week. In advance of that meeting, I sent Justin a questionnaire. Every questionnaire I develop is a little bit different, but they all aim to accomplish the same goals—namely to define the character of the product, service or organization being represented, gain insight into its culture and set reasonable criteria by which the success of the project will be judged. If there are multiple stakeholders involved, each of them gets to fill out their own questionnaire. The first thing I do is

reconcile any differences among them. You'd be surprised how often players on the same team have radically opposing views as to the nature of their business or the role design will play in their marketing. In Paradox's case, Justin and his business partner were aligned from the beginning. Gift number one.

Among the questions I posed to the partners were: How was the name arrived at and what does it mean? Are there any associations with the words paradox or media that you particularly wish to foster? Are there any you particularly wish to avoid? What are the essential reasons your clients choose to work with you? What are your short- and long-term growth plans? I also asked questions pertaining to the company's structure, areas of specialization, current marketing vehicles and so forth. The answers I received back were thorough and thoughtful—an indication

that the two had a focused business plan, shared vision and a mutual commitment to the success of their venture.

After reviewing their responses, the three of us met to discuss the answers in greater detail. Although the answers were thorough, there's no substitute for real discussion. Sometimes it helps clarify a previous response, and sometimes it raises new questions. In almost all cases, it leads to some unexpected discovery that just can't be anticipated on a questionnaire. There is a richness and depth of understanding that can only come from dialogue. This understanding helps inform the work and establishes a bond of partnership between designer and client. There have been projects where I've never met the client face-to-face, and more often than not those projects have fallen short of expectations or suffered under a laborious process. With Paradox, the big takeaway from our

# THE PARADOXICAL P:

I thought this direction had a lot of merit—until I discovered that Elixir had come up with the solution for a company named Perspecta. They did it first—and better—so this direction was scrapped.

face–to-face confab was the realization that the term media was misunderstood and ultimately less important to their positioning than originally thought. On the questionnaire, the name was neatly justified, but the more we actually talked about it the more it seemed to encumber the conversation, so by mutual consent it was dropped. Gift number two.

The other thing we talked about was how far they were willing to go conceptually. Some clients—even creative clients—have very conservative notions when it comes to their identity. It may be that they want the exact nature of their business or services to be represented, or they become uncomfortable with the abstraction of a metaphor. Justin was past any such reservations from the beginning and encouraged me to explore design concepts with total freedom. Gift number three.

With the design parameters wide open, I began looking at what I had to work with. First and foremost, there was the name. Paradox is a wonderfully enigmatic word that immediately conjures up fanciful Escher-esque geometric constructions, literary conundrums, the fabled ouroboros and of course the age-old riddle of the chicken and the egg. Of these, the first and last seemed to carry the most promise. There was a time when I would have temporarily shelved these ideas while I pushed for the harder, more obscure solution. Increasingly, however, I've come to trust my intuition on things. The first ideas come first for a reason—not because they're easy but because they're true. It becomes a matter of trusting your instincts, committing to an idea and then pushing that idea to its formal and conceptual limit.

Another direction might have been to represent the company's services or areas of interest, but because Paradox Media was involved in a variety of activities—including event production, promotion and management of a range of fine and performing artists—a service-specific logo didn't seem feasible. There was simply no reasonable way to cover all the bases from a representative standpoint. Instead, I recommitted myself to illustrating the concept of a paradox as a means of building name recognition through iconic association. This posed a second problem: Paradoxes, by their nature, contain an element of impossibility. As such, they are tricky little devils to put on paper. I managed to narrow my options to a few, including a mobius strip, an irrationally constructed P and the ultimate finalist, the chicken and the egg. [ART 18-3]

# STARTING BY HAND:

I almost always start on paper. I draw on tissue so I can trace the good parts of one design quickly and easily. Once I get the sketches to a level that's close to what I'm looking for, I scan them in and refine them in Illustrator. I may print the digital files out a second time and refine them by hand again if I'm not resolving the details fast enough electronically.

# FINE TUNING:

Just a few of the countless iterations of the tail section of the paradoxical bird.

I knew from the start that the chicken was the right solution, and it would just be a matter of how it was rendered. Sure enough, it was the hands-down favorite when I presented it to Justin and his business partner over a pint of Guinness. I've never been a big fan of boards and try to present on simple printouts whenever possible. If you're dealing with a small group, as I was, it's much easier to just share loose pages. I'm also usually loathe to let the client take the presentation away with them, as it too often leads to input from uninvolved parties—spouses, friends and the like. The more tightly you can control the process the better. One thing I do to prepare for the eventuality of the client's request to keep the presentation is to caption each direction with a few choice words. I've found that it helps remind the client of the context in which we originally considered each concept. When they

ask to take the presentation away and mull it over for a few days, I'm usually ready with a small bound version, one concept per page, each with its own caption explaining the idea. For the chicken I wrote:

"The Classic Paradox. Which came first, the chicken or the egg? This solution takes is multilayered approach, representing the word and the concept and conveying a sense of ongoing success. The enigmatic egg—the nascent talent—both confounds and compels the nurturing hen. In this way the logo almost wrestles with itself, drawing the viewer into its endlessly cyclical debate. This is the mark that lingers with you, makes you smile, makes you think and leaves you happy."

It's a little whimsical, I know, but design is a romantic endeavor and deserves to be talked about in colorful terms.

With the client committed to a single direction, the task remained to render the mark in a distinctive and compelling way. I Googled a lot of chicken pictures and created a kind of hybrid from the various poses I was able to find. I must have redrawn that bird a hundred times, starting on tissue then scanning the best of the hand-drawn versions in to Adobe Illustrator and refining it digitally. I spent a lot of time refining the tail—to the point of obsession. I'd work on it for a few hours in the evening then print it out and put it beside my bed at night. When I'd get up in the morning it would be the first thing I looked at, hoping to discover the secret of what wasn't working in the design. When I finally got the tail to a point where I was satisfied—somewhere between a squirrel's tail and a circular saw—I started obsessing over the feet, the

# BUSINESS CARD EXPLORATIONS:

Early exploration of possible business card designs
These versions were created before it was revealed that
the client would relocate within months of the initial
printing.

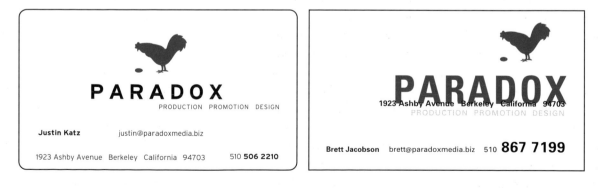

# A FLEXIBLE SYSTEM:

Studies for a modular system of stickers. The goal was to create a flexible and cost-effective solution. Knowing that the company would soon be relocating, the stationery is comprised of a system of one-color stickers that contain all the variable information. When it came time to relocate, simply printing new stickers enabled Paradox to completely update their system with minimal waste and expense.

size, shape and position of the egg, etc. At some point I just had to stop myself.

The last phase of the project was to design a system of business papers. As a startup, Paradox was budget conscious but still wanted a compelling design that made a strong creative statement. Compounding the problem was the fact that the company was using a temporary address while they searched for a permanent space. My solution to both issues was to design a system of one-color stickers for all of the variable information. These were then applied to a preprinted letterhead and unprinted business cards and envelopes. The same sticker was used to create the letterhead and envelopes, which

not only unified the system but also made it very inexpensive to produce. The client performed the handwork themselves, and for less than six hundred dollars had a complete business system for four people.

The entire process lasted just a few weeks and was one of the most efficient and rewarding design experiences I've ever had. The resulting mark is memorable, witty and a simple and airtight metaphor for an otherwise complex concept. Beyond representing the meaning of the word paradox, it captures the spirit of the client's business and subtly alludes to the complex relationship between art and artist.

As with nearly all the case studies featured in this book, its success is the product of a number of key ingredients. First among them is a working partnership between client and designer in which the roles and responsibilities are clearly defined, and which was entered into from a position of mutual respect. Second is a commitment to a working process based in actionable research and that supports and promotes creativity and risk and leaves room for the unexpected. Lastly, but of no less importance, is a commitment to the highest levels of craftsmanship.

## CONTRIBUTORS:

**CHAPTER 1:**
## TAYLOR GUITARS
Mires > Design For Brands
2345 Kettner Blvd.
San Diego CA 92101
www.miresbrands.com

**CHAPTER 2:**
## GRANDCONNECT
Werner Design Werks, inc
411 First Ave North #206
Minneapolis MN 55401
www.wdw.com

**CHAPTER 3:**
## GEORGIA MUSIC HALL OF FAME
Deep Design
5901 Peachtree-Dunwoody
Road, Suite 200c
Atlanta GA 30328
www.deepdesign.com

**CHAPTER 4:**
## NYC2012 OLYMPIC BID
Brand Integration Group,
Ogilvy & Mather
Worldwide Plaza
309 W. 49th Street
New York, NY 10019

**CHAPTER 5:**
## BLACKWOOD STUDIOS
Watts Design
2nd Floor 66 Albert Road
South Melbourne 3205
Victoria Australia
www.wattsdesign.com.au

**CHAPTER 6:**
## CONVERSE
Sandstrom Design, Inc
808 SW Third Ave. Suite 610
Portland OR 97204
www.sandstromdesign.com

**CHAPTER 7:**
## CINESOUND
Faux Koi
3853 14th Ave. S
Minneapolis MN 55407
www.fauxkoi.com

**CHAPTER 8:**
## NGI COMMUNICATIONS
NOON
10 Cleveland Street
San Francisco CA 94103
www.designatnoon.com

**CHAPTER 9:**
## NOCHE
Louise Fili Ltd
156 Fifth Avenue
New York NY 10010
www.louisefili.com

## CHAPTER 10:
## ESTRUS RECORDS

Art Chantry Design Company
P.O. Box 63275
St. Louis MO 63163
www.artchantry.com

## CHAPTER 11:
## GILEAD SCIENCES

Marcus Associates
96 Hillside Avenue
San Anselmo, CA 94960
www.marcusassociates.com

## CHAPTER 12:
## THE NINTH VINE

Manic Design
64 Jalan Kelabu Asap
Singapore 278457
www.manic.com.sg

## CHAPTER 13:
## RYAN ASSOCIATES

Elixir Design
2134 Van Ness Avenue
San Francisco CA 94109
www.elixirdesign.com

## CHAPTER 14:
## KROGER

Gardner Design
3204 E. Douglas
Wichita KS 67208
www.gardnerdesign.com

## CHAPTER 15:
## THE HOUSTON TEXANS

Verlander Design
PO Box 370156
Montara CA 94037
www.verlander.com

## CHAPTER 16:
## QUEER EYE FOR THE STRAIGHT GUY

Shrine Design
60 Beacon St. #3
Chelsea MA 02150
www.shrine-design.com

## CHAPTER 17:
## ZWEITES DEUTSCHES FERNSEHEN (ZDF)

Simon & Goetz
Rotfeder-Ring 11
Westhafenpier 1
60327 Franfurt Am Main
www.simongoetz.de

## CHAPTER 18:
## PARADOX MEDIA

MINE™
190 Putnam Street
San Francisco CA 94110
www.minesf.com

# PERMISSIONS:

**CHAPTER 1:**
pages 10-17 © Mires > Design For Brands, 2005.

**CHAPTER 2:**
pages 18-25 © Werner Design Werks, Inc.

**CHAPTER 3:**
pages 26-31 © Deep Design

**CHAPTER 4:**
pages 32-37 © Ogilvy & Mather Brand Integration Group

**CHAPTER 5:**
pages 38-43 © Watts Design

**CHAPTER 6:**
pages 44-49 © Sandstrom Design

**CHAPTER 7:**
pages 50-57 © Faux Koi Design

**CHAPTER 8:**
pages 58-63 © NOON

**CHAPTER 9:**
pages 64-69 © Louise Fili Ltd.

**CHAPTER 10:**
pages 70-79 © Art Chantry Design

**CHAPTER 11:**
pages 80-87 © Marcus Associates

**CHAPTER 12:**
pages 88-93 © Manic Design Pte. Ltd.

**CHAPTER 13:**
pages 94-101 © Elixir Design, Inc.

**CHAPTER 14:**
pages 102-109 © Gardner Design

**CHAPTER 15:**
pages 110-117 © Verlander Design

**CHAPTER 16:**
pages 118-123 © Shrine Design

**CHAPTER 17:**
pages 124-131 © Simon & Goetz

**CHAPTER 18:**
pages 132-139 © MINE™